RULING CONGRESS

This book is printed on 100 percent recycled paper

A Study of How the House and Senate Rules Govern the Legislative Process

Ted Siff and Alan Weil, directors

The Ralph Nader Congress Project

Grossman Publishers

A DIVISION OF THE VIKING PRESS
NEW YORK 1975

RULING
CONGRESS

First published in 1975 by Grossman Publishers
625 Madison Avenue, New York, N.Y. 10022

Published simultaneously in Canada by
The Macmillan Company of Canada Limited

Printed in U.S.A.

Library of Congress Cataloging in Publication Data
Ralph Nader Congress Project.
    Ruling Congress.

    Includes bibliographical references and index.
        1.   United States.   Congress—Rules and practice.
2.   Legislation—United States.   I.   Siff, Ted.
II.   Weil, Alan.   III.   Title.
KF4937.R34   327'.172'0924   75-6669
ISBN 0-670-61040-2

Contributors

Ted Siff, Project Director and Editor
A.B., Harvard College, 1970; J.D., University of Texas Law School, 1974
Law Clerk, Attorney General of Texas

Alan Weil, Project Director and Editor
B.A., University of Texas, 1970; J.D., University of Texas Law School, 1973
Law Clerk, Judge Homer Thornberry, U.S. Circuit Court of Appeals, Fifth Circuit

Researchers:

Alan Austin
A.B., Harvard College, 1970; J.D., Stanford University, 1974
Law Clerk, Justice William O. Douglas, U.S. Supreme Court

Dan Goldstein
A.B., Amherst College, 1970; J.D., University of Texas Law School, 1973
Law Clerk, Judge Howard Kaufman, U.S. District Court, Maryland

Bruce G. Rosenthal

Tom Walsh
B.A., Texas Technological University, 1970; J.D., University of Texas Law School, 1973
Legal Aid, State of Oregon

Sara Glazer

Deanna Nash

Contents

Introduction

First-year law students spend some of their early days distinguishing between "substance" and "procedure." By the time they finish law school they have learned that "substance" and "procedure" are features of a seamless web, which in the operating world of the courts makes them inextricable components of advocacy power.

In the intense inner world of the Congress, strategic use of *rules, precedents, customs, and courtesies* spells power—who has it, who keeps it, who uses it and to what substantive ends. For decades these procedures served to concentrate power within the House and Senate in senior barons who further concentrated their power by almost never challenging each other's jurisdiction or territory. Although the exercise of these rules was very much enmeshed with ideologies, personalities, and the diverse corruptions of special interests, invocation of the rules also served as a buffer to depersonalize conflicts so as to further avoid accountability.

The power of Congressman Jamie Whitten (D., Miss.) illustrates how the rules and customs of the House of Representatives literally determined what was and what was not done in agriculture and pesticide policy for many years. By the unwritten seniority rule Whitten became chairman of the Subcommittee on Appropriations for the Department of Agriculture in 1947. Like Whitten, other subcommittee members either came from agricultural districts or were close to agribusiness, as was the full Appropriations chairman, George Mahon, of Lubbock, Texas. The same characteristics prevailed in the House and Senate legislative committees on agriculture. Although food policy affects all areas of the country—rural and urban—its shaping or blockage was in the hands of this small coterie of representatives. So, too, was the power to conduct oversight of federal agricultural agencies or investigative hearings into the vast domain of agribusiness. The absence of democratic rules accorded the committees and their chairmen this enormous concentration of power and consequently denied this power to other legislators.

Groups or individuals working for more consumer-oriented food policies, fewer agricultural subsidies, limitations on dangerous pesticides and food additives, food stamps for the poor, and other such goals had very little leverage on these committees. They had little success in appealing to the much larger audience of legislators in the full House of Representatives, because this audience was too remote a source of accountability for the agriculture committees. A subcommittee chairman like Whitten had only to work harmoniously with the powerful agribusiness lobbies to cement his power over these matters in the House and to be crowned the unofficial "Secretary of Agriculture" by Department of Agriculture officials themselves.

Other rules and traditions solidified this hegemony. On the floor of the House, the comity extended to chairmen severely reduced the chances of amendments or opposition to Whitten's legislative package, especially under Chairman Mahon's additionally powerful aegis. The rare revolts on the House floor which succeed do so because blocs of votes signaled or controlled by veteran legislators join with the House speaker and majority leader for majority action. Since chairmen do not like to be challenged, they rarely challenge other chairmen, a custom fortified by the prospect of long and entrenched tenure provided by the seniority system. Wilbur Mills (D., Ark.), the long-time chairman of the House Ways and

Means Committee, had it even easier than other chairmen. He routinely obtained a closed rule from the Rules Committee, so that tax bills were reported to the House floor for voting up or down, with no right of amendment. Power, concentrated by rules, has had a long reach indeed in both the House and the Senate.

Such are examples of the old order which recent events have begun to change. In many unpublicized ways, the intensifying changes trace back to 1968, when Richard Conlon, formerly a newspaper reporter and after that a legislative aide to Senator Walter Mondale, became staff director of the Democratic Study Group, in the House of Representatives. The DSG was an unofficial group of over 100 (over 200 in 1974) liberal Democrats formed in 1959 to foster liberal legislation and reform. Conlon's main mission, as outlined by the handful of activist members who recruited him, was to work with them to democratize the rules of the House. The unsung Conlon took a long view of his job and combined it with enough impatience, political savoir-faire, and common sense to work in tandem with outside citizen and labor groups and make his anticipated tenure worthwhile for reform. In late 1970 and early 1971 the House approved a modest legislative reform package that included the recording of teller votes. Previously the legislators could file past the clerk and be counted for or against a bill or amendment on the House floor without their names being recorded. This anonymity permitted them to avoid being held to account by their voters or the press, unless a sharp-eyed reporter recognized a legislator in the yea or nay line from the press gallery.

Another key change—limiting a member to the chairmanship of only one subcommittee—immediately spread the leadership positions and their policy perquisites among more and younger members. For the first time roll-call committee votes were made mandatorily available to the public, breaking the secrecy curtain that had permitted members to act in committee without account-ability. Most of the committee chairmen and staffers disliked this requirement and still refuse to publish the votes—sticking strictly to the letter of the requirement that the votes be available at the committee offices. Any interested citizen must copy the information by hand at the committee files in Washington, D.C.

In a concomitant reform, the Legislative Reorganization Act of 1970 required that business meetings of committees be open unless the committee in a public session voted to close the business meeting. By these two moves the Congress took the first important steps to open up the critical legislative decision-making activity seldom seen by the public. Circumvention of the open-committee rule by secret votes to close the meeting before it ever opened was shortcircuited in early 1973 with an additional requirement that the vote to close must be by roll call in a public meeting. Also covered by the rule in 1973 were subcommittee meetings and hearings, and a clarification that the rule covered executive legislative sessions, in which bills are "marked up" by the members before being sent to the House floor.

In 1971, at the beginning of the Ninety-second Congress, the Democratic caucus, prodded by the DSG reformers, instituted several other instruments of democracy. It required that at the request of ten members of the caucus there must be a separate ballot for the election of a committee chairman. Previously there had been one slate, and caucus approval of all the chairmen simultaneously was pro forma.

The chairman election requirement was further refined in the Ninety-third Congress, to require an automatic separate vote on each committee chairman by secret ballot. Although all the committee chairmen were reelected in 1973, the seeds of change had been sown. It was this reform which led to the upheaval of January 1975, when two chairmen, F. Edward Hébert (D., La.) of the Armed Services Committee and W. R. Poage (D., Tex.) of the Agriculture Committee, were deposed, in large measure because they had egregiously violated Democratic caucus rules. The caucus also broke another tradition in replacing veteran Chairman Wright Patman (D., Tex.) of the Banking Committee with Henry Reuss, fourth in seniority on the committee, thereby bypassing the second and third members in line. These defeats put all committee chairmen, a number of whom consistently violate caucus rules and vote more often with the Republican majority than with the Democratic, on notice that they will be accountable to the Democratic majority. In the Ninety-fourth Congress, Appropriations subcommittee chairmen were also required to stand for election by the whole Democratic caucus.

In 1973 the Democratic caucus established a twenty-four-person steering committee to help guide party policies in the Congress. Half of the committee members were appointed by the speaker and half elected by the caucus from various geographical regions for a four-year term. Although given limited authority initially, within two years the steering committee was catapulted into the powerful role of appointing members to committee assignments. The principle of rotating membership established by the steering committee was subsequently adopted, during the Ninety-third Congress, for the design of the new Budget Committee. In addition, the 1973 House Democratic Caucus adopted a "Subcommittee Bill of Rights" that gave a committee's majority caucus—not the chairman—the right to determine subcommittee jurisdiction; allowed subcommittee chairmen—not the chairman of the full committee—the right to set subcommittee meeting dates (in consultation with the chairman, to avoid conflicts); required that all legislation be referred to the appropriate subcommittee within two weeks unless the committee's majority caucus decides the full committee should handle it; required that the ratio of Democrats to Republicans on a subcommittee be no less favorable than for the full committee; and gave each subcommittee, subject to the control of the committee's majority caucus, an adequate budget to discharge its duties for legislation and oversight (each subcommittee has a minimum of one staff person). It was the violation by autocratic chairmen of many of these protections that was highlighted in early 1975 in the successful campaign to unseat several committee chairman.

The one formal House attempt to initiate reform in recent years was perhaps the least successful. In January 1973 Speaker Carl Albert (D., Okla.) created a Select Committee on Committees to study the House congressional committee system and recommend changes. Reform advocate Representative Richard Bolling (D., Mo.) was appointed chairman and given a million dollars and a ten-person committee of five Democrats and five Republicans. The major recommendation of the Select Committee, to limit most members to only one committee assignment and reduce the size of committees, was defeated on the House floor in the fall of 1974, in part because some members did not want to lose their jurisdictions and in part because of opposition to committee realignments that could have significantly reduced the influence of the liberal voting bloc.

Other Select Committee recommendations were adopted, however, with additional recommendations from the Democratic caucus reform committee, headed by Congresswoman Julia Butler Hansen (D., Wash.). Every committee of more than fifteen was required to have subcommittees. This was aimed at the Ways and Means Committee, which for years, despite its broad jurisdiction, would move only one bill at a time because it operated only as a full committee. This arrangement served as an automatic deterrent to passage of bills through the committee.

Other Bolling/Hansen reforms included a requirement that the majority of a conference committee must support the House position on a bill, and permission for the speaker to jointly refer bills. One small but key addition was the requirement that the speaker complete compilation of the precedents of the House by a date certain—January 1, 1977—and that the precedents be updated and reprinted every two years thereafter. This was necessary because, despite special appropriations for the job since 1966, a full compilation of House precedents still has not been published. The most recent published precedents stop at 1936. Previously, loud complaints among House members, especially among newer ones, had led to a provision in the Legislative Reorganization Act of 1970 that the House parliamentarian must publish and maintain currently and in cumulative form, commencing with the Ninety-third Congress, a condensed, up-to-date version of all parliamentary precedents which have current use and application. The House parliamentarian, Louis Deschler, retired in 1974 and his volume, *Procedure in the House of Representatives* (1959–1974), was published in December 1974, a few days before the end of the Ninety-third Congress. In the Ninety-fourth Congress, members will for the first time be able at least to refer to information about the key precedents since 1959 in their own offices. Previously Deschler kept only one chronological notebook with the precedents from each day the Congress was in session. Members who wanted to look at the precedents were forced to do so in Deschler's office. Staff members were seldom allowed even this small privilege. Deschler's attitude was the epitome of unaccountability. First appointed by the speaker in 1928, he learned his job so well that he became indispensable, autocratically influencing legislative policies more than most democratically elected members. The legislatively set deadlines culminating in the Bolling/Hansen requirement is finally putting an end to the secretive power of the House parliamentarian.

With the election in November 1974 of seventy-five new Democratic House members—one-fourth of the entire House Democratic Caucus—other long-desired reforms became possible under the guidance of the shrewd, liberal activist chairman of the Democratic Caucus, Representative Philip Burton (D., Calif.).

After the 1974 elections, previously unassailable Wilbur Mills initiated the new members with escapades in the company of an Argentine strip-tease dancer that made him the laughingstock of the country and forced his resignation as chairman of the powerful Ways and Means Committee. These events miraculously occurred only days before the scheduled vote to strip the committee assignment function from the Ways and Means Committee, a move whose success was assured by Mills's incapacitation. Ways and Means Democrats had used this power to proliferate their ideologies to other committees or to obtain commitments of support, as for the oil depletion allowance, in return for a favored committee slot. Of all the rules changes of recent years, removal

RULING CONGRESS

1

Tools of
the Trade

Members of Congress rely on several sources to recount their deeds to constituents. Newspapers announce the latest dam or federal highway brought to the district, and emblazon a photograph of a smiling member of Congress shaking hands with a local leader over the victory. Members' newsletters, sent to every mailbox in the district,* put each representative's activities in a favorable light. And congressional letters of congratulations on high-school graduations, fiftieth wedding anniversaries, new births, and centennials may arrive in the mail (again at taxpayers' expense) to greet a surprised constituent. In addition, constituents who write their members of Congress for information or guidance in getting service from the local Veterans Administration, refunds

* Under the franking privilege, official congressional correspondence may be mailed "free"—i.e., at the taxpayers' expense.

from the Internal Revenue Service, or cuts in Social Security red tape, may also get a sense that their representatives are working for them.

But a member's ability to function inside Congress—to know how it works and how to make it work—is rarely advertised. Representative Don Riegle (D., Mich.) discussed this distinction between image and reality at House Rules Committee hearings on legislative reorganization in December 1969:

> I would think very often a man's political success in his district relates to the image he has in the district in serving his constituents and so forth. It may well be a guy could do a very good job and be elected in perpetuity and not be an effective man in the terms of the interworkings of Congress, and his constituency would have no way whatever of finding that out.[1]

The inner workings of Congress involve complex interactions among members, constituents, lobbyists, executive-branch personnel, and many, many others. The whole elaborate system inside the Capitol—with its own TV and radio recording studios; catering, check-cashing, and medical services; cafeterias, barbershops, and gymnasiums—is intended to help members meet the needs of the electorate. Constituent casework is one way to meet these needs. Congress' oversight powers (to monitor executive-branch administration of its programs) are another. But the members' legislative work includes more than drafting bills, amendments, and resolutions; they must then see each one through the complex legislative circuit to enactment.

HOW A BILL BECOMES LAW

To get legislation through Congress, members have to be familiar with the long, arduous path that a bill must follow to become a law:

· A member *introduces* a measure to the clerk of the House or the secretary of the Senate. The bill is given a number and is printed overnight. (Copies are available to the public, either from the office of the member who introduced the proposal or from the documents room.)

· The parliamentarian, acting on behalf of the speaker of the House or the presiding officer of the Senate, *refers* the bill to a standing or select committee. The Legislative Reorganization Act of 1946, incorporated in the House and Senate manuals, spells out committee jurisdictions over bills.

· *Hearings* on the bill are held by the subcommittee, the full committee, or both. Members of Congress, executive-branch personnel, and citizens may be invited to testify. (Transcripts of open or public hearings are available through the committee considering the bill or in depositories for government documents around the country.*)

· At a *"mark-up"* session, members consider the bill section by section and vote on changes.

· The committee *reports* the bill for floor consideration. They provide a *committee report*, which concisely summarizes the proposal and defines the arguments pro and con. (Committee reports are available through the documents room.)

· The bill is placed on a *calendar*. The Senate has one calendar listing bills in the order that they are reported out of committee, but, by obtaining unanimous consent or making a motion, the majority leader may call up a bill out of order. The House has five calendars: the union calendar (for all revenue and appropriations bills), the house calendar (for nonrevenue measures), the private calendar (for all private bills), the consent calendar (for noncontroversial bills transferred from the house or union calendars), and the discharge calendar (for bills that have not been reported by a committee; it requires a petition signed by a majority of House members).

---

* Each congressional district has at least two libraries that representatives have designated as depositories for government documents. Land-grant colleges and state libraries are automatically designated as depositories, and, in addition, senators may select two depositories in their states.

· Nonprivileged, controversial bills in the House go next to the Rules Committee for a *special rule*. A majority of the committee must report such a resolution before the bill can go to the floor.

· On the floor, the bill is *read* aloud at several points (though the time-consuming reading of bills is often dispensed with), *debated*, and *amended*. Amendments are voted upon; the bill is read again, and the entire bill is voted upon. (Proceedings are published in the *Congressional Record*.)

· The bill is then sent by message to the other house for the same procedure (introduction, committee hearings, mark-up sessions, committee report, calendar placement, and so on).

· The bill returns to the first house, which decides whether or not to *accept any amendments* attached by the other house. If there is a disagreement a conference between the houses may be called to work out the differences. (Again, the *Congressional Record* transcribes the floor debate and votes leading to these decisions.)

· If a conference is called, and if a majority of conferees from each house reach agreement, they write up a *conference report* listing the changes agreed to. They send it to the floor of both houses for a vote. Both houses must accept the conference report before the bill can be *enrolled* on parchment paper. (Unless the conference is open, there are generally no public transcripts of conference committee debates or votes.)

· If both houses agree without a conference meeting, the bill is *enrolled* on parchment paper.

· After the speaker of the House and the president of the Senate (the Vice-President of the United States) *sign* the bill, it is sent to the President of the United States for signature into law. If the president refuses to sign the bill, a two-thirds vote of each house is needed to override the veto.

At every point in the legislative circuit, bills meet obstacles which can halt their further movement. To get around these obstacles (or to put them up around other members' legislation) a member of Congress must know the parliamentary rules and procedures of Congress.

THE FORMAL RULES

The rules of the House and Senate are an immeasurably complex body of written law, rulings from the chair during floor debate, and unwritten but traditionally binding codes of behavior. The written rules include the United States Constitution; forty-four standing rules for each house; Thomas Jefferson's *Manual of Parliamentary Practice*; and over forty thousand precedents (rulings from the chair) for the House and about ten thousand for the Senate. The unwritten rules are just as formal, and members learn them even as they enter the halls the first day: "If you're new here, speak when spoken to," "Don't challenge rulings from the chair," "Shy away from rules fights unless you can win," "What you do will be done unto you" (the reciprocity principle), and many others.

1. The Constitution lists the qualifications of representatives and senators; delegates certain areas to one house alone (such as assigning the power of impeachment and the right to initiate revenue-raising bills to the House); provides that members may punish a member "for disorderly behavior, and, with the Concurrence of two-thirds, expel a Member";* and defines a "quorum" to do legislative business as a majority of a chamber.

2. Both the House and Senate use Jefferson's *Manual* wherever it does not conflict with their current standing rules. Jefferson compiled the rules while he was Vice-President of the United States and therefore President of the Senate (1797 to 1801). Jefferson explained in his preface that he took up the task for two reasons—because the Constitution provided that each branch of Congress "determine the rules of its own proceedings and because

* See House Parliamentarian Lewis Deschler's annotation of the use of this clause in *Rules of the House of Representatives* (House *Manual*), 92nd Congress, pp. 24–25.

the Senate deferred to its President for questions of order arising
out of rules it has made." Jefferson's stated purpose in his preface
was to lay the groundwork for a code of rules that would continue
to develop, with the effect of "accuracy in business, economy of
time, order, uniformity, and impartiality."[2] His basic sources for
the *Manual* were the United States Constitution and English parliamentary law. With House Parliamentarian Lewis Deschler's
annotations, it runs about 184 printed pages.

3. Since the Senate is a continuous body, its standing rules*
carry over from Congress to Congress. But the House rules are
modified and adopted at the beginning of each Congress, with
Jefferson's rules in effect until the House adopts its standing rules.
The majority party writes the new standing rules in its party
caucus before the first day of the session. The rules thus reflect
the majority decision on how the House should be governed. In
closed caucus, by secret ballot, members vote on the rules, which
are then brought to the full House for a final vote. Though party
dissidents may join minority members in objecting to a particular
rule, in the main, the rules are usually accepted as the caucus
wrote them. The majority party could conceivably change any
rule—even the entire committee system—as long as the new rules
conformed with the Constitution and a majority adopted them on
the House floor. Representative Thomas Rees (D., Calif.) says
that freshmen members of Congress are at an immediate disadvantage, for they have barely had time to read the rules, let alone
to master them enough to analyze suggested changes before the
caucus vote.

All members were at a disadvantage during the floor debate on
the adoption of the rules at the beginning of the Ninety-second
Congress: the proposed changes were not printed in time to give
members the opportunity to read or examine them before a vote.[3]
Yet some important changes had been made in the majority par-

---

* Standing rules are those orders governing the conduct of business which
are listed in the House and Senate manuals and reprinted each Congress.

ty's caucus that affected even the Legislative Reorganization Act of 1970. For example, Rule XI of the act had authorized the hiring of two minority-party staff members for each committee. But the Democratic caucus chose to strike that language and insert in its place a weaker clause calling for the fair treatment of the minority party in committee.[4]

The rules reforms passed by the Democratic caucus at the beginning of the Ninety-third Congress (1973) have been called "the biggest change in the way the House operates since a revolt of 63 years ago stripped a 'czar' speaker of most of his powers."[5] In a bid to strengthen party leadership, a policy committee was set up to recommend legislative priorities; its members were to include party leaders and a cross section of members. The reign of seniority, an unwritten but binding rule, was broken when the caucus provided for a periodic caucus vote on committee chairmen. And committee meetings were to be open to the public, unless the members—in a public vote—voted to close the meeting. So the onus shifted to *voting to close* a meeting, an action members might find difficult to justify. The Senate permits open meetings *if* the committee choses to do so, a less dramatic change.)

The forty-four standing rules are important because they define the jurisdictions that committees have over bills, the prerogatives of committee chairmen, the powers of the speaker or presiding officer, the duties and qualifications of members and congressional officers, general floor procedure and decorum, and the administration of the chamber. They define where radio-television correspondents may sit, what times Capitol sweeping and cleaning may be done, and whether or not the doors of the Senate or House chamber may be closed during floor sessions. They also permit confidential communications between Congress and the president, whereupon the chamber may be "cleared of all persons except the Members and officers thereof" (House Rule XXIX).

Members must follow prescribed rules from their oaths of office to their last days in Congress: getting office space, hiring staff, introducing bills to committee, working in committees, getting their bills on a House calendar or Senate schedule, winning a favorable rule from the Rules Committee (House) for floor debate, and negotiating in a conference committee with the other house.

The House standing rules run about 253 pages, including the parliamentarian's annotations. The Senate standing rules fill about 110 pages, without annotations.

4. The standing rules, however, form only the base of the parliamentary structure of both houses. For whenever a member raises a point of order on the floor,* the parliamentarian issues a ruling (through the speaker or the presiding officer) that sustains or rejects it. The ruling becomes a precedent for future decisions by the chair. The House precedents to 1936 alone fill eleven books. Since the first Congress, over fifty thousand rulings have been handed down. There is no compilation of *all* these precedents available to members, so that the total written corpus of procedural law is quite unwieldly, complex, and in some cases, mysterious.

THE CODE OF COURTESY

Perhaps the overriding rule in Congress is the code of courtesy—partly written in scattered portions of the standing rules and partly unwritten, but very powerful and binding just the same. Throughout the written rules are specific directives about decorum and courtesy. The rules attempt to set a tone of order where conflicts—geographical, personal, temperamental—could reign. Fisticuffs within the halls of Congress were not rare during the nineteenth century. One day in 1838, Henry Clay no sooner resumed his seat on the floor than "without the slightest warning, he received a blow in the face," and "in the fight that followed a pistol was discharged wounding an officer of the police."[6] On May 22, 1856, Representative Preston Brooks (S.C.) entered the

---

* A member on the floor may raise an objection that the rules governing conduct of business have been violated. If the objection is correctly cited, the chair sustains it.

United States Senate and beat Senator Charles Sumner (Mass.) senseless with a cane over differences of opinion on the slavery question.[7][*] Rules were also developed to handle certain kinds of impropriety, like John Randolph's insistence on bringing his hunting dogs onto the floor of the House.[8] Members of the House could wear hats in the chamber until the 1830s and were permitted to smoke until the 1870s.[9] But written rules soon prohibited both, and do to this day.

The House has seen fit not to change such admonitions in the standing rules as "while the Speaker is putting a question or addressing the House, no member shall walk out of or across the hall, nor, when a member is speaking, pass between him and the Chair" (House Rule XIV, 7). In debate, "No Senator . . . shall, directly or indirectly, by any form of words impute to another Senator or to other Senators any conduct or motive unworthy or unbecoming a Senator," and "No Senator in debate shall refer offensively to any State of the Union" (Senate Rule XIX). Furthermore, in neither house is a member allowed to name another member; one may only say the "representative from Iowa," not "H. R. Gross."

For the occasion when one member offends another in floor debate, there is a provision known as "taking down the words." It is an official reprimand of the discourteous member. At the offended member's request, the words are read aloud for the speaker to determine if they are in order. Should a member deny having spoken the words read aloud, the House must decide what exact words were spoken. If the speaker rules the words out of order, the member who spoke them may offer an apology or may be prohibited from speaking the rest of the day. The offended member may move that the words be expunged from the *Congres-*

---

[*] Brooks resigned July 15, 1856, even though the attempt to expel him failed to win the necessary two-thirds vote. He was re-elected to the same Congress (84th) to fill the vacancy left by his own resignation. Meanwhile, his injuries caused him to be absent until December 5, 1859. See *Biographical Directory of the American Congress 1774–1961* (Washington, D.C.: Government Printing Office, 1961).

sional Record. As interpreted by the code of courtesy, the *mere demand* that a member's words be "taken down" is a very serious matter; it indicates the height of personal conflict.

Because members are allowed to "revise or extend" their remarks before the government presses print the *Record* for the day, many samples of congressional tempers, discourtesy, or insults (as the slightest word may be taken to be) do not appear for public eyes to study. In their place may appear a formal sentence, such as, "At this point, a portion of the debate was deleted by order of the Senate."

Under the rule allowing the *Record* to be edited, members may erase words they find damaging or insulting; they can add words which suggest that they are participating in floor debate; and they can extend their remarks (at a cost of more than $140 per page to taxpayers) to give the impression that they are imparting knowledge to the public.

The formal courtesies required by the written rules have been cause for complaint. When the Ninety-first Congress stayed in session until New Year's Eve, members were cranky, attacking each other and "the other house." According to Senator Edward Brooke (R., Mass.), congressional sessions would be at least ten days shorter if members would "stop calling each other distinguished." And Mike Mansfield (D., Mont.) replied, "I appreciate the remarks of the distinguished senator from Massachusetts."[10]

The code of courtesy pervades all congressional activities—whether or not it is specified by the standing rules. According to House Standing Rule V, "The Doorkeeper shall enforce strictly the rules relating to the privileges of the Hall and be responsible to the House for the official conduct of his employees"; William M. (Fishbait) Miller is paid forty thousand dollars a year, to manage "thirteen ladies' restrooms, five men's restrooms, thirty-three janitors, fifty-one pages, fifty-five doormen, two snackbars, the document room and the folding room."[11] The sergeant-at-arms is delegated to "maintain order" and gather a quorum when the houses are in session, according to Rule IV. Part of his duties, however, have evolved into determining dress codes for members of Congress and their staffs on the chamber floor. According to John Coder, a staff member of the Senate Rules Committee, the Senate has no formal written rules to govern clothing worn on the floor. Neither does the House, said a spokesman in the House parliamentarian's office. "We have no written set of clothing regulations directed at one sex." However, women staff members wearing trousers have been stopped on their way to the floor by the sergeant-at-arms.

In fact, courtesy rules often win in conflicts with standing rules. As the curbs on a chairman's powers illustrate, the self-imposed rules of courtesy can overcome rules reforms. Prior to the Legislative Reorganization Act of 1970, chairmen had the power to refuse to call committee meetings, thereby holding up or destroying legislation that they did not like. Rules Committee Chairman Howard Smith, for example, went on fishing trips whenever he did not like a piece of legislation coming before his committee, according to Representative Spark Matsunaga (D., Hawaii). In his absence, the committee could not call meetings on bills. Now chairmen are required to adopt regular committee meeting days, and there is a procedure that allows a committee majority to call meetings against the chairman's will or in his absence.[12] But few members can overcome the power of the code of courtesy to dare challenge and offend a chairman who prefers not to follow the rules. At an organizational meeting of the House Government Operations Committee in 1970, members voted away their rights by accepting revised committee rules that say: "The chairman is authorized to dispense with a regular meeting or to change the date thereof, and to call and convene additional meetings, when circumstances warrant."[13] They also voted to give other powers to Chairman Chet Holifield (D., Calif.), such as keeping the press corps out of the meeting and combining two major subcommittees. Bella Abzug (D., N.Y.) has published her version of the meeting:

> Holifield's plan to combine the two subcommittees passed with a tie vote. Conyers, Moss, Reuss, and Rosenthal voted

for it. Why? I think because they feel a need to survive in the Club. Unfortunately. They think they have to kowtow to the chairman, because they think that's the way to get power. What they don't understand is that by kowtowing they are giving up their power. Think about it: Had any one of those four guys I mentioned voted against Holifield, we could have had the press inside the committee room to report about what he was doing.[14]

Members have occasionally made the choice to break the code of courtesy, counting the risk worth the legislative results. Former Senator Fred Harris (D., Okla.) held up his colleagues at nine o'clock one evening when he tried to stress the importance of the Sugar Act Amendment that he and Senator Edward M. Kennedy (D., Mass.) supported. Even though he had agreed with Majority Leader Mansfield to vote on the 1971 Sugar Act that night, he changed his mind when he saw how close the vote might be. He wanted to postpone the vote so that he could muster support overnight, and threatened to keep everyone up all night by introducing amendments and quorum calls to achieve this delay. Senator Russell Long (D., La.) was furious at this break in folkways. "I object," he said. But Mansfield broke in, saying, "For God's sake, no, Russell, we'll be here all night."[15] Harris won his ground by ten o'clock, but his discourtesy caused some grumbling.

One member who has not hesitated to break both written and unwritten Senate rules of courtesy is Senator Mike Gravel (D., Alaska). One Gravel foray beyond the pale of congressional courtesy was quite dramatic. It began when Senator Robert Griffin (R., Mich.) used his right to object to a unanimous-consent request to prevent Gravel from making a speech on the Senate floor. It was June 29, 1971, and Gravel wanted to read parts of the still-secret Pentagon Papers into the *Congressional Record*. There were few Senators on the floor, and Gravel needed unanimous consent to rescind a quorum call so that Senate business (his speech) could go on. Since Griffin had objected to the unanimous-consent request, a quorum had to be gathered before

Gravel could begin. But the sergeant-at-arms searched fruitlessly for three hours for members to form a quorum; the Senate adjourned at 9:28 P.M. without hearing Gravel's speech. But Gravel did not give up his search for a public forum. That evening he called a meeting of his Buildings and Grounds Subcommittee and invited the news media, his first step beyond the pale of courtesy in this episode. In front of TV cameras he read portions of the secret Pentagon Papers, possibly breaking written Rule XXXVI requiring members to keep secret any confidential communiqués from the president to Congress. At 1:12 A.M., Gravel broke Senate decorum by bursting into tears while reading from documents. The next day Stephen Rich reported in the *Washington Post*, "One senator after another said privately that he was 'amazed,' 'surprised' or 'astounded'" by Gravel's daring expression of emotion and his daring act of calling a late-evening committee meeting at such short notice and on such a controversial topic.

Senator Lowell Weicker (R., Conn.) called the meeting "illegal"; Senator Jennings Randolph (D., W. Va.), chairman of the Public Works Committee, parent to this subcommittee, did not consider the Pentagon materials "germane" to the committee's business, would not recognize the meeting as legitimate, and would not allow the full committee to pay for a transcript of the event. Gravel's legislative assistants argued, however, that calling a subcommittee meeting did not break any rule. Such meetings are often held on short notice, they explained. Besides, they said, they delivered notices to every member and had Congressman John Dow (D., N.Y.) as a witness. They handled the jurisidictional problem by saying that the United States did not have enough money for public buildings and grounds because of the war. There is no "germaneness" rule regarding committee jurisdiction, the aides said; there is only "jurisdictional jealousy" when one committee handles what another wants.[16] The next day, Majority Leader Mansfield stood behind Gravel: "He will not be censured or made to apologize; I don't know what rule, regulation or code he's broken."[17] Gravel did not return to the Senate floor until July 5, when he offered a two-minute speech which alluded to senatorial rules of courtesy:

> Perhaps, I did not approach the matter with the same degree of *delicacy* another would employ. . . . What I did I felt and continue to feel, will bring credit to the United States Senate, not embarrassment. I would never be party to any act that would bring discredit to this august body. [Emphasis added.]

A year later, Gravel discussed Senate decorum in a Congress Project interview:

> You need decorum because Senators are in conflict, otherwise the situation could erupt. The problem is that some Senators get more involved in the shell of decorum than in the substance inside the shell. They like the emoluments of the office too well.
>
> For instance, in the case of the Pentagon Papers—I felt reading them was the important thing to do. I believed it was important that an elected official be giving the information to the people. The people can then share in legislative responsibility.

The code of courtesy also serves as a useful strategy for members of Congress. Using a general tactic of "you leave me alone and I'll leave you alone," members of Congress are able to remain conciliatory toward each other.

SENIORITY—A RULE OF CUSTOM

In addition to the huge body of congressional rules—the Constitution, Jefferson's *Manual*, the standing rules, the precedents, and the code of courtesy—is still another major law, a law based on custom. It is the one-word answer to the many-sided riddle: What is the deciding factor for assigning Capitol office and parking spaces to members of Congress? What is a major guideline in determining which member on the floor wins the chair's recognition to speak? What determines where members sit at a committee hearing? What makes a bill introduced by a senior member of Congress more likely to get serious consideration than one introduced by a junior member? What has been the absolute criterion for selecting committee chairmen since World War II? The answer: seniority.

Seniority is the unwritten law by which Congress allocates among its members privileges, responsibilities, and powers. By this system, members of Congress turn over control of the legislative process to their colleagues who have managed to survive the electoral process—and life itself—the longest. The average age of committee chairmen in 1972 was over sixty-seven; half of the chairmen were seventy or over. Also by this system, *men* run Congress. Of the twelve women elected to the Ninety-second Congress, none chaired a full *standing* committee. The House and Senate each have well over a hundred subcommittees, but in the Ninety-second Congress only three were chaired by women.* Furthermore, districts or states where the two-party system is least vigorous—often rural southern states and districts—held the positions of leadership. In the Ninety-second Congress, southerners chaired nine of the seventeen standing committees in the Senate and eight of twenty-one in the House. Even more important, they controlled the major ones—the House Appropriations, Armed

* In the 92nd Congress, Margaret Chase Smith (R., Me.), the only woman in the Senate, was ranking minority member of the Appropriations Subcommittee on State, Justice, and Commerce, the Judiciary, and Related Agencies; and of Armed Services' subcommittees on Nuclear Test Ban Treaty Safeguards; Reprograming of Funds; and Center for Naval Analysis.

In the House, these women chaired subcommittees: Julia Butler Hansen (D., Wash.), (Appropriations' Subcommittee on Interior); Lenore K. Sullivan (D., Mo.), (Banking and Currency's Consumer Affairs); and Edith Green (D., Ore.), (Education and Labor's Subcommittee No. 1). Martha Griffiths chaired the Select Committee on the House Beauty Shop. Women ranking minority members included Florence P. Dwyer (R., N.J.), (Banking and Currency's Consumer Affairs and Government Operations' Intergovernmental Relations) and Margaret M. Heckler (R., Mass.), (Veterans' Affairs Subcommittee on Housing).

Services, and Ways and Means committees, as well as the Senate Judiciary and Finance committees. As of the Ninety-third Congress, Arkansas could boast three chairmen of Congress' strongest and most-desired committees: John L. McClellan of Senate Appropriations, J. William Fulbright of Senate Foreign Relations, and Wilbur Mills of the House Ways and Means Committee. Texas could boast four: Wright Patman of House Banking and Currency, George Mahon of House Appropriations, W. R. Poage of Agriculture, and Olin Teague of Veterans' Affairs.

Seniority is only a custom: there is neither legal nor constitutional basis for it. Nowhere in the hundreds of pages of Congress' standing rules does the word "seniority" appear.* The Senate first adopted seniority sometime after the Mexican War—to choose committee chairmen. Historians are not quite sure when or why the Senate did this, but it probably wanted to keep appointments out of the alien hands of its presiding officer—the vice-president.[18]

Seniority came to the House over half a century later as a "reform" measure. In the early 1900s, representatives quaked under the iron rule of Speaker "Czar" Cannon (R., Ill.). Tiring of intimidation, they revolted in 1911 and stripped him of his powers. Rather than ever allow any speaker to appoint and remove chairmen again, they opted for seniority.[19] Before reform, speakers appointed chairmen, considering seniority as one factor; in the revolt's wake, members with seniority perpetuated their own power by passing chairmanships to other senior members. Champ Clark (D., Mo.), Cannon's successor, later explained seniority's appeal:

* It does appear in some of the rules adopted by individual committees, however. One 92nd Congress rule for the Senate Committee on Commerce, for example, reads: "Subcommittees shall be considered *de novo* whenever there is a change in the chairmanship and seniority on the particular Subcommittee shall not necessarily apply." See *Rules Adopted by the Committees of Congress*, compiled by the Joint Committee on Congressional Operations, 92nd Congress, October 27, 1971.

That seniority always has been and always will be an important factor in making committee assignments is absolutely certain and no mortal man can give any philosophic or tenable reason why it should not be. . . .

No sane man would for one moment think of making a new graduate from West Point a full general, or one from Annapolis an admiral, or one from any university or college chief of a great newspaper, magazine or business house. A priest or preacher who has just taken orders is not immediately made a bishop, archbishop, or cardinal. In every walk of life men "must tarry at Jericho till their beards are grown."[20]

But seniority has not worked out as Clark envisioned. On some occasions, the seniority system ignores experience altogether. When members transfer from one committee assignment to another, they start at the bottom of the seniority ladder in the new committee. Or when members lose elections or leave Congress for other reasons and return later, they start at the bottom of the seniority ladder. This happens even if the member has gained valuable experience in the interim. Hubert Humphrey (D., Minn.) served as Senator for fifteen years before he spent a term as Vice-President. When he was re-elected to the Senate in 1970, he ranked only as a freshman.

In the last two decades or so, violations of the unwritten rule of seniority have been rare: only twice since 1949 has it been violated in the assignment of committee chairmen. (See Table 1.) Seniority's status as custom, however, in no way diminishes its force: few written laws have been as religiously observed. The Senate has faced such tempting cases for breaking tradition as the deaf and inaudible Chairman Capper or the permanently absent Chairman Glass;[21] but it has resisted all enticement to ignore seniority's command. Committee chairmanships are automatically awarded to the members with the longest continuous service on the committee. And once comfortably ensconced as chairman, a member is likely to remain. Since it began following the seniority

TABLE 1.

Violations of Seniority in
Appointment of Committee Chairmen
U.S. House of Representatives—1881–1969*

Congress	Year	Speaker and party	Seniority followed	Seniority violated	Total committees
47	1881	Keifer (R)	2	37	39
48	1883	Carlisle (D)	8	30	38
49	1885	Carlisle (D)	21	19	40
50	1887	Carlisle (D)	20	21	41
51	1889	Reed (R)	20	27	47
52	1891	Crisp (D)	12	35	47
53	1893	Crisp (D)	25	24	49
54	1895	Reed (R)	13	39	52
55	1897	Reed (R)	36	16	52
56	1899	Henderson (R)	42	15	57
57	1901	Henderson (R)	49	8	57
58	1903	Cannon (R)	43	11	54
59	1905	Cannon (R)	51	8	59
60	1907	Cannon (R)	45	13	58
61	1909	Cannon (R)	42	18	60
62	1911	Clark (D)	25	27	52
63	1913	Clark (D)	33	20	53
64	1915	Clark (D)	50	6	56
65	1917	Clark (D)	45	10	55
66	1919	Gillett (R)	35	22	57
67	1921	Gillett (R)	44	15	59
68	1923	Gillett (R)	40	17	57
69	1925	Longworth (R)	37	22	59
70	1927	Longworth (R)	43	1	44
71	1929	Longworth (R)	38	7	45
72	1931	Garner (D)	27	18	45
73	1933	Rainey (D)	38	7	45
74	1935	Byrns† (D)	32	13	45
75	1937	Bankhead (D)	42	4	46
76	1939	Rayburn (D)	37	9	46
77	1941	Rayburn (D)	39	7	46
78	1943	Rayburn (D)	34	11	45
79	1945	Rayburn (D)	37	9	46
80	1947	Martin (R)	9	4	13
81	1949	Rayburn (D)	19	0	19
82	1951	Rayburn (D)	18	0	18
83	1953	Martin (R)	17	1	18
84	1955	Rayburn (D)	19	0	19

TABLE 1. (*continued*)

Congress	Year	Speaker and party	Seniority followed	Seniority violated	Total committees
85	1957	Rayburn (D)	19	0	19
86	1959	Rayburn (D)	19	0	19
87	1961	Rayburn† (D)	20	0	20
88	1963	McCormack (D)	20	0	20
89	1965	McCormack (D)	20	0	20
90	1967	McCormack (D)	20	1	20
91	1969	McCormack (D)	21	0	21

* Data from 1881 to 1963 is from the previously cited article by Polsby, Gallagher, and Rundquist. Data from 1963 on is from DSG.
† Byrns died in office and was succeeded by Bankhead; Rayburn died in office and was succeeded by McCormack.
SOURCE: *Congressional Record*, "The Seniority System in the U.S. House of Representatives," Democratic Study Group, introduced by Donald M. Fraser (D., Minn.), February 26, 1970, p. H.2553.

custom the Senate has ousted only five chairmen—the last nearly fifty years ago.[22] Since 1943, the House of Representatives has replaced only one chairman—Adam Clayton Powell (D., N.Y.), who lost his House membership in 1967 after living on Bimini, a Carribean island, for two years, and continuously flouting House rules.

Far from being mere technical phrases, the rules and their codes, precedents, and customs have a powerful impact on the number and nature of the bills that become law. In 1971, 535 members of Congress introduced over eighteen thousand bills: about seven per cent of these actually passed. Rules—as weapons of delay, obstruction, obfuscation, and manipulation—played a part in this culling process. While every democratic body must have rules outlining orderly procedures, the time-encrusted machinery of the House and Senate are too easily and often used to subvert majority rule, choke off floor debate on vital issues, and allow members to obscure their actions and their votes through parliamentary maneuvering that is often incomprehensible to the public.

For many reasons, the majority party, which is in a position to stop abuses of the rules, has not done so; its leaders, who are in control of the rules, enjoy the discretion of interpreting them. Absenteeism is rampant and members have not taken rules seriously enough to learn them for themselves. And the will for order and courtesy has too often surpassed any desire for real advocacy on the floor of Congress.

TOO MANY APPRENTICES

Rules are meaningless until they are used by people. But few members of Congress have learned the rules well enough to be able to use them—indeed, estimates of the number of knowledgeable representatives range from only ten members to ten per cent of the House.[23] The power of manipulating rules and procedures to win legislative positions has fallen into the hands of a few, often self-taught experts on rules. In both houses, these members form a small, informal, but powerful group. This cadre overlaps, but does not coincide with another group comprised of high-seniority representatives formally recognized, nurtured, and protected by the committee system. The rules experts are the leadership,* the parliamentarian and his assistants, rules committee members, committee chairmen (fifty-seven in the Ninety-third Congress) and ranking members, and any member who takes

---

* The list of leadership positions is short: speaker of the house, president pro tempore of the Senate, majority leaders, minority party leaders, majority whips, and minority whips.

Rarely is an incumbent leader thrown out of office (see Appendix 1). Since 1970, however, a trend of challenging leaders has grown. For two days before the 92nd Congress convened, each party in each house caucused to choose its leaders and several positions were hotly contested. Hale Boggs (La.), Morris Udall (Ariz.), B. F. Sisk (Calif.), Wayne Hayes (Ohio), and James O'Hara (Mich.) were pitted against each other in the biggest House Democratic leadership contest in thirty years. At the same time, Sam Devine (Ohio) challenged John Anderson (Ill.) for chairmanship of the Republican Conference. In the Senate, Edward Kennedy (Mass.) and Robert Byrd (W. Va.) were opposed for majority (Democrat) whip, and Hugh Scott (Pa.) fought Howard Baker (Tenn.) over the minority-leader (Republican) position.

great pains to learn the rules and uses them daringly on the floor.[24]

What makes this powerful establishment different from the high-seniority group is that freshmen members can join its ranks. This potential for power through knowledge of rules and procedures is vital to newcomers. Otherwise, freshmen are the least able to benefit their constituents because their activities are dominated by the seniority tradition and political party bonds.

When it comes to gaining power through knowing the rules, however, freshmen are on their own. They have no single manual or set of books to depend upon for a full understanding of the use of rules. They are hard pressed to find the out-of-print volumes of precedents to 1936, and rulings from the chair have not been codified since then; Senate precedents have not been updated since 1964. Even manuals or textbooks on the rules do not illustrate how rules might be used or how they interrelate.

The congressional establishment has made few attempts to disseminate information about procedure to members. In the early 1960s, a bipartisan committee in the House, assisted by the American Political Science Association, began to offer seminars for freshmen members. But the seminars were brief and undetailed. The 1965 seminar lasted only about five days. The syllabus, printed in the 1965 Organization of Congress hearings, shows a bias toward socializing members into the routines of accepted codes of courtesy. By just the second day, members were learning about the seniority system and congressional decorum. On the *last* day, House Parliamentarian Lewis Deschler was present to answer questions about rules; and freshmen learned the basics about the various kinds of calendars involved in moving a bill from committee to the floor; kinds of debate on the floor; various motions; and voting procedures.[25] Senate and House party leaders occasionally hold educational sessions for staff members, where the parliamentarians and their assistants conduct classes on floor procedures. But these are generally futile efforts. The Democratic Study Group also sponsors seminars for House freshmen. Following the 1972 election, Harvard University's John F. Kennedy School of Politics held a week-long seminar for House freshmen.

At the 1965 hearings on the organization of Congress, Jonathan Bingham (D., N.Y.) suggested more formal, lengthy "orientation and indoctrination" for freshmen. He suggested that the dead space after the election and before January oaths of office would be an appropriate time, and staff members should also attend. Bingham said that orientation should meet a need he perceived for *intensive* training on the rules and procedures. Members were not getting in-depth training:

> Speaker McCormack has properly advised every freshman to master the rules and we did have limited instruction on how some of them operate. However, they are long, involved, and obscure.
>
> No doubt, they have great virtue when viewed in perspective, but it is difficult to tell which ones are important, and which ones are the product of ritual and are more lightly regarded. For example, Rule XV states that when a rollcall is underway, the doors of the House will be shut. However, there is easy access to the floor through the Speaker's lobby. The freshman needs to know what other rules are similarly treated.[26]

And Representative James Mackay (D., Ga.), while a freshman in 1965, suggested an official school for freshmen members of Congress that might go beyond the excitement of inauguration and orientation in January to later months in the year, when members had a chance to settle down and learn what to ask.[27]

Without adequate classes and books on how rules can be used, freshmen members must learn by socialization. To become rules experts, then, they must stay on the floor to watch older hands; they learn by making mistakes and spending long hours studying the rules. As Representative Charles Vanik (D., Ohio) put it, "You learn one of the rules each time you get kicked in the head with it. After a while, you know a few rules, but you pay for it."

This extremely haphazard, time-consuming method costs

American constituents as well. Their representatives are dependent on established members (who have many reasons to support the *status quo*) for vital information—how to get legislation through Congress. They must rely on the parliamentarians, the House or Senate leadership, and a handful of self-taught experts to work the rules for them.

This dependence of many members on a few affects the substance of the legislation that Congress ultimately passes. In a book about her experiences as a new representative, Bella Abzug (D., N.Y.) expressed her high estimation of the power of rules and her dismay about members' dependence on others to invoke that power. Although she limited her concern to "liberals," her words actually apply to all political persuasions in Congress:

> I'm convinced that the only way to fight the inflexibility of Congress is to turn the system against itself. There must be a way, somehow, to take all these damn rules and regulations and limitations—which the power structure now uses to squelch anything that sounds too liberal—and turn them around to our advantage.
>
> As far as I can tell, there are very few experts on procedure in the House. Those few experts we do have are old-timers, and not liberals. The average liberal thinks up what he wants to do and then runs off to somebody else to ask, "Now what procedural step do I take in order to do this?" Consequently, liberals rarely get anything significant accomplished.[28]

Dr. Walter Kravitz, senior specialist in government at the Congressional Research Service, explained the lack of knowledge about the rules:

> Members do not seek the skillful use of rules: they seek a legislative end. The rules are not the end objects: they rather help to achieve the end cure.[29]

So members notice rules as they affect the movement of their own legislation through Congress. But they do not tend to draw an accurate picture of the power of the rules in every phase of the legislative circuit—from introduction of a bill to passage of a conference report.

For whatever complicated reasons—limited access to informative books on rules in action, few competent congressional teachers, minimal time to expend on rules—members have grown dependent upon others, especially the parliamentarian. Former Democratic member Glen H. Taylor (who ran for Vice-President as a Progressive) explained; "There is no compulsion to learn the rules. The Parliamentarian is always at your elbow when you are in the Chair."[30]

2

The
Parliamentarians

THE EDGAR BERGEN–
CHARLIE McCARTHY ROUTINE

There are two ventriloquists in Congress: Lewis Deschler,* House parliamentarian (who earned $42,191.88 in 1971, making him the highest-paid official in the Congress), and Floyd Riddick, Senate parliamentarian (who earned $35,793.66). Each sits close to a leader on the floors of Congress: to the right of the speaker or presiding officer in the House, in front of but below the presiding officer in the Senate. Each has immediate access to the eyes and ears of the command post, the chair.

Presiding officers over noncontroversial bills and amendments

* On July 1, 1974, Lewis Deschler retired. William H. Brown, Deschler's assistant for about twenty years, was appointed as his replacement. Brown is expected to run the office in the same manner as his mentor.

are usually inexperienced members of Congress in the process of learning the rules. But even long-term members do not know the rules thoroughly enough to make rulings without the parliamentarian's aid. Representative Thomas Rees (D., Calif.) described this ventriloquist arrangement to the Congress Project:

> Chairmen of Committees of the Whole are generally in the position of not knowing how to rule. It's an Edgar Bergen—Charlie McCarthy routine. Once I was in the Chair and a Member rose to be recognized and I didn't know what to say. From my right I heard a still small voice whispering in my ear, "For what purpose does the gentleman from Montana rise?" And this happens all the time.

The institution of the parliamentarian is young. Deschler and Riddick are only the second people to hold these powerful posts. Deschler has ruled since 1928; Riddick since 1964. In the congressional world of bills, resolutions, amendments, rules, precedents, and parliamentary maneuvering, these two men hold a vast treasure. They give it up to members of Congress only a coin at a time. Their treasure is the official, complete compilation of rules and precedents for the United States Congress and the expertise in legislative maneuvering that comes with their job: an immeasurable private treasure, assembled from a public document—the *Congressional Record.*

Precedents, those rulings on points of order by the speaker or presiding officer, are the interpretations of the standing rules of the House and Senate and they bind as rules. As of the Ninety-second Congress, there were more than forty thousand such rulings in the House and about ten thousand in the Senate. Senate precedents up to 1964 are published in *Senate Procedures: Precedents and Practices* by Charles L. Watkins and Floyd Riddick. The ten thousand House precedents up to 1936 were published in the massive eleven-volume *Precedents of the House of Representatives* by Hinds and Cannon. There is no complete, published compilation of precedents after 1964 for the Senate or

1936 for the House. The unpublished, but complete sets of the nation's congressional rules and precedents are locked in the private offices of the parliamentarians. The American people and their 535 elected representatives are dependent upon these two men for the formal and informal interpretations of the rules and procedures of Congress.

These two influential men are not elected by members of Congress. There are no congressional rules governing them. The House parliamentarian serves "at the pleasure of the speaker," while the Senate parliamentarian gets his job and pay from the secretary of the Senate.* They are invisible to the American public; they need not worry about re-election.

Both Deschler and Riddick were assistants to the parliamentarians who preceded them, Lehr Fess in the House and Charles L. Watkins (who served for more than forty years) in the Senate. And Deschler, scheduled to retire in 1974, seems to have already chosen his successors (contingent upon the agreement of the speaker of the House). The ages of his assistants indicate something of Deschler's master plan. Assistant Parliamentarian Bill Cochran, who handles all usual bills† on the floor, is about ten years younger than Deschler; Bill Brown, who handles all appropriations bills on the floor, is about ten years younger than Cochran; Charles Johnson, Deschler's legal assistant, is about ten years younger than Brown.

The position of parliamentarian has evolved considerably beyond its origin in the clerkship system, in which clerks took notes, delivered papers in Congress like postmen, and read bills aloud to the houses of Congress. Specialization has led to the creation of

* The secretary of the Senate is appointed by the majority party caucus. A vote on the Senate floor confirms the appointment. It is a "strictly political" appointment, according to the Senate Rules and Administration Committee. The secretary of the Senate usually remains in office until there is a change in the majority party. The present secretary of the Senate, Francis Valeo, has held office since October 1966 and had a 1972 salary of $36,000.
† Deschler himself handled the most controversial bills or those that probably involved intricate parliamentary maneuvering.

powerful roles—bona fide parliamentarians. Riddick was handed a wand of power by his predecessor. Deschler has fashioned his own wand. And few outside of Congress appreciate the power the two men command, power that is seemingly hidden in the most mundane activities.

THE INVISIBLE HOUSE ENGINEER

Deschler is running the House.
—Representative Thomas M. Rees

The fate of a bill is constantly in Deschler's hands.
—David Cohen, Common Cause

As parliamentarian for more than forty years, Lewis Deschler has served under nine speakers of the House.[1] He came to the House as a messenger at the speaker's table, became assistant to Parliamentarian Lehr Fess a year later, and, the following year, 1928, at the ripe age of twenty-two, Deschler became parliamentarian himself.

Deschler was born March 3, 1905, in Chillicothe, Ohio. At seventeen he entered Miami University in Oxford, Ohio, and distinguished himself as a tackle on the varsity football team. He graduated from George Washington University, Washington, D.C., in 1925. At the age of twenty-five he served as assistant secretary of the American group at the Interparliamentary Union Conference in London, England. While serving as parliamentarian, he received the Juris Doctor and Master of Patent Law degrees from National University in Washington, D.C., and passed the D.C. bar examination with the highest score ever.[2]

Throughout his service in the House, Deschler has been an invisible engineer. He researched thousands of House rulings to find in President Andrew Jackson's era the legislative key that opened the door for President Roosevelt's "100 days of reform legislation."[3] At the same time, he gave parliamentary advice to Republicans who sought to use the rules of the House to block the

President's programs.[4] And it was Deschler who found the precedent which helped both the Alaska and Hawaii statehood bills bypass a Rules Committee that intended to block them forever.[5]

Deschler was a charter member of Speaker Sam Rayburn's "Board of Education," a small group of Rayburn's most trusted friends and advisers. Behind closed doors, the board mapped the strategy for such controversial measures as the civil rights bill of 1957, which Deschler guided from introduction through final passage. Behind the cloak of the speaker, he advised the chair on all points of order: he warned it of potential procedural roadblocks and how to maneuver around them. Deschler once remarked that he had been parliamentarian for so long that he "can walk out on the floor and feel it when something is going to happen."[6] Lobbying groups, who understand as few do the importance of Deschler's work, realize that Deschler's unparalleled mastery of the rules, his ability to do almost anything with the legislative machine, would make him an invaluable asset to any interest group. But Deschler has rejected several offers to become a high-paid lobbyist.[7]

During the nearly half a century that Deschler has been in office, the duties of the parliamentarian have greatly expanded. They now include referring all bills to the proper committee; advising the speaker or chair on all points of order or parliamentary inquiries; checking for procedural problems all legislative drafts of bills, resolutions, and rules coming out of the Rules Committee; and offering members of the House technical assistance for preparing motions and other legislative measures.

All House paths lead to Deschler's office for the final word on any parliamentary question. Ten feet away, in the speaker's (and the parliamentarian's) reception room, behind white curtains on glass doors, are the complete precedents of the United States House of Representatives. This treasure is safely hidden from both the public and representatives' personal staffs. Scrapbooks, one volume for each year since 1936, contain slips of paper clipped from the *Congressional Record*. Some thirty to forty thousand precedents on slips of paper, carefully clipped and annotated by the parliamentarian's assistants, fill the pages.

Apparently, the task of cutting up the *Record*, adding a few words to summarize what was happening in the House at the time of the ruling, and pasting that precedent and summary on a piece of paper in a loose-leaf binder transforms the public ruling into a private work accessible to a privileged few, and then only in the parliamentarian's office.

Deschler allows no one but his own staff to research precedents collected in his scrapbooks—not even members, their staffs, or committee staffs. Members with a parliamentary question may see a precedent or two, but only in the presence of the parliamentarian. The space of the parliamentarian's office, which is actually one of the speaker's rooms crammed with desks, is too small to allow for extra researchers such as members or their staffs, says Deschler. And if any parts of the scrapbooks were removed from the area, they might get lost, he explains. Neither the parliamentarian nor his staff readily give advice to a member's staff, according to Assistant Parliamentarians Bill Brown and Charles Johnson, because Deschler says people on a member's staff have a tendency to misunderstand and mislead the member for whom they work.

Deschler has said that an indexing system was begun in 1963 so that the precedents—arranged chronologically in the scrapbooks—could be grouped and analyzed by subject matter.[8] But this index is not available to the public, members of Congress, or their staffs. Johnson and Brown contend that the index system is rough and incomplete, with only a few scrapbook cards actually indexed.* More often than not, Deschler's memory is the index. His staff recalls many instances when Deschler referred them to a

---

* Yet Mike Reed, Speaker Albert's administrative assistant, has indicated to Congress Project researchers that the parliamentarian's office has a very sufficient index system, which aids the parliamentarian and his assistants to find the proper precedent on two minutes' notice during debate of a point of order on the floor.

particular day in the *Congressional Record* and a particular ruling off the top of his head.

Congress has not frequently faced the question of the inaccessibility of its own rules and precedents. But in 1970, during floor debate over the Legislative Reorganization Act, some members were dismayed with the parliamentarian's control over the precedents. Representative Chet Holifield (D., Calif.), for one, offered his view:

> It is almost unbelievable and, in my opinion, it is inexcusable that the Members of this House do not have access to a printed compilation of the rules and precedents since the year 1936. That is 34 years. Many of us who have handled bills on the floor have been faced with parliamentary situations and questions as to whether what we were doing was contained in the rules and the precedents and have been embarassed many times. Our only recourse, of course, is to go to the Parliamentarian's office. The very exhibition of that book of clippings . . . , how many of the Members have ever tried to go through a thing like that. It is in such a condition that it is in inaccessible form, from a realistic standpoint, to the Members of the House.[9]

And Representative Thomas M. Rees (D., Calif.) complained:

> We have printed precedents up to 1936. These are the Cannon and Hinds precedents. If you wish to do any research in the precedents of the House of Representatives, you find that you have to go to Cannon and Hinds, but then you have an impossible task to research precedents between 1936 and 1970. They have not been kept up to date and have not been printed.[10]

In the seven Legislative Branch Appropriations Acts from 1966 to 1972, Congress voted the House parliamentarian's office a total of $88,675 (plus funds for additional staff) to update the precedents.* But no results have been forthcoming. To force

---

* For the fiscal year ending June 30, 1966, the office received $10,000 for the compilation of the precedents; June 30, 1967, $10,000; June 30, 1968,

some action, Representative Andrew Jacobs (D., Ind.) unsuccessfully tried to amend Section 342 of the 1970 Legislative Reorganization Act. Any precedents not printed and available to members, Jacobs argued, should not be used in rulings from the
chair.* Jacobs said on the floor that his amendment was designed
"to accomplish that which all law is supposed to accomplish;
namely certainty in the anticipation of the affairs of whatever
body is being governed." Without a printed collection of the rules
and precedents in each member's office, a member cannot antici-
pate all the possible modes of action to achieve legislation, Jacobs
declared. He told his colleagues in floor debate: "Whatever law is
depended upon—and precedents in the House of Representatives
certainly take on the very fundamental force of law—to govern
any body should be a law that is written down and should be a
law which is certain."

Rees supported Jacob's amendment:

> This is a good amendment; with this amendment it will
> mean that the office of the Parliamentarian will have to
> supply up-to-date printed precedents. This office has to be
> expanded so that every Member of this House can have at
> the beginning of every legislative session an up-to-date com-
> pilation of the precedents of the House. If the precedents are
> developed week by week, we can then be furnished pocket
> supplements or loose-leaf supplements so that every Member
> will have in his own office his important and necessary tool
> if he is to be an effective Member of the House.[11]

But House Speaker John McCormack objected to the amendment, stating that the precedents were being compiled, but that "it

---

$12,000; June 30, 1969, $12,540; June 30, 1970, $13,210; June 30, 1971,
$14,540; and June 31, 1972, $16,385. Deschler was authorized to hire
such staff as he determined necessary and at salaries he deemed reasonable
subject to the approval of the speaker. Deschler first hired his daughter,
Joan Deschler Eddy, at a yearly salary of $13,399.20. Several other per-
sons have also been hired at similar salaries.

* Sec. 343. Any parliamentary precedent from any previous Congress which
has not been printed, indexed, and distributed to all Members, as provided

takes years to make a careful compilation of the precedents."[12] Representative Chet Holifield, though supporting the concept of the amendment, stated that he did "not believe . . . , however, that this amendment should be passed."[13] The amendment was rejected by a voice vote.

Five years later, Deschler was yet to publish a compilation of precedents. He did not foresee a finished compilation for three years, perhaps ten years, if the precedents were integrated with the Hinds and Cannon volumes, which were last updated in 1936.

AT THE TOGGLE SWITCH

Control over the precedents brings the parliamentarian tremendous influence over the legislative process: of the forty thousand precedents, there is at least one—sometimes many—that can support a certain legislative position and one that can oppose it. In a conflict, Deschler says, the latest precedent governs. Yet, as Deschler has told others, some cases are "like the edge of a knife." And even in these instances, Deschler makes the decision. The result, Representative Rees contends, is "like out of Kafka— we don't know what the law is until the ruling is made, based on the precedents we've never seen."[14] Representative Richard Bolling (D., Mo.) recalled that sometimes when he was in the chair, Deschler would hand him alternative rulings on a particular point of order.

One illustration of Deschler's effect on the substance of legislation is his 1955 decision that scotched one form of monitoring appropriations of taxpayers' money. An appropriations bill requested a $25,000 study of the need for a third House office building. After turning the chair over to Representative Clark

---

in either Section 341 or Section 342 of this title shall, be considered without effect as a precedent and may not be cited as the basis for any parliamentary ruling in the House of Representatives." (*Congressional Record,* September 16, 1970, p. H.22211.)

Thompson (D., Tex.), Speaker Sam Rayburn introduced an amendment on the floor to replace the $25,000 study with a $2-million appropriation and "such additional sums as may be necessary" to construct what later became the Rayburn House Office Building,[15] a project that had an estimated cost of $87,358,953 by 1967.[16] Since the proposed construction had not been authorized by any previous legislation, the amendment constituted legislation on an appropriations bill. Thus, it violated House standing Rule XXI, Clause 2,* and Representative Clare Eugene Hoffman (R., Mich.) raised a legitimate point of order while the Rayburn amendment was being read to the House. The chair informed Hoffman that he would have to wait until the reading had been concluded before raising his point. Hoffman sat down in the front row and engaged himself in conversation with another member. After the clerk had finished reading the amendment, Representative Clarence Cannon (D., Mo.), managing the supplemental appropriation bill that Rayburn wanted to amend, was recognized by the chair. He stated that the amendment was proper and that his committee had accepted it. Suddenly Hoffman jumped to his feet and reiterated his point of order. On Deschler's advice, Chairman Thompson ruled that, since another member had been recognized and had spoken on the merits of the amendment before Hoffman sought recognition, the point of order under House rules and precedents came too late.

Some years later, responding to criticism of the ruling, Representative Thompson disclaimed responsibility. Lew Deschler was the man in charge, Thompson said: he made the decisions; he guided the chair.[17]

While members of the House wait for a published form of the

* Standing Rule XXI, Clause 2, reads: No appropriation shall be reported in any general appropriation bill, or be in order as an amendment thereto, for any expenditure not previously authorized by law, unless in continuation of appropriations for such public works and objects as are already in progress. Nor shall any provision in any such bill or amendment thereto changing existing law be in order, except such as being germane to the subject matter of the bill shall retrench expenditures. . . .

House precedents, they have three major sources of information: conferences with the parliamentarian, in-House documents that contain only selected precedents, or outside consultants.

Conferences at the parliamentarian's office are probably the most dependable source on parliamentary questions for members. Indeed, Deschler ranks giving advice and information to all members seeking it as one of his prime responsibilities. He considers the parliamentarian's job as facilitating discussion, debate, and action on the merits of proposed legislation. Conferring with members before floor debates, Deschler says, reduces discussion of procedural questions on the floor and allows more time to wrangle out the real issues. These conferences, he claims, have accelerated the activities of the House, where, before he inherited the office, as much as two hours could be spent on one point of order. Now, the questions are often ironed out ahead of time.

If a representative plans to present an amendment and wants to know if it will be in order, or if a member wants to present a point of order in response to an offered amendment, Deschler must be consulted. A member is expected to come to Deschler with any parliamentary maneuver, and thus, he has said, over 90 per cent of the parliamentary arguments presented on the floor have previously been worked out in conference by the member and the parliamentarian.

A member's advance conference with Deschler reduces conflict on the floor and sometimes prevents humiliation. Members will try to avoid the disgrace of losing a battle publicly before their colleagues at almost all costs. Those who are convinced by Deschler that they cannot win a point of order may forsake their positions to save face.

Some members have been scalded by conferences, however. They maintain that they merely show their hand to the House leadership when they ask specific questions before debate. They often use the parliamentarian's tactics only to find that the leadership has mapped out a battle plan to counterattack, complete with documented typed sheets of rules and precedents for the presiding officer or speaker.* A member who springs a parliamentary request on the floor, without having checked with Deschler first, is likely to be punished. If the parliamentarian has not been informed of the point of order beforehand, the Chair may be disposed to rule the point out of order without so much as a sentence of explanation, according to Wes Barthelmes, administrative aide to Senator Frank Church (D., Idaho).

In certain circumstances, however, surprise may be the best resource. Christine Sullivan, legislative assistant to Representative Michael Harrington (D., Mass.), believes that "Deschler should be the last person to [ask about] a parliamentary question if you want to make your point on the floor. Surprise is probably your best bet." She referred specifically to an effort by Representative Harrington to tack on an end-the-war amendment to a Military Procurement Bill then before the House. Although she questioned whether the amendment was germane, she was more concerned that if Harrington had conferred with Deschler in advance he would have keyed the opposition. The minority counsel to the House Agriculture Committee, Hyde Murray, has explained the occasional need for surprise:

> Lew loves this House and would never do anything to hurt it. But sometimes I know viscerally that if I show this to Lew he's going to knock it down and rebut it. Only in that kind of situation is surprise an alternative.

Representative Rees has said that a visit to Deschler for an opinion on the appropriateness of any legislative measure is like "a defense attorney going to the prosecuting attorney and asking him, 'Is this a good case or not?'"

Those who end up on the losing end of a bout with Deschler have few other sources for procedural advice. No other source is

* According to John Kraemer, once a tactician and antipoverty lobbyist, Representative Tom Foley (D., Wash.) checked with Deschler on December 29, 1970, and was assured that an amendment to the 1964 food-stamp bill would be in order when the bill came up. The next day the Foley amendment was introduced, an objection was raised and the speaker, with Deschler's advice, sustained the objection.

as complete as Deschler's horde of precedents in his scrapbooks or as knowledgeable as Deschler himself. Alternatives include the following:

· The *Congressional Record*, which has the precedents buried in it. Be your own parliamentarian; clip out the rulings and save them. Available to the public.

· The Democratic Study Group, started in 1964, which is a potential rival to the parliamentarian by working on a set of precedents. Staff people go through the *Congressional Record*, using the inadequate index and clip rulings. An on-again-off-again operation. Available to DSG members.

· The House Republican Policy Committee's *Committee Staff Manual on Legislative Procedure in the U.S. House of Representatives* (1973), a description of the most important rules and procedures of the House provides some advice. Available to Republican members of Congress.

· A weekly summary of the rulings of the chair, compiled by Mel Miller, minority counsel to the House Administration Committee. He began in 1970. Available to Republican staff members.

· The American Law Division of the Congressional Research Service, at the Library of Congress, answers members' requests for interpretation of laws, assembles legal bibliographies, and writes legal histories. Available to members of Congress. (None of the sixty million items in the Library of Congress in 1971 contained the complete compilation of the precedents of the House of Representatives, because the parliamentarian's office has the only set.)

· *Jefferson's Manual of Parliamentary Practice* contains the House rules plus selected precedents. Updated to 1972. Available to the public.

· *Hinds' and Cannon's Precedents of the House of Representatives* contains ten thousand precedents in eleven volumes, to 1936. Available to the public but now out of print.

· *Cannon's Procedure in the House of Representatives* was

prepared by former member and parliamentarian Clarence Cannon. It has a topical index and synopsis of precedents *up to 1936*. *Deschler's Procedure in the U. S. House of Representatives* brought the synopsis of precedents up through 1973.

· Robert Luce's *Legislative Procedure*, a four-volume 1922 study, is standard though dated.

· Floyd Riddick's *The United States Congress, Organization and Procedure*, a 1949 study of House procedure by the present Senate parliamentarian, has some procedural information.

· Morris K. Udall's *The Job of a Congressman* (1966) is an introduction for freshman representatives.

· *Cleaves' Manual* on conferences and conference reports is standard on this narrow range of rules. Available to the public.

None of these sources, of course, is complete and up-to-date. None can substitute for the codified precedents themselves. And currently only the parliamentarian has access to all the precedents.

WHEN THE HOUSE
PARLIAMENTARIAN GOVERNS

Only in rare instances does Deschler's power become visible. In 1971, for example, it materialized during maneuvering on the conference report to H.R. 6531, involving pay increases for American military personnel. The Senate had approved a pay increase of more than $2.8 billion, while the House had authorized increases of $2.7 billion. According to the House rules on conferences between the houses to settle differences in the laws they have passed, the conferees could agree to a pay increase somewhere *between* the House and Senate figures.[18] But the conferees agreed on a figure *below* both the House and Senate increases, $2.4 billion. In addition, the conference committee decided to postpone enactment of the increases, in direct contravention of both the House and Senate bills.[19] According to Rule

XXVIII, Clause 3, of the 1970 Legislative Reorganization Act, the conference report violated two parts of the House rule which stipulates that a conference report

> shall not include matter not committed to the conference committee by either House, nor shall their report include a modification of any specific topic, question, issue or proposition committed to the conference committee by either or both Houses if that modification is beyond the scope of that specific topic, question, issue or proposition and so committed to the conference.[20]

So, if it was brought to the floor of the House for final passage, the bill could be struck down on two points of order. Before the bill could be considered on the floor, the conference report had to get a rule from the Rules Committee, which, except under certain calendars or extraordinary procedures, is required before any legislative measure may be considered on the floor by the full House. The House conferees, headed by Representative F. Edward Hébert (D., La.), knew they were flaunting the conference report rule.[21] They planned to request a special rule from the Rules Committee waiving points of order against the conference report. With such a rule, no member of the full House could object to considering the report on the grounds that it violated the rules of the House. For the conferees, it would be the best of all possible worlds. They could legislate in a conference, overruling the majority of both the House and Senate, without fearing that the conference report would be thrown out for breaking a House rule.

Hébert, representing the conferees, and William Steiger (R., Wis.), an opponent of the conference report, testified before the Rules Committee. The effective-date provision of the conference report, Steiger claimed, broke Rule XXVII, Clause 3, by altering something not presented to the conference—an issue that the houses had agreed on.[22] Steiger also indicated that the $2.4-billion figure violated the standing rule by going beyond the scope of the topic committed to the conference. The Rules Committee voted nine to six against Hébert and against a rule waiving points of order.[23]

Enter Lewis Deschler. During his tenure as parliamentarian, Deschler had assumed a special duty, not prescribed in any written rules of the House. For the sake of efficiency, a major goal of his definition of the House parliamentarian's duties, Deschler assists the Rules Committee when it drafts rules. He informed the committee members that a rule for consideration of the conference report could *not* be written if it did not waive points of order against the report.[24] He cited no precedent; he gave no authority for his ruling. Without the rule from the Rules Committee, Deschler argued, the conference report would die, and with it months of work by both houses. The very next day the Rules Committee reversed its vote and granted the rule that Hébert and the conferees had requested.

On a previous occasion, Deschler's interpretation of Rule XXVIII had evoked criticism even from the Senate. The Senate had passed and sent to the House S. 575, an extension of the Appalachian Regional Development Act of 1965 and of the Public Works and Economic Development Act of 1965. The House changed the Senate bill with an amendment to the Accelerated Public Works Act of 1962, authorizing a $2-billion appropriation for public-works projects throughout the country. Having changed the original Senate bill, the House asked for a conference with the Senate. But, according to Senator John Sherman Cooper (R., Ky.), the Senate conferees could not be allowed to present their alternative to the House amendment because "[the House conferees] had received an opinion from the House parliamentarian" which said that the Senate alternative violated Rule XXVIII.[25] Although both Cooper and Senator Howard Baker (R., Tenn.) spoke against this opinion, they argued in vain. Once Deschler had made his ruling, the decision would not be changed.

Deschler was again cited in the November 1971 debate on the rule for the conference report for the military-procurements bill of

1972.[26] At the heart of the controversy over the report were two clauses of Rule XX: Clause 3, under which House conferees cannot accept nongermane Senate amendments in conference unless they have prior authorization from the full House and the House has to vote on each separate nongermane amendment;* and Clause 1, which provides that each nongermane amendment of the Senate must be disposed of separately on demand of any member by a vote on the floor.[27] No precise definition of "germaneness" is available; the precedents under that heading form a byzantine maze. But amendments that were not considered by the House committee with jurisdiction over the original bill are often held to be "nongermane." According to the House Republican Policy Committee's *Committee Staff Manual on Legislative Procedure*:

> Because of the underlying rationales that the rule of germaneness is designed to preclude consideration of subjects which were not before the appropriate committee, it is said that the rule of germaneness will be applied strictly against amendments which are in nature complete substitutes for the bill under consideration.[28]

The Senate had taken the House-passed military-procurements bill, had stricken everything after the enacting clause, and had inserted its own language. This insertion is called "an amendment in the nature of a substitute." In the Senate version of the military-procurements bill were six amendments, which, if they had been

---

* This clause was added by the 1970 Legislative Reorganization Act to prevent a few House members from defeating or bypassing the majority of the House. It had been common for the Senate to vote "riders" or amendments onto unrelated large tax or appropriation measures. The House, with its stricter rules, could not attack or vote upon nongermane amendments. When the final version was hammered out in a conference committee, the few House delegates usually controlled by a committee chairman could accept Senate-added provisions that could never pass the House. Although irrelevant to the tax or appropriations matter, the House would be forced to cast a single vote on the entire measure, thus enacting provisions that a large majority might not favor.

offered in the House, would have been declared out of order under House rules as nongermane to the bill.[29]

In the bargaining between the House and Senate conferees, several of the Senate nongermane amendments remained in the conference report. One amendment limited United States military and economic assistance to Laos. Another called on the President to set a specific date for the cessation of all United States military involvement in Indochina. This was a modified, weaker version of the Mansfield Amendment that had been adopted by the Senate. And the third authorized the United States to import chrome from Rhodesia, violating the United Nations embargo on trade to which the United States was a party with racist Rhodesia.[30]

Again, Representative Hébert as chairman of both the House Armed Services Committee and the House conferees, asked the Rules Committee for an unusual rule to insure that points of order would be waived against the bill. The rules on conferences were clear, as Representative H. Allen Smith (R., Calif.) explained on the floor later: "No conferees of the House may agree to nongermane language until and unless the House tells them to do so." By accepting these three nongermane amendments, the conferees had broken the House rules. They asked that their actions be sanctioned by a special rule from the Rules Committee. The committee did grant a waiver of points of order, and, following the Legislative Reorganization Act, they ruled that any member could demand a separate vote on any one or all of the three nongermane Senate amendments. The measure could then return to conference with the House having been heard.

Smith explained the rule during the floor debate on the report:

> This rule represents the first effort by the House to insist that this provision of the rules of the House Clause 3 of Rule XXL be abided by. This is the first time that the House will have an opportunity to require a separate vote on nongermane language added by the other body. If we do not stand up here, we are giving notice to the other body that they can continue to run over the House whenever the notion strikes

them and they can think up a nongermane rider to add to a House bill. It does no good to pass rules providing for the handling of nongermane amendments if we do not use the procedure provided by our rules. If every time a hard case comes up we say that it should be an exception to the rule and a waiver of the rule should be granted, we shall have taken a major step along the road of waiving our constitutional right to determine our own rules of procedure.[31]

Representative Durward Hall (R., Mo.) made a parliamentary inquiry about the outcome of votes on the nongermane amendments: "In the event that such a vote was demanded on those separate sections and it was not agreed to by this body, would the entire conference report be rejected and returned to the conferees or the other body?"[32]

At this point the chair made a surprising ruling. The speaker cited a provision of Jefferson's *Manual* adopted in 1796.[33] He cited precedents decided before 1906.[34] His answer thus canceled the key provisions of the Legislative Reorganization Act of 1970 on conference reports which had been incorporated into the standing rules, and the rule by the Rules Committee. The chair ruled:

> A provision of *Jefferson's Manual*—found in sections 542 and 549 of the House Rules and Manual—holds that conference reports must be acted on as a whole, being agreed to or disagreed to as an entity.
>
> The House by its action in rejecting any one of the sections on which a separate vote may be demanded would nullify the agreement between managers on the part of the House and the Senate, and the conference report would therefore fall.[35]

Some members of the House were quite surprised by the speaker's ruling. William Steiger said, "I must admit to be amazed, frankly, by what I understood to be the ruling of the chair." And Smith declared,

I do not intend to get into any argument here on the floor of the House with the Speaker, who has answered the parliamentary inquiry, nor do I speak for all the members of the Rules Committee.

I will state my opinion that if one, two or three is voted down I believe we can get back to conference on one, two or three. I believe the Rules Committee can write any rule it wants to so long as it is not unconstitutional and so long as the members sitting on this floor agree with what we send to them.[36]

The next procedural question was raised by Representative John Dellenback (D., Ore.):

I am left with one question, which is, in the event that there should be a rejection by the House of item No. 1, for example, will we then proceed to item No. 2 anyway, or will the defeat of item No. 1 and thus the defeat of the conference report by the ruling of the Chair and the statement of the chairman, make us stop at that particular point?[37]

Hébert provided this answer:

If we lose the first amendment it is all over as far as the conference report is concerned. If we are sustained, we will go to the second item.[38]

The speaker's answer to the parliamentary inquiry and Hébert's statement had canceled not only the provision of the Legislative Reorganization Act but also this unusual action by the Rules Committee. Indeed, a central purpose of the unusual rule granted was to insure that the conference report might be accepted while a nongermane amendment was not. The result was that the House and Senate conferees would resume the conference, not over the conference report which was accepted, but over the disagreed-to amendment.

Under such circumstances, few members were so cavalier or so committed to one principle that they would vote down an entire conference report to weed out a very small part of it. The only nongermane amendment to be challenged was the Rhodesian chrome issue. Representative Don Fraser (D., Minn.) whose Subcommittee on International Organizations and Movements had rejected such an amendment earlier in the session, demanded a teller vote. But the speaker's answer to parliamentary inquiry had already dictated the outcome. The vote of 251 to 100 was anticlimactic; the amendment was accepted.

It is difficult, of course, to know how much of the ruling was Deschler's and how much was Albert's. In such important matters, Deschler could hardly act against the speaker's wishes. Yet, unless Albert was entirely opposed to the reforms enacted by the Legislative Reorganization Act of 1970 concerning conference procedure, Deschler's advice had great influence. For it was Deschler who found the precedents. And Deschler opposed Clause 3 of Rule XX in the Legislative Reorganization Act. He still opposes it. He believes that it interferes with the legislative prerogatives of the Senate. He explained the ruling on the Military Procurements Bill this way: in writing the Legislative Reorganization Act, neither the House nor the Senate considered the parliamentary tool called "the amemdment in the nature of a substitute." In this case, the conference report was an amendment masquerading as a substitute. When the Senate strikes everything after the enacting clause of the House-passed bill and inserts its own language—an amendment in the nature of a substitute—as it did in this case, that language must be accepted as is. It cannot be divided. Thus, the chair ruled that when a nongermane amendment is defeated, so is the entire conference report: the part of the conference report which is an amendment in the nature of a substitute cannot be rejected without rejecting the whole. But this interpretation allows 1796 rules and pre-1906 precedents to overrule both the intent of a 1970 standing rule and the intent of a 1971 Rules Committee rule agreed to by a majority of the House. In this case, the latest precedent did not govern, but the parliamentarian did.

The House parliamentarian serves "at the pleasure of the speaker." The speaker's needs—rulings based on the precedents of the House—and the parliamentarian's knowledge make the two officers intimate legislative cronies.

Deschler has said that his duty to the speaker is paramount. When he decides that a matter brought to his attention in a consultation with a member is important he tells the speaker about it. He also occasionally suggests a conference between the member and the speaker. Though Deschler admits that he must always be nonpartisan, he believes that he has a simultaneous responsibility to serve the speaker to his fullest. Everything Lewis Deschler does is, by rule, under the aegis and scrutiny of the speaker. He can never act against the speaker's wishes.

This close relationship between Deschler and the speaker sharply contrasts with that of Deschler's counterpart in the Senate, Floyd Riddick. The Senate parliamentarian has neither a powerful protector nor a single director: the secretary of the Senate scares no one; the president of the Senate (the vice-president) is an outsider and is treated like one. Riddick has his friends in the Senate, but none can compare with the House speaker. A disgruntled House member must first go through the speaker to attack Deschler, but any senator can go directly after Riddick's jugular vein. This simple difference in the hierarchy largely explains, according to Church's aide, Wes Barthelmes, why Riddick is "amiable" with members and staff while Deschler is not, and why Deschler wields so much more power than Riddick.

For all his "brusque" ways, Deschler is trusted by the speaker. His loyalty to the speaker is never doubted, asserts Congressional Research Service staffer Walter Kravitz. Speaker Carl Albert has said that there are "not enough metaphors in the book to describe Lew. He is the anchor of the House; he is an indispensable instrument in the efficient and wise operation of this great organization."[39] And Speaker Sam Rayburn once responded to a member's reference to his long term and undoubted knowledge of the rules: "One of us knows the rules: that fella . . . Lew."[40] John McCormack, another former speaker, observed:

He is not only a brilliant gentleman as we all know but dedicated to the service of the House of Representatives. He is the No. 1 Parliamentarian of the world. He serves all members impartially and fairly. However, over and above everything his dedication to the House will always be a very prominent part of this great body.[41]

Sitting beside the speaker or chair, Deschler or one of his assistants is always prepared for any point of order or parliamentary maneuver. Since he took office, there have been only six appeals on a ruling by the speaker or the chair.[42] Only one of them was successful, and Deschler himself actually orchestrated it. It was 1928, Deschler's first year as parliamentarian. Representative Fiorello La Guardia (R.-Prog., N.Y.) consulted with Deschler and raised a point of order on a reference of a bill to a House calendar—it was a precedent set by Speaker Nicholas Longworth that Deschler wanted to change. Once La Guardia appealed the ruling, the House overruled the speaker.

Ordinarily, only when communications and negotiations off the floor have broken down completely would a member even consider appealing a ruling by the speaker. This kind of challenge under the informed folkways of the House is considered a personal attack on the speaker's leadership. So a symbiotic relationship has developed between the parliamentarian and the speaker. Deschler protects the speaker or the chair or the floor leader with his expertise, and the speaker's power insulates Deschler's rulings from either attack or close scrutiny by the membership.

The influence that Deschler has exercised over speakers of the House has depended upon the speaker's experience and character. Several members noted that Speaker Rayburn would say, "Lew, find a precedent for this position. This is what I'm going to do and I want the precedent to support it." But Representative Bolling says that Speaker McCormack would merely ask Deschler for "the correct position to take" on a given parliamentary issue. As Speaker Albert has become more and more accustomed to the office, he has increasingly asserted control over the affairs of the House under his jurisdiction.

Deschler's loyalty to the speaker is easily transferred to any presiding officer or floor leader in Congress. His loyalty reflects his love for the House. It remains transfixed to the symbol of power and leadership—the chair—even at risk to his life. And two such occasions did occur. In 1932 a man waving a .38 revolver burst into the House galleries. As members of the House began to run from the floor, Deschler stopped the presiding officer, saying, "You can't leave—you're presiding." And the two men stayed put until the gunman, having fired no shots, was removed. In 1954 Deschler had a closer call when several armed Puerto Ricans broke into the House gallery. As they began shooting indiscriminately at the members on the floor, Deschler pushed members (even the chairman this time) out doors and under seats, although he himself was in the line of fire. Several members were seriously injured, Deschler was not hit.

So it is not surprising that members have praised Deschler's dedication highly. In 1970 Representative Mendel Rivers (D., Miss.) paid tribute to the second official House parliamentarian on the floor:

> Lewis Deschler is the embodiment of our rules of order. He is the embodiment of law and order. He is the right hand of the Speaker, and he is the image of Congress.[43]

YOU DON'T QUOTE UMPIRES

Notwithstanding occasional praise, Deschler has cultivated anonymity during his nearly fifty years in office. To him, anonymity is a proper prerequisite for his job. After all, he says, he is not a member of the House; he considers himself a servant, one who aids elected representatives. He stays out of the limelight by allowing no reporters to quote him and never speaking for the record.

Reporters have learned to respect his wish to remain behind the scenes. If a novice reporter quotes Deschler, he does not get an interview with the parliamentarian the next time he needs information. As one reporter put it, "Deschler is an umpire. You don't quote umpires."

Though Deschler has almost as much power as most congressional leaders, he remains unaccountable to the press and the public, and even most members do not know him well.

> It is startling to circulate among Members of long service and realize that the great majority do not faintly realize Deschler's stature either on the floor or in his . . . office.[44]

Those who have had uncomfortable experiences with Deschler's parliamentary advice and decisions feel the pressure of his power, in spite of his anonymity. They usually refuse to give specific examples of Deschler's possible unfairness—even when they are guaranteed nonattribution—but they do not hesitate to say that they believe Deschler has occasionally been unfair. So any story involving the parliamentarian is extremely difficult to verify.

Of course, members of the House could legislate rules to limit the parliamentarian's duties and his control of the precedents. But they have abdicated their responsibility to keep tabs on appointed officers of Congress and on the rules of the House. They may feel secure in the insight Deschler gives them into a precedent—the particular gold coin they need to win a point of order or other parliamentary procedure on the floor. They may sense the defeat of a bill by a parliamentary maneuver if they complain aloud about the parliamentarian's rulings. They may even underestimate Deschler's influence. No matter how they may justify their inactivity in monitoring the parliamentarian, the question of the compilation of precedents should lurk throughout their daily legislative activities. How can they accept the fact that there is only one set of complete precedents for the United States House of Representatives in the whole world, and that set is in the exclusive, inaccessible possession of the parliamentarian?

Deschler works hard; he has a huge daily task. He may be the sum total of all that friends and critics have called him: "the minister without portfolio," "Rasputin of the American Congress," "the J. Edgar Hoover of the House," "the anchor of the House," "the image of Congress," "the invisible engineer," "the third most arrogant man I ever met," or "not only a great man but a good man." He is likely to be much more than this, but his insistence on a low profile guarantees that we cannot know exactly who he is or what he believes or what he is doing. The only thing that we can know for certain is that he is a power to be reckoned with.

The few academic books on rules barely deal with the parliamentarian's power. Their indexes rarely mention his existence. When he is cited, he is praised as the authority of trust. For instance, Charles Clapp assesses Deschler's power favorably:

> The presence of the parliamentarian in the House chamber when that body is in session and the unobtrusiveness of his assistance to presiding officers as well as congressmen on the floor makes it less important that even legislators entrusted with chairing sessions of the Committee of the Whole be thoroughly steeped in the parliamentary rules of the House.[45]

The almost absolute power that an appointed officer holds over elected representatives is rarely examined. That members have abdicated their responsibility for knowing the tools of their trade —the rules—is not questioned. That the parliamentarian's unobtrusiveness could still be a kind of incredible power is not often considered by most academicians.

In sum, Deschler is satisfied with the rules as they were before the Legislative Reorganization Acts of 1946 and 1970. He prefers the old *status quo*. Members of the Legislative Reorganization Subcommittee of the Rules Committee, which drafted the 1970 act, have seen their intentions twisted by Deschler. He opposed the provision in the 1970 act that authorized recorded teller votes in the Committee of the Whole. He opposed the reform measure that allows members to cosponsor pieces of legislation. And he opposed almost any change in House organization and procedure. He opposed the limitation of standing committees in 1946. In their place, Deschler says, are now hundreds of subcommittees. In the preface to the Ninety-second Congress edition of the *House Manual*, Deschler gave the House rules unqualified praise:

> Today they are perhaps the most finely adjusted, scientifically balanced, and highly technical rules of any parliamentary body in the world. Under them a majority may work its will at all times in the face of the most determined and vigorous opposition of a minority.

The rules *are* highly technical, they *may* be finely adjusted, but they are certainly not scientifically balanced. But the more important issue is how these rules are interpreted and applied and who can have access to them. They are not self-executing. The application of parliamentary rules requires judges who are visible and accountable to a public that has free access to printed, codified rules. There must be publicly available copies of their interpretations—the precedents. By closely examining the parliamentarian's job and considering all of the questions of accountability, it is apparent what a tight grip the parliamentarian—regardless of how nonpartisan, thorough, and hard-working he is—can have on Congress and the laws it enacts.

It must be recognized that two factors have contributed to the parliamentarian's immense influence: the parliamentarian's drive for power and the members' failure to utilize their own rights to meet their own needs. It is the great majority of the members of the House who have failed to adequately recognize the importance of the precedents, and who have failed to find ways to overcome the parliamentarian's ingrained reluctance to make his work public. It is up to members of the House to follow through on their several requests that the parliamentarian also codify the precedents. They can no longer allow themselves to be bound by unwritten congressional rules of courtesy that inhibit them from challenging the parliamentarian for not completing the task assigned to him—the codification of the precedents from 1936 to the present.

THE SENATE'S MEDICINE MAN

Dr. Floyd Riddick inherited his focal position at the hub of legislative procedures from the first official parliamentarian of the Senate, Charles L. Watkins, in 1965. And, with a nod from the secretary of the Senate,* Riddick will choose his own successor, most likely from among his three assistants, when he retires.

After earning a Ph.D. in political science from Duke University in 1935, Riddick served as a statistical analyst for the Rural Resettlement Administration, an instructor of political science at American University, a legislative analyst for the United States Chamber of Commerce, and a Senate editor of the *Daily Digest*. He assisted Watkins for thirteen years before becoming parliamentarian himself. Parliamentarian Riddick is every bit Deschler's counterpart in guarding a treasure; he possesses the only set of complete precedents of the United States Senate. This world's only set is kept in files in the parliamentarian's office. The precedents are filed and cross-filed by subject. Senators do not have access to these files, except to ask a few questions relevant to their daily needs. *Senate Procedure*, a book Riddick coauthored with Watkins, contains only *selected* precedents to 1964† (and it

* The secretary of the Senate is appointed by the majority party for the duration of its stay in power. Riddick says that the secretary of the Senate asks for parliamentary points, but he does not influence or even ask about the parliamentarian's rulings.
† The foreword to Watkins and Riddick divides precedents into two classes—those with no prefixes (which carry the most weight) and those

has not been updated). Riddick denies that the complete precedents are inaccessible:

> We're not trying to keep the precedents secret. We have the
> precedents but they've just never been printed. The 1964
> volume cites all these precedents and you can go read them.
> If you question a ruling, you would go read them in the
> [*Congressional*] *Record* anyway. The rest are notes to sus-
> tain us.[46]

While Riddick is not restricted by specific Senate rules defining
his position as parliamentarian, his powers do not equal
Deschler's. Like Deschler, he guards the organized, complete
precedents, but unlike Deschler, he does not have the shield of the
speaker's office protecting him from the onslaught of any attacking knights of the House. Riddick must ride with a number of
knights, who sometimes agree upon little more than that they are
the powers-that-be. As a result, he avoids making decisions in
controversial areas.

On the Senate floor, Riddick formally speaks through the president of the Senate (the Vice-President), who usually attends just
those sessions where a tie vote, which he has the authority to
break, might occur. The president pro tem, who sits in the absence of the president of the Senate, is not prone to while away
hours in the chair either. So, as often as not, the Senate parliamentarian is speaking through the acting presidents pro tempore
of the Senate, a position that rotates among freshman members.
Riddick is virtually a ventriloquist in such instances, whereas a
compilation of precedents handily indexed could give the members the tools they need to act independently.

Obviously, no power rests with acting presidents pro tempore,
unless they know the rules as the parliamentarian does. Otherwise, he makes their decisions for them. The powers-that-be who

---

with "see" or "see also." Those without prefixes are rulings of the chair on
points of order (whether appealed or not). Those with "see" or "see also"
are responses to parliamentary inquiries.

might set limits on the parliamentarian are more often the Senate committee chairmen, the party leaders, and the handful of senators who are experts on the rules.

It is these men in power who help Riddick use the other important part of his power—referring bills to committee. Even though the 1970 Legislative Reorganization Act set out the jurisdictions of Congress' committees, some bills do not neatly fall into one particular jurisdiction. Riddick says that he consults with the powers-that-be on these occasions. After advising the chairmen, he lets them hash out their territorial boundaries; then he recommends that the Senate refer the bill by unanimous consent. So Riddick avoids controversy by not assigning such bills on his own.*

Deschler says that, as House parliamentarian, he plays a part much earlier in the process of referral, however, by consulting with staffers and members about "where a bill might go if . . ." or "what can and cannot be done." Riddick says that he refers bills on the "predominance of the subject matter," so these consultations test whether the bill's short title and description will send it to the committee desired. After the bill has been introduced, committee chairmen let Riddick know about their "interest" in a bill, in hopes that the bill will come their way.

In addition to Riddick's powers to refer bills to committees and to command the only complete set of Senate precedents is his right of interpretation, his rulings, on the Senate floor. Riddick is aware that his knowledge gives him an edge: "No one might know what [a precedent] is, unless they were there at the time. There are a lot of double-edged swords: all kinds of angles and you must know them." In any kind of ambiguous procedural problem on the floor, then, the parliamentarian can lift the sword and place it on one side or another of a question. Riddick de-

---

* Such fragmentation of bills presents problems later, for each committee turns out its own bill. Staff members then do groundwork trying to negotiate whose bill will become an amendment or whether Congress will simply pass two or three separate bills to cover one problem.

scribed his expertise in locating the right precedents by saying that he had "a feel for it like fishing." At the 1965 hearings before the Joint Committee on the Organization of Congress, reform-minded Senators Clifford Case (R., N.J.) and Joseph Clark (D., Pa.) testified that the parliamentarian's interpretations might sometimes be affected by his deference to the more prestigious Senate leaders.[47]

The parliamentarian's power to make rulings is subject to appeal by members of Congress. But rarely has a parliamentarian's decision been overnturned.* In his six years as Riddick's assistant, Bob Dove has seen a yearly average of six or seven appeals from the ruling of the chair, but he has seen Riddick overruled only once. Appeals from rulings are rare, for they are not considered to be a "courteous" procedure, according to the informal rules of Congress. The appeals procedure provides that a senator who disagrees with a ruling may appeal the ruling, argue his case to his colleagues, and let the forces of reason, truth, and justice produce the correct answer. But in practice, members are not always equipped with enough information to be able to appeal effectively. Nor have they equipped themselves through legislation: they have not even ordered their parliamentarian, as the House did, to codify the precedents; they have authorized or appropriated less than seven thousand dollars to enable their parliamentarian to complete such a task. (Of course, the House has not seen full results of its orders.) Consequently, without spending days to search back issues of the *Congressional Record*, where precedents are set down as they happened, a member of the Senate has little prospect for victory over the chair's rulings, the parliamentarian's words. Clark summed it up at the 1965 hearings:

---

* The parliamentarians' rulings are technically the rulings of the speaker or the presiding officer since those officers can make their own decisions if they choose to ignore the parliamentarian. Decisions of the speaker or presiding officers can be overturned by a vote of two-thirds of the members present.

This is a comment that may be unpopular among parliamentarians, but I do think they exercise a kind of tyranny based upon a rather mechanical approach to the interpretation of rules. I know we are scared to death of our Parliamentarian. I suspect that you are, too, in the other body [the House]. They exercise an authority which I do not think is sound. There are not always Members of either body who are going to make themselves familiar with the rules that they can stand up and argue with the Parliamentarian if they think he is rendering a decision which is not entirely correct.[48]

Without simple access to the codified precedents, senators and their staffs have grown dependent upon the parliamentarian's office to advise them on procedure. These consultations are virtually mandatory if senators want their bills to go to the most favorable committee or to be victorious on the floor. At Dr. Riddick's office, senators may discuss their own legislation in the draft stage to assure its committee assignment, and they may ask questions about proper maneuvers on the floor to get their work passed or to stop someone else's legislation.

But indications are that he does not dispense information equally: some senators must ask very specific questions to get a usable response, while others may ask very open-ended questions. And, except for his rulings through the chair, Riddick does not make note of his advice, he explains, so no one can say "but you told me such and such." When senators complain to him after a parliamentary outcome on the floor, he says he is able to reply that the issue has changed since the time of the consultation. Riddick also tries "to avoid absolutes until the issue actually comes up on the Senate floor—I cannot always give a clear-cut answer."

Dr. Riddick and his staff do not count senators' consultations as a form of lobbying to get a favorable parliamentary decision on the floor. But when asked if senators try to lobby him, Riddick wryly replied, "They want to win their case."

All in all, consultations with Riddick are important, if only to give senators a sense of parliamentary security. Carey Parker, legislative assistant to Senator Edward M. Kennedy (D., Mass.), summarized the power of the parliamentarian's advice: "If you know the parliamentarian, you're two-thirds of the way home on any [floor] fight, though it helps to know the parliamentary points."

STRONG PRESCRIPTIONS

Senators have rarely publicly questioned the parliamentarian's right to hand out advice piecemeal in lieu of printing the codified precedents—only Clark and Case did so at the 1965 hearings, and Senate Resolution 75, passed in 1965, excluded consideration of the rules, procedure, and precedents of the Senate from the jurisdiction of the investigating Joint Committee on the Organization of Congress, whose recommendations eventually led to the 1970 legislative reorganization and House rules reforms. The parliamentarian, unhampered by Senate rules to limit his duties, has the power to offer solution upon solution to a procedural problem. The rules and precedents of the Senate, which he alone delivers through the chair, sometimes cause surprise by their seeming arbitrary appearance on the floor. At the 1965 hearings, Senator Clark likened the situation to "a real Augean stable in terms of the kind of nutty—and I use the word advisedly—precedents, outdated, having no real relationship to the modern world, by which we tie ourselves up in knots."[49]

In selecting a precedent and delivering it to the chair's attention, the parliamentarian rules. Even if he chooses not to rule—that is, to let the Senate decide for itself—he is wielding a kind of power. The ways he has handled Senate Rule XVI provide examples of this power: his choices, or failure to choose, have affected the fate of amendments on sending jets to Israel; increasing funds for the Antitrust Division of the Justice Department; and increasing funds for the Civil Rights Commission. In each case, the amendments brought up on the floor faced points of order. But each faced a different kind of debate over Rule XVI.

Rule XVI, Clause 1, states that no appropriations bills can be allowed if they are greater than what was authorized, *except* in three cases: (1) if the bill is "made to carry out the provisions of some existing law, or treaty stipulation, or act, or resolution previously passed by the Senate during that session"; or (2) if "the same be moved by direction of a standing or select committee of the Senate"; or (3) if the bill has been "proposed in pursuance of an estimate submitted in accordance with law." As carried out on the floor, this rule provides the Senate parliamentarian with discretionary powers. Riddick may decide whether an increase in appropriations fits any of these three exceptions.

When questions about this rule arise, Riddick says, he decides "by sitting in counsel with the staff and study[ing] the matter." He explains that Rule XVI means "you can't change the law by increasing appropriations. You can restrict, but that is not considered changing the law." If a bill restricts appropriations already authorized at a higher figure, it still raises problems. According to Riddick, "If the restriction says, 'None of the funds may be used for X purpose,' then it's O.K. If it says, 'All but Y amount may not be used for X purpose,' then there are problems and I must examine the situation."*

Here are three cases where the Senate parliamentarian has ruled on the exceptions in Rule XVI that permit appropriations increases from the floor.

Case One: Riddick stood aside from a senatorial battle and avoided making a decision on a point of order on November 23, 1971.

Senator Henry Jackson (D., Wash.) had introduced an amend-

---

* According to the *Senate Manual*, no amendments may be placed on appropriations bills that have the effects of "legislating" (Rule XVI). But the boundary between "restricting" and "legislating" is fuzzy. The parliamentarian judged that Senator Curtis' (R., Nebr.) amendment to the 1972 Occupational Health and Safety Bill was a restriction and therefore acceptable. Yet this amendment set new policy, for it provided that no funds could be used for inspecting, regulating, or controlling employers with fewer than fifteen employees. It had the effect of legislating that these employers would not be subject to federal health and safety regulations.

ment to the 1972 Department of Defense Appropriations bill. This amendment, proposing to appropriate funds for the sale of jets to Israel, was presented as an extension of previous legislation:

> Sec. 901. For expenses, not otherwise provided for, necessary to enable the President to finance sales, credit sales, and guarantees of defense articles and defense services to Israel, as authorized by section 501 of Public Law 91–441 (84 Stat. 909), $500,000,000 including $250,000,000 for sales, credit sales, and guarantees of F-4 Phantom aircraft to Israel.[50]

Senator Allen Ellender (D., La.) raised a point of order challenging Jackson's amendment; he argued that a more recent law, the Foreign Military Sales Act of 1971, took precedence:

> Section 10(a): Notwithstanding any provision of law enacted before the date of enactment of this section, no money appropriated for foreign assistance shall be available for obligation or expenditure unless the appropriation thereof has been previously authorized by law.

Jackson used a "Memorandum for the Parliamentarian," written by Hugh C. Evans, senior counsel for the Office of Legislative Counsel, to support his case that the amendment was in order. Senator J. W. Fulbright (D., Ark.) challenged Jackson's interpretation of the legal passage upon which the amendment had been justified. Fulbright argued that a key phrase meant an "authorization to transfer funds," where Jackson took it to mean an "authorization for appropriations."

Rather than decide between the arguments, the chair ruled as follows:

> The Chair is aware and has carefully studied the memorandum of the senior legislative counsel supporting the contention that section 501 is authorization for an appropriation such as this. However, the Chair would point out that the point of order is addressed to an interpretation of the law.

> The Chair knows of no provision or precedent authorizing
> the Presiding Officer to interpret the law.[51]

The Senate accepted Jackson's arguments, failed to sustain Ellender's point of order, and went on to pass the whole appropriations bill.

Case Two: On June 15, 1972, Senator John Tunney (D.,
Calif.) used the precedent of Jackson's amendment to argue on
behalf of his amendment to the 1972 Appropriations Bill for the
Departments of State, Justice, and Commerce, the Judiciary and
related agencies. The Antitrust Division of the Justice Department, Tunney argued, needed an extra two million dollars to
enforce antitrust laws. Senators Muskie, McGovern, Kennedy,
Mondale, and Humphrey, all Democrats, spoke in favor of his
amendment on the floor. But Senator Marlow Cook (R., Ky.)
raised a point of order that the amendment violated Rule XVI.
The parliamentarian decided that the precedent set in the Israel
jet case was not sufficient to sustain the proposed increase. The presiding officer ruled:

> The Chair is advised that this amount proposed is in excess
> of the budget estimates and is not authorized by law. There-
> fore, under rule XVI, paragraph 1, the amendment is not in
> order. The point of order is sustained.[52]

Tunney used his right to appeal the ruling of the chair. A "terribly bad precedent" would be set, Tunney declared, if the
ruling of the chair was sustained. First, in spite of the chair's
ruling to the contrary, "there has been an authorization in setting
up the Department of Justice, in setting up a system where we
have an assistant attorney general for the Antitrust Division, and
where we have passed the Sherman Antitrust Act, the Clayton
Antitrust Act, the Robinson-Patman Act—all designed to enforce
the antitrust policy of this country." Second, the chair's ruling
"would mean that the decision of the Appropriations Committee
on the size of the budget for any executive department is always

final." Cook argued that precedents would be shattered if Tunney won his appeal, for it would reverse the normal order of appropriations bills—putting changes in too late, where they could have been made at the proper time on the original bill. Tunney lost his appeal 51 to 17. (Rarely do the members of Congress override chair-parliamentarian decisions.)

Case Three: In 1971 Senator Philip Hart (D., Mich.) introduced an amendment to increase the Civil Rights Commission appropriation by $560,000. This amount exceeded what had been authorized, Senator John McClellan (D., Ark.) warned. Hart based his case on the third exception clause of Rule XVI that reads "or proposed in pursuance of an estimate submitted in accordance with law." Hart inferred that an increase may be in excess of the existing authorization if it is within the president's budget estimate, and he read a letter from Charles Schultz, Director of the President's Bureau of the Budget, as confirmation that the increase met this criterion. If one cannot exceed the existing authorization, Hart reasoned, there would be no need to have this exception to the rule. This time the chair, with Riddick's aid, ruled as follows:

> The Chair feels that the language cited by the Senator from Michigan as the exception in Rule XVI, "or proposed in pursuance of an estimate submitted in accordance with law," would be language that would come into play if the authorization was, perhaps, for the Department of Defense in giving it duties and saying it should have those funds as shall be necessary and required to carry out its duties. In that instance, estimates would be submitted in accordance with law. But in the act in force here, we have a specific appropriation with specific language. The authorization was for $3.4 million. That is further referred to, as stated by the Senator from West Virginia, in the budget estimate itself, when it says, "Additional authorizing appropriations will be proposed in the amount of $400,000." That is the language before the Congress, and there would be no need for the

additional authorizing legislation at all if the amendment would be in order.[53]

Riddick's ruling through the chair directly contradicted numerous precedents. By this ruling, the third exception of Clause 1 of Rule XVI was negated, for it made the budget estimate dependent upon the authorization clause. The history of Rule XVI shows that the exception clauses have been kept separate and distinct:

> an amendment to make an appropriation is in order, if it is authorized by law *or* submitted pursuant to a budget estimate. [Emphasis added.][54]

Riddick's decision determined the amount of FY 1972 appropriations for a government agency, the Civil Rights Commission.*

Another procedural question—the interpretation of the unanimous consent agreement—gives the parliamentarian powerful leverage. During the Rhodesian chrome debate, opponents to Fulbright's position made a motion to reconsider the bill after it passed. The tactic threw the Fulbright forces into disarray, what few were left on the floor—the rest had left the building thinking they had won. Senator Kennedy made a parliamentary inquiry on behalf of Fulbright's side of the controversy. He asked the chair whether the motion to reconsider was debatable. The chair ruled:

> Under the unanimous-consent agreement, where time has been agreed to, there would not be additional time for debate on the motion to reconsider.[55]

Next, Kennedy inquired whether the unanimous-consent agreement applied just to the amendment or to the amendment and any motion to reconsider. And the chair ruled:

* Hart had introduced his amendment to increase the commission's funds with these words:

> Mr. President, one of the most effective ways of thwarting progress in this Nation, and of suggesting to the American people that we in the Federal government lack sincerity in trying to do something about the problems confronting us, is to deny adequate funds to those agencies given the responsibility for moving us forward. (*Congressional Record*, July 19, 1971, p. 11461.)

The purpose of the unanimous-consent agreement would be to limit time on the final consideration of amendments. Otherwise, there would be no purpose for the unanimous-consent agreement. A quorum call would be in order, but no further debate.[56]

Only when it was too late, after the result of a vote on the motion to reconsider, which Fulbright's side lost by one vote, did Fulbright locate the right passage in the Watkins and Riddick book to show that the chair had ruled incorrectly:

I happen to think, according to my rule book, that the Chair misinterpreted the parliamentary inquiry a moment ago with regard to debate on a motion to reconsider. His ruling, I think, is not in accord with at least the rule book I have before me, which on page 687 of my book states: "A unanimous consent agreement limiting debate on a bill and amendments does not apply to a motion to reconsider the vote on an amendment."[57]

The parliamentarian's decision in this case was not the result of researching the precedents or interpreting the rules. It was a value judgment as to which precedent should apply. It demonstrates the discretionary powers of the parliamentarian and their effects on the course of legislation. It shows the members fumbling to locate rules so that they might argue with the chair. And it illustrates the weakness of using parliamentary inquiry in the place of outright point of order to test challengers.

One further example of how the parliamentarian profoundly affected the legislation that Congress passed: on February 24, 1972, a dramatic moment unfolded over the order of debate and votes on amendments to the Higher Education Act of 1965 and the Vocational Education Act of 1963. Senators Mansfield, Scott, Mondale, Griffin, and Allen had proposed amendments dealing with the degree to which school children should be bused. Senators Mansfield and Scott bid to be recognized ahead of Griffin. The chair's decision would favor the first amendment to be recognized, because the first amendment that is passed precludes consideration of the others. To persuade the chair to recognize the Senate majority leader first, Senator Mansfield cited precedents, back through common law, where the majority leader of the English House of Commons was always recognized first. The chair did accept Mansfield's right to be recognized first, and thereby the debate and vote upon the Mansfield-Scott amendment came first.

For a moment several southern senators vied for the chair's attention, in hopes of delaying the rush into debating the Mansfield-Scott amendment. But the chair recognized only the Mansfield-Scott team, and Scott immediately began debate on the amendment. He would not stop to allow parliamentary inquiries until he could describe the nature of the amendment. Critics on the floor labeled the whole legislative procedure—the order of amendments, the nature of the amendment, the refusal to yield to a parliamentary inquiry—"strong-arm tactics." Following the debate on the busing issue, the Mansfield-Scott amendment passed.

From Senator Allen's vantage point, the chair should have followed an entirely different order of amendments:

> An antibusing amendment was introduced, and then a probusing amendment was introduced by the Senator from Pennsylvania and the Senator from Montana. Then an antibusing amendment was offered by the distinguished Senator from Michigan (Mr. Griffin), and then a probusing amendment was offered by the distinguished Senator from Minnesota (Mr. Mondale).
>
> You would think, Mr. President, that in order that no attempt would be made by the leadership to get recognition the next time because recognition had been alternated—antibusing, pro busing, antibusing, pro busing—you would think, Mr. President, that the Presiding Officer would have recognized an antibusing Senator, the Senator from Michigan (Mr. Griffin), to offer the last amendment; but I guess there are some prerogatives of leadership in the Senate.[58]

Allen, who opposed busing, gave the Senate his interpretation of the precedent that recognized the Senate leadership first:

> Possibly I have been under an illusion that these prerogatives were exercised with regard to general legislation and not exercised with regard to legislation or proposed legislation in which the leadership had a definite interest by reason of sponsorship of the legislation.

The minority, the antibusing senators on this day, was upset about the way the Senate leadership had used the rules. Senator David Gambrell (D., Ga.) got the minority's dismay across with humor. He took Senator Scott's word from a national interview— Scott had said that Congress would "waffle" on the busing issue— and applied it to the procedure Mansfield and Scott used to get their amendment up first:

> It was my impression, from watching the parliamentary procedure here, that waffling was where the joint leadership caught the distinguished Senator from Michigan (Mr. Griffin) between themselves and the chair.[59]

As an appointed, not elected, official; as the chief adviser to the chair on parliamentary order and procedure; as the comptroller of the official precedents, never published in complete, codified form; and as the most informed consultant on parliamentary matters, Dr. Floyd Riddick is a very powerful Senate official. But for a number of reasons Riddick is not as powerful as Deschler:

· He has ruled ten years as parliamentarian (and thirteen as assistant parliamentarian); Deschler has ruled forty-six years as parliamentarian (and two as assistant parliamentarian).
· He has no constant leader like the speaker of the House to protect himself and the chair from motions to overrule.
· He has fewer precedents to watch over, about one-fourth those of the House.

· He has a slightly smaller, less centrally located staff than the House parliamentarian.

But like Deschler, Riddick holds these powers, among many:

· He is, of course, not answerable to the American public through the election process or through exposure in testimony before a Congressional committee.
· He has the only official codified set of Senate precedents in the world.
· He is an invisible power, remaining anonymous.
· His job has not been clearly defined by Senate rules.
· Few recognize how powerful his position is.

A few proposals have been suggested to whittle down the parliamentarian's duties, and therefore his power. For one, Senator Clark proposed to the Joint Committee on the Organization of Congress in 1965 that all the Senate precedents be cast aside:

> The Presiding Officer shall construe these rules so as to give effect to their plain meaning. Precedents and rulings in force prior to the adoption of these rules shall not be binding in the construction of these rules.[60]

But so far, Clark's comparatively radical proposal has not been accepted—or even debated on the Senate floor. When reminded of Clark's proposal, Riddick said, "Clark and I didn't always agree." Riddick explained that precedents are needed to interpret rules. For example, Riddick said, when does a roll call begin? When the chair has so ordered? When the clerk calls the first name? When the first member has responded? A precedent is required to give the rule meaning.

A second proposal can be found in the study done by the Senate Subcommittee on Computer Services on the feasibility of putting legislative records on computers. The report suggests that the automation of the parliamentarian's precedent file is worth future investigation. The subcommittee's purpose, however, was to "permit the Parliamentarian to provide more rapid response to the Chair in matters requiring advisement,"[61] rather than to make the precedents available to all senators and their staffs.

In the meantime, Dr. Floyd Riddick answers to "the powers that be" and hands out advice to rank-and-file senators as he judges most fair. He does not use his power in a partisan way. Rather, his philosophy of avoiding controversy and sudden changes in the interpretation of rules pervades his parliamentary decisions. His is the power of the *status quo*, just like Deschler's. Officials who so directly and significantly affect the substance of legislation must be visible and accountable to the public.

In 1927, after the House adopted a resolution to create an office of assistant parliamentarian, Speaker Longworth described the increasing responsibilities of the parliamentarian:

> The duties of the Parliamentarian of this House are many and various, and they are among the most important duties performed by any man in the Capitol. They are growing daily; they are becoming more important and multifarious, and the situation at present is that it is almost impossible for one man to do all the routine work necessary; and, more important still, if that man resigns or anything should happen to him, there is no one qualified to take his place. We have been very fortunate, I think, certainly during the time I have been in Congress, in always having capable parliamentarians, none of whom resigned or died suddenly or were ill for a day, so that there has been time to train another man to fill that position. However, I do not exaggerate when I say no man, however able he may be, can in less than two years of intense study become entirely capable of fully carrying out the duties of the Parliamentarian.[62]

Since Longworth spoke, parliamentarians in both houses have become even more busy. Their staffs have grown, and they have trained assistants. And they both now have substantive decision-making powers.

Now that the House and Senate parliamentarians near their retirement, Congress should reassess the role of parliamentarians. Should unelected officials—no matter how ethical and honest they have been—make *substantive* legislative decisions? Should they alone hold the world's only complete set of precedents? Should they be able to continue the traditions of anonymity and consultation as means of remaining out of public view while advising on procedures to get legislation through Congress?

3

Twentieth-Century Lords and Fiefdoms: Chairmen and Their Committees

Officially the House and Senate legislate, but in reality they do little more than approve or disapprove what the committees respectively report to them.

— *Floyd Riddick*, Congressional Procedure*

The standing committees are the vital organs of Congress and their chairmen are the dominant voices.

Committees hold this pre-eminent position as a result of the congressional practice of referring all bills to committee for hearing.† Every year torrents of bills (25,354 in the Ninety-second

---

* Boston: Chapman and Grimes, 1941, p. 112.
† Parliamentarian Lewis Deschler's annotation of Jefferson's *Manual*, Section 446, says: "In the House of Representatives, it is a general rule that all business goes to committees before receiving consideration in the House

Congress) swamp Congress. In addition to this workload, there are many problems—often technical—requiring highly specialized knowledge and investigation. In response to this inundation, Congress uses committees to channel its concerns, to filter out unnecessary or ill-advised matters, and to refine needed legislation.

This flood of proposals forces Congress not simply to use committees but to rely on them heavily. Since even legislators of boundless energy cannot hope to research the thousands of bills introduced, they must rely on the committees for expertise. In addition, members are dependent upon other committees for legislation of local interest to constituents—air bases, dams, roads, and the like.

Congress does not affirm every committee decision. But the committees' negative powers are nearly absolute: the bills they do not report to the floor usually die.

To overturn a committee's negative judgment, members of Congress have only a few tools at hand. The Senate can attach a committee-buried bill to legislation already on the floor. In the House, however, this countermeasure is stymied by the rule that

---

itself. Occasionally a question of privilege or minor matter of business is presented and considered at once by the House." House Rule XI, "The Powers and Duties of Committees," reads: "All   proposed legislation, messages, petitions, memorials, and other matters relating to the subject listed under the [twenty-one] standing committees . . . shall be referred to such committees, respectively."

Senate Rule XXV, "Standing Committees," reads: "The following standing committees shall be appointed at the commencement of each Congress, with leave to report by bill or otherwise." But Senate Rule XIV, Clause 3, does not require that all bills be referred to a standing committee: "No bill or joint resolution shall be committed or amended until it shall have been twice read, after which it *may be* referred to a committee." (Emphasis added.)

According to Larry Baskir, aide for Senator Sam Erwin's Subcommittee on Constitutional Rights, one senator can block a bill from going to committee by objecting to its automatic referral the day it is introduced. But it takes an extraordinary reason and the support of the leadership to be successful. (Interview July 5, 1972.)

riders must be germane to the main bill.* Groups of senators can also try to pressure a committee through multiple sponsorship of a bill. The list of sponsors is designed to impress the committee with the quantity of floor support. Formally, the House puts some restrictions on this move, but representatives can accomplish the same end—with considerable waste—by each supporter introducing the same bill independently.† In all, little in the way of committee power over legislation has changed since Woodrow Wilson observed,

> It is evident that there is one principle which runs through every stage of procedure and which is never disallowed or abrogated—the principle that the committees shall rule without let or hindrance. And this is a principle of extraordinary formative power. It is the mold of all legislation.[1]

COMMITTEE ASSIGNMENTS

The methods and criteria used to assign members to standing committees—twenty-one in the House and seventeen in the Senate—are quite important to constituents, members' re-election potential, and national policy-making. Representative Morris Udall could make little use, back on the hustings in landlocked Arizona, of an assignment to Merchant Marine and Fisheries. But if his constituents lack interest in the high seas, they do have one concern about water: they do not have enough. For Udall to promote his electorate's needs, he has to land a position on the Interior and Insular Affairs Committee. Representative Pierre S. DuPont

* Jefferson's *Manual*, Section 495, once provided for House riders: "When an essential provision has been omitted, rather than erase the bill and render it suspicious, they add a clause on a separate paper, engrossed and called a rider, which is read and put to the question three times." But Parliamentarian Deschler's annotation of this section says, "This practice is never followed in the House of Representatives."
† House Rule XXII, authorized by H.R. 42 on April 25, 1967, puts a limit on sponsorship: "Two or more but not more than twenty-five members may introduce jointly any bill, memorial, or resolution to which this paragraph applies."

IV, a Republican from Delaware, arrived in Washington with strong feelings about drug abuse. For him to take significant action in this area, he had to find a seat on the House Interstate and Foreign Commerce Committee. Representative Bella Abzug wanted an opportunity to represent women constituents by winning a position on the House Armed Services Committee:

> One of the basic reasons I'm claiming a right to a seat on the [House] Armed Services Committee is that I'm a woman. A woman hasn't served on it since Margaret Chase Smith, and that was twenty-one years ago. . . . Do you realize that there are 42,000 women in the military? Do you realize that about half of the civilian employees of the Defense Department are women—290,000 of them at last count? And if that isn't enough there are one-and-a-half million wives of military personnel.[2]

Udall got assigned to Interior and Insular Affairs. DuPont, however, did not get the spot he sought in the Ninety-second Congress. And Bella Abzug was assigned to Government Operations and Public Works instead of the committee she had requested.

How were these assignments made? Most members have no concrete idea. When asked how he ended up with seats on the Merchant Marine and Fisheries Committee and on the Foreign Affairs Committee, Representative DuPont explained, "Assignment of committees is a mystic process. It's one of the most important things that happens to you as a legislator and before you know what's happened to you, it's over."

Altogether four unofficial committees, called committees on committees, determine *standing committee* assignments and reassignments of those who want to transfer from one standing committee to another.* Two of these committees—one Republi-

---

* Every session some members are dissatisfied with the seats they previously held and want to transfer. (See Appendix 2 for a list of transfers to and from the standing committees. Those with the lowest number of transfers away indicate what members consider to be the most desirable or influential committees to be on.) The party leader has almost absolute independence in assigning members to joint, special, and select committees; commissions; and international delegations.

can and one Democratic—are in the House and two in the Senate. They meet in closed session; their deliberations and the reasons behind their decisions remain known only to themselves.[3] Final committee assignments become public record, but otherwise, these committees exercise their great power undisturbed even by Congressional scrutiny.

All four committees-on-committees have no official status. Congress never voted them into creation. Congress did not adopt a rule assigning them to their task. Rather, they are only the creation of each of the major parties in each chamber.

Nor do the various committees-on-committees fill a rules vacuum. Each house of Congress has rules that lay out other procedures for selecting committee members. Since 1884, Senate standing Rule XXIV has provided:

> The Senate, unless otherwise ordered, shall proceed by ballot
> to appoint generally the chairman of each committee, and
> then, by one ballot, the other members necessary to com-
> plete the same.

The rule clearly states that the Senate shall entertain nominations for the chairmanships, and then elect them and their committee members.

But a citizen in the Senate gallery would hear nothing on the Senate floor vaguely resembling this activity. Instead, the majority leader presents a resolution listing all majority committee assignments and chairmanships. "Is there objection to consideration of the resolution?" the president pro tem intones. After the silence which invariably follows, the resolution is adopted. The minority leader then submits the minority assignments with the identical results. The president pro tem does not call for nominations for each chairman. No senator endorses a candidate. Neither committees nor chairmen are considered individually. The Senate does not even trouble to vote on the assignments.

The Senate is able to void the intent of Rule XXIV by invoking its loophole clause: "unless otherwise ordered." The loophole has become the only operative part of the rule. The Senate no longer bothers to suspend the regular order of the rule before submitting the resolution.

Requests to honor the intent of the rule are rare. When there was such an attempt at the beginning of the Ninety-second Congress, it produced mild confusion and surprise. The majority leader had just submitted the resolution when Senator Fred Harris (D., Okla.) addressed the chair:

> Under Rule XXIV, if a Senator requests it, will there be individual votes on the several chairmen, individually and separately?
>
> PRESIDENT PRO TEM: When the resolution is adopted, it is acted upon as a whole.
>
> HARRIS: Mr. President, a further parliamentary inquiry? . . . Does not Rule XXIV provide that there be a vote by ballot on each of the chairmen, if that is requested by a Senator?
>
> PRESIDENT PRO TEM: If it is demanded, of course.
>
> HARRIS: That can be by voice vote.
>
> PRESIDENT PRO TEM: Yes.
>
> HARRIS: Mr. President, I do so require, saying in advance that I do not intend to vote against any chairman, but I do think it is important to point up this procedure for the future. No effort has been made by anyone to make a case against any individual chairman, but I think the procedure is important. . . . To point up the fact that the Senate does elect its chairmen and is responsible for them, and they to the Senate, I think this procedure should be undertaken.
>
> I do require, if I may, under Rule XXIV, an individual vote on each chairman listed in the resolution.

Then Mike Mansfield, the majority leader, admitted that he

> had not anticipated that this would come up in this fashion. . . .
>
> The Senator, of course, as the Chair has indicated, is perfectly within his right. . . . But I wonder whether the two Senators at this time would consider the possibility of a

unanimous-consent request that all the chairmen be voted on en bloc.

Mr. HARRIS: Let me say, Mr. President, that I do not think it would take long to put those individual questions to the Senate. I certainly do not intend to surprise the majority leader. . . .

The majority leader withdrew his request. A voice vote was taken. Apparently, no dissenting voices were heard, not even from the Republican side.[4] (By precedent, each party stays out of the other party's affairs.) When the minority committee assignments were submitted the following day, the Senate resumed its customary procedure. So much for the powers of pure custom.

The rules of the House pose even more obstacles to reform. Standing Rule X, Clause 1 stipulates that the lower chamber's standing committees "shall be elected by the House." Rule X, Clause 4 adds, "at the commencement of each Congress, the House shall elect as chairman of each standing committee one of the members thereof." Unlike the Senate rule, these have no loophole through which the camel can pass. The House, therefore, has interpreted these rules piecemeal in rulings (precedents) until true election of committee members has become impossible. By precedent, the House—like the Senate—may consider in one resolution committee members and their chairmen. Unlike the Senate, the resolution is indivisible, so that the House has no alternative but to consider all chairmen and members en bloc. Attempting separate votes by permitting amendments to the resolution is also out of order.[5] Even debate on the slate cannot be accomplished unless the sponsor of the resolution cooperates.

One attempt to return to the basic spirit of the House rules on appointments of committee chairmen and members was made at the beginning of the Ninety-second Congress.* Insurgent Demo-

---

* In Jefferson's *Manual*, "Every Committee [has] a right to elect their own chairman." Deschler's annotation of Jefferson's *Manual*, Section 317, explains how chairmen get their positions: "Prior to the Sixty-second Congress, standing as well as select committees and their chairmen were ap-

crats tried in caucus to oust John McMillan (D., S.C.) from the chairmanship of the District of Columbia Committee. When this failed, Jerome Waldie (D., Calif.) was determined to force a floor fight on the challenge.

To permit debate, Wilbur Mills, chairman of the House Democratic Committee on Committees, first introduced the resolution naming the committee appointments. He then moved to suspend the reading of the resolution. Waldie then presented his plan. He explained that to defeat a single chairman, the House would first have to defeat Mills' entire resolution—that is, it would have to refuse to appoint any Democrat to any committee or chairmanship. The original resolution would then return to the Democratic Committee on Committees for a new recommendation for the chairmanship of the District of Columbia. Waldie did not actually suggest that the House implement Rule X, Clause 4 and elect its chairmen. He was instead attempting to defeat one chairman within the restrictive confines of the rule's present interpretation. But the slightest chance that the Waldie proposals would eventually revive the rule horrified the House leadership. Hale Boggs, the majority leader, asked Waldie whether he agreed

> that we would be establishing a precedent here that could be carried to any length and in truth and in fact, if the majority party voted unanimously we could displace any committee member or every committee member nominated by the minority. . . .
>
> Is it not accurate that if a minority on the Democratic side and a majority on the minority side get together they could take over control over the entire committee system in the House? Is that not correct?

The minority leader, Gerald Ford, also adamantly opposed allowing the House to elect its own committee members:

pointed by the Speaker, but under the present form of Rule X, adopted in 1911 and continued as a part of the Legislative Reorganization Act of 1946, Committees and their respective chairmen are elected by the House."

The Democratic caucus made a decision on a committee chairman. Whether we on our side agree with it or not, by *precedent* that is a matter within the ranks and prerogatives of the majority party. . . . By precedent and otherwise, we on our side should not get into procedures and prerogatives of the majority party. . . .

As Republicans, we should exercise our option to vote "yea" or "present" on the previous question, because the matter is one for the Democrats to decide and not for us.

When the vote was finally taken, the House overwhelmingly endorsed the party leaders' viewpoint and trounced Waldie's proposal 258 to 32.[6]

THE COMMITTEES-ON-COMMITTEES JIGSAW

In place of House Rule X and Senate Rule XXIV, each party in each house has generated its own unwritten procedures for making appointments. All are variations on a basic theme: first, the party leaders jointly determine the size of the committee and the ratio of Democrats to Republicans. Second, the committees on committees each meet to match members with empty seats. Matching committee vacancies with members is a complicated patchwork of factors, some of which are totally divorced from a candidate's merit or competence to do the job. Seniority, party ratio, geographical origin, political safety in future elections, and lobbyists' opinions all enter into committee assignment decisions.

The House has a relatively simple system for determining congressional seniority. Members are ranked by length of service in the House; members who have served equal lengths of time rank alphabetically.

But the Senate's measures of seniority rival the Tax Code in complexity. First, it ranks senators by continuous service, so that a senator who served two terms, lost, then returned will rank during his third term, not with the three-termers, but with the freshmen.[7] Further, the Senate measures congressional seniority to the day. Senators Warren Magnuson (D., Wash.) and J. William Fulbright, for example, were both elected on the same day in 1944, but Senator Magnuson swore the oath of office on December 14, 1944, twenty days before Senator Fulbright, and therefore outranks him. Senator Jacob Javits (R., N.Y.) ranks below all other members of the class of 1956 because he was sworn in six days late. Date of the oath is not always controlling for members elected in a special election or appointed to fill an unexpired term. If election or appointment occurred when the Senate was not in session, for example, then the date of election, or certification of appointment by the governor controls.[8] This special rule allowed former Senator George Murphy (R., Calif.) to give his successor, Senator John Tunney, a head start by resigning before his term ended. Tunney, appointed by Governor Ronald Reagan to serve the last day of Murphy's term, thus ranked ahead of his fellow freshmen by virtue of one day's seniority.

To rank senators sworn the same day, the Senate distinguishes according to previous political experience. Former senators rank first, followed by former governors, then former representatives.[9] Novices bring up the rear. As former Senator Joseph Clark discovered to his chagrin, mayors, even mayors of Philadelphia, are not credited with political experience.[10] Finally, those senators still ranking equally are catalogued either alphabetically, or according to the date their state entered the union, or by lot.[11] When all criteria for ranking have been applied, seniority has transformed the Senate from a body of equals to a hundred-tiered hierarchy.

That seniority is a primary factor in placing members on committees is not surprising. Seniors dominate three of the four committees on committees. In the House, a host of other seniors —deans of state delegations, committee chairmen, and party leaders—play significant roles as power brokers. Nor is it surprising that they perpetuate their own kind of power—seniority of males. In the House, for example, there is evidence that women are being assigned to the Education and Labor Committee rather than the more powerful or influential Judiciary, Rules, or Armed Services committees. Bella Abzug, during the Ninety-second Congress, commented on this phenomenon, which virtually ensures that women will not accede to the chairs of such committees:

> The more I look at this committee system, the more outrageous I realize it is. Of the grand total of twelve women in the House, five have been assigned to the Education and Labor Committee, which, for some reason or other, the gallant men around here are shaping into a female repository. Maybe they figure if they get us all in one place we'll cause less trouble.
>
> Only one woman will serve on the powerful Ways and Means Committee and two on Appropriations. None of us has been assigned to the Rules Committee, the Judiciary Committee,* or, of course, the Armed Services Committee.[12]

Representative Martha W. Griffiths (D., Mich.) has said, "I don't think Congress discriminates against anyone once you get there. All you have to do is to get on a committee and outlive everyone else. It's automatic."[13] Griffiths chairs the Select Committee on the House Beauty Shop. However, Representative Julia Butler Hansen (D., Wash.), who chairs Appropriations' Subcommittee on the Department of the Interior and Related Agencies, has told of a tentative movement against seniority—where a woman is involved:

> The Chairman of the Appropriations Committee went around to ask everyone on the committee if they were sure a woman would do a good job as subcommittee chairman before I was appointed. They did this even though I had more experience than any of them.[14]

---

* In the 93rd Congress, Representatives Elizabeth Holtzman (D., N.Y.) and Barbara Jordan (D., Tex.) were assigned to the House Judiciary Committee.

In making committee assignments, these committees on committees also consider party ratio. By *custom*, all standing committees are bipartisan. Except for two House committees—Ways and Means and Rules—the party ratio on each committee approximates the party ratio of the chamber as a whole. For some years an agreement between the parties has fixed the membership of Ways and Means at 15:10 and Rules at 10:5.[15] However, party leaders generally desire to avoid the unpleasant contingency of bumping a member off a committee;* instead, to satisfy the party ratio, the leaders usually agree to enlarge the committee so that the underrepresented side can be brought up to strength.[16]

Once the committees on committees have determined committee assignments, the appointments for the House are then ratified by the party in a caucus. In the Senate they go straight to the floor.

Senate Republicans

The Senate Republican committee assignment process is the simplest of the four. Its setup has no power brokers and no politicking; lobbyists play no part. But its single criterion—seniority—also fails to appoint members on the basis of interest and competence. Members of the Republican Committee on Committees ask Republican senators in their order of seniority which vacancy they desire to fill, leaving scraps to the juniors.[17] A freshman Republican senator with experience as an urban mayor,

* Senate Rule XXV, clause 6(c) specifies: "By agreement entered into by the majority leader and the minority leader, the membership of one or more of the standing committees . . . may be increased temporarily from time to time by such number or numbers as may be required to accord to the majority party a majority of the membership of all standing committees."

The 1946 Legislative Reorganization Act fixed the total number of members on each committee, but a House resolution can change the number. In the House some committees are regularly more desirable than others, so that party leaders have increased their size to accommodate some who want positions on them. All the appealing committees except Rules and Ways and Means have ballooned in size over the years. (See Appendix 3.)

for example, could get stuck with Veterans' Affairs if a more senior member had taken the last open slot on Banking, Housing, and Urban Affairs.

The Republicans close out all possibility for flexibility by measuring seniority to the most minute detail until no two senators rank equally. In 1972, Charles Percy (Ill.) and Edward Brooke (Mass.) competed for a seat on Foreign Relations. Since both had equal service in the Senate, they flipped a coin.[18] The political judgment of a Jefferson nickel decided that Percy may someday chair one of the Senate's most powerful committees.

Until recently, the Republican system permitted seniors to completely dominate the committee assignments on the "big four" —Foreign Relations, Armed Services, Finance, and Appropriations. Seniors often sat on two and sometimes three of these. Then, in 1959, the Republicans adopted the "Johnson Rule,"* which forbade any Republican senator from taking an additional committee seat before those with only one had gotten their preferred vacancy.[19] While the "Johnson Rule" did not altogether prevent a Republican senior from serving on two major committees, it at least gave juniors a fighting chance.†

In 1971, Senate Republicans took another tentative step toward breaking the fetters of seniority. At the urging of Senator Charles McC. Mathias (R., Md.), they decided that a senator could serve as ranking minority member on only one committee at a time.[20] As a result, Margaret Chase Smith (Me.) and George Aiken (Vt.) each had to surrender their seniority on one committee to retain the top spot on another. This reform did not circumvent seniority since the next most senior member succeeded Aiken and

* The Republicans took Majority Leader Lyndon Johnson's Democratic reform measure (1956) as their model.

† In 1970, the Senate amended Senate Rule XXV to limit senators to service on only one of the big four. In addition, the amendment limited senators to two seats on second-ranking committees. While this reform will spread power more widely in the future, it does not cure past ills, for senators serving on more than one major committee before 1970 were permitted to retain their seats.

Smith, but the move is symbolic of recent dissatisfaction with seniority's hammerlock on committees.

Senate Democrats

On the other side of the aisle, Senate Democrats have a committee on committees called the Steering Committee. Members of the Steering Committee are nominated by the floor leader and hold their positions for the duration of their tenure. Despite recent attempts by Majority Leader Mike Mansfield to give juniors greater representation, the Steering Committee is mostly comprised of seniors. In the Ninety-second Congress, only one of the committee's fifteen members had entered the Senate within the last decade. Including the ex officio members (the Democratic whip and the secretary of the Democratic Conference), the average Senate tenure of Steering Committee members is about seventeen years.

The Steering Committee has full discretion to make committee appointments, subject to approval by the whole caucus. But the composition of the Steering Committee—seniors, often chairmen —may turn discretion from an attribute into a vice. Seven Steering Committee members in the Ninety-second Congress chaired their own committees and were thus in a position to bolster their own power. They can choose appointees who agree solidly with their point of view, and they can make appointees feel indebted for the assignment. For example, former Senator Joseph Clark found that once the "Johnson Rule" opened major committee assignments to juniors, the Steering Committee used these plums to reward juniors who opposed changing the filibuster rule and to punish those who tried to alter it.

Despite the Steering Committee's independent strength, a strong floor leader can bring it under single-person party control. Lyndon Johnson, for instance, had almost incontrovertible influence on committee assignments when he served as majority leader. This power can be abused: as majority leader, Johnson often used the secretary of the Senate, Bobby Baker, as a conduit to express his views to senators seeking committee seats.* And it did not go unnoticed:

> One senator described Baker's influence on committee as-
> signments for freshmen under Johnson: "Bobby is the one
> you asked how things went and where you went and who
> you talked to and he said, 'There is no chance of Appropri-
> ations, just forget that.' He said the same about Foreign
> Relations. He said, 'Don't mention that at all, but look
> around and list any others you want,' and then he made a
> few suggestions. As it came out, three other members of the
> class went directly on Appropriations in their freshman year,
> but I have been kept off."[22]

House Democrats

House Democrats seeking committee appointments must look to the Ways and Means Committee, whose fifteen Democrats double as their party's committee on committees. House Ways and Means members won their double hats in 1911 when the House stripped the speaker of the power to appoint committees.† At that time, the Ways and Means Committee, composed of loyal party regulars, appeared to be the natural repository for a task requiring party loyalty. Today, it consists mainly of party veterans, chosen only after they have performed long and loyal congressional ser- vice. Only with a reform in the Ninety-third Congress did the speaker, majority leader, and whip become *voting* members on this committee.

---

* After Johnson left the Senate for the vice-presidency, and Mike Mans- field took his old slot, Baker continued this role—apparently on his own. According to Randall Ripley, "When Mansfield became majority leader in 1961, Baker . . . continued this phase of his activities, until his [forced] resignation in 1963, but his relationship to Mansfield was far different from his relationship to Johnson. Some Senators felt he was operating on his own, or at least in response to important Democrats other than the ma- jority leader. Baker's successor [J. S. Kimmett] does not give this kind of advice."[21]

† In late 1974 the committee on committees' function was given to the elected Democratic Steering and Policy Committee.

To win appointment to the appointment-making committee, members have to meet their major criteria. First, they have to prove their ability to win elections. They usually represent safe districts—where the party and the members are sure of re-election. More than half the members on the committee in the Ninety-second Congress had to wait a decade before they won the key appointment. (See Table 2.)

TABLE 2.
Committee on Committees: Democrats
92nd Congress

Members	House Tenure		Committee Tenure	
	Year Entered	Terms Served	Year Assigned	Terms Served
Mills	1939	17	1943	13
Ullman	1957	8	1961	6
Burke	1959	7	1961	6
Griffiths	1955	9	1963	5
Rostenkowski	1959	7	1965	4
Landrum	1953	10	1965	4
Vanik	1955	9	1965	4
Fulton	1963	5	1965	4
Burleson	1947	13	1969	2
Corman	1961	6	1969	2
Green	1964	5	1969	2
Gibbons	1963	5	1969	2
Carey	1961	6	1971	1
Waggonner	1961	6	1971	1
Karth	1959	7	1972	1

Second, members must demonstrate "legislative responsibility" by deferring to House rules and traditions, to win appointment to this House appointments committee. It has been said that this committee—comprised of "senior members in an institution that respects seniority"—is "ill-designed for flexibility and responsiveness to electoral changes and public opinion trends. Rather, it is more analogous to a firmly-entrenched bureaucracy capable of considerable resistance to any pressures placed upon it."[23]

Still another requirement for a seat on this appointment-assigning committee is geographic distribution. For reasons long forgotten, certain states claim a right to seats on the committee.[24]* The committee maintains an odd geographical balance: members from six states, Alabama, Georgia, Florida, Tennessee, Texas, and Louisiana, represent the South; the remaining 60 percent of the committee's membership represents 75 per cent of the nation's population, the Midwest has four, the East three, and the West merely two representatives.

Each House Democratic committee on committees member is responsible for a zone (see Table 3) comprising from one to seven states (twelve to twenty-five representatives).†

> As nominations are opened for each committee, members of the Committee on Committees proceed in order of their seniority to nominate candidates from their zone. Discussion of individual candidates takes place as they are nominated, and their names are written on a blackboard. Once the junior member of the Committee on Committees has completed his nominations for the committee under consideration, secret balloting takes place without further delay.[25]

Procedure of the House Democratic committee on committees offers members seeking new assignments no single formula to follow. Candidates have to move on all fronts: they submit a résumé that defines how their background fits the committee they

---

* The "reserved states" tradition is not consistently applied to every seat on Ways and Means; but where tradition is operable, it may even override other criteria for office. In 1965 Tennessee's seat became vacant, and no senior, "safe-seated" Tennessean stepped into the breach. Richard Fulton, who had only begun his second Congressional term, was appointed to preserve Tennessee's seat.

† While the states within one member's zone are supposed to be geographically contiguous, this does not always occur. For instance, in the 92nd Congress, Sam Gibbons represented not only Alabama and his home state of Florida, but also states as distant as Hawaii and Alaska.

When it is not politically wise to let a member continue to represent a state in his or her zone, it is usually assigned to Chairman Wilbur Mills to handle.

TABLE 3.

Zones of the House Democratic Committee on Committees
(92nd Congress)

Member	States	Number
Mills (Ark.)		16 (total)
	Arkansas	3
	Oklahoma	4
	Missouri	9
Ullman (Ore.)		12
	Oregon	2
	Washington	6
	Colorado	2
	Arizona	1
	Nevada	11
Burke (Mass.)		25
	Massachusetts	8
	Connecticut	4
	Rhode Island	2
	Maine	2
	New Jersey	9
Griffiths (Mich.)		17
	Michigan	7
	Wisconsin	5
	Indiana	5
Rostenkowski (Ill.)		12
	Illinois	12
Landrum (Ga.)		20
	Georgia	8
	South Carolina	5
	North Carolina	7
Vanik (Ohio)		17
	Ohio	7
	W. Virginia	5
	Maryland	5
Fulton (Tenn.)		14
	Tennessee	5
	Kentucky	5
	Virginia	4
Burleson (Tex.)		22
	Texas	20
	New Mexico	1
	Utah	1
Corman (Calif.)		20
	California	20

TABLE 3. (*continued*)

Member	States	Number
Green (Pa.)		14
	Pennsylvania	14
Gibbons (Fla.)		16
	Florida	9
	Hawaii	2
	Alaska	*4
	Alabama	*4
Carey (N.Y.)		24
	New York	24
Waggonner (La.)		13
	Louisiana	8
	Mississippi	5
Karth (Minn.)		12
	Minnesota	4
	Kansas	1
	Wyoming	1
	Iowa	2
	Montana	1
	North Dakota	1
	South Dakota	2

* One vacancy

want to be on and explains how the assignment would benefit their constituents; they seek the favor of the dean of their state delegation, the chairman of the committee they want to join, and their party leader; and they sometimes obtain letters of recommendation from lobbyists working with the desired committee.[26]

The most senior members of the state delegations—the "deans"—act as advisers to freshmen, explaining the elaborate, unwritten custom of committee assignments. They also act as intermediaries, introducing members to the leadership, and to the chairman and members of the desired committee.[27] In 1958, when the Connecticut Democratic delegation was all freshmen—with no dean to act on their behalf—they landed what members of Congress rank as the least influential committee assignments: the District of Columbia, Post Office and Civil Service, and Science and Astronautics Committees.

Chairmen are so important in the assignment process that when they object to a candidate, the House Democratic committee on committees rarely overrides their veto. Even presidents will defer to the chairmen on committee appointments. When President Franklin Roosevelt decided to help Representative Lyndon Johnson win a seat on Naval Affairs, the President invited its chairman, Carl Vinson, to dinner at the White House.[28]

Support for certain appointments can, on occasion, be enlisted from outside Congress—as, for example, when community leaders from a representative's constituency besiege a chairman with personal visits and phone calls.

Organized lobbies play their part too. The American Farm Bureau has long had a voice in appointments to the House Agriculture Committee, and one former representative, Harold McSween (D., La.), even submitted letters of recommendation from the Farm Bureau to the committee on committees.[29] Other representatives have recounted their tales:

> When I first came to Congress I requested and got a good committee. When the assignments were made they ended up with one vacancy on Education and Labor. The first I knew of it was when some labor lobbyists came to me and asked whether I would go on if they could get me on. I'm sure they had checked me out and knew what my general point of view was. They went ahead and got me on. I neither asked for it nor lifted a finger for it.

> Some business people came to me and pointed out there would be a vacancy on Ways and Means. They told me they hoped I would consider serving on the committee and asked whether I would mind if they wrote letters suggesting me for service there.[30]

On the other end of the scale, to free a member from a committee assignment that has no direct bearing on constituent needs, just plain well-directed complaints have worked on occasion.

It often happens that two members of Congress have a justifiable claim to the same committee assignment—on the basis of constituent interest, speaking to the right people, and soliciting the right letters. At this point, the relative seniority of the two applicants comes into play.*

The House Democratic committee on committees' power over committee assignments is slowly being gnawed away—by a body that is growing teeth, the House Democratic Caucus. For most of the century, the caucus had been steadily losing power—to the point where members were not even reviewing the appointment committee's recommendations. Until 1965, when the caucus regained its right to participate in the committee selection process, the slate of nominations had gone directly to the House floor. But the 1965 reform was a bare formality: the caucus had to consider the recommendations as a single slate.

In 1971 the caucus further reformed itself. Upon the recommendation of the reform committee headed by Representative Julia Hansen (Wash.), the caucus agreed that individual nominations could be debated and approved by the entire group if ten or more members requested such a procedure. There were forty major challenges to committee appointments that year.

By 1973 a committee assignment reform was victorious. Committee members are still voted as a slate, but the 1973 caucus decided to vote on every nomination for chairman by automatic secret ballot (without need for petition).[31]

House Republicans

First-term Republicans are advised about the committee-assignment process by the House Republican floor leader and give their

---

* Political scientists disagree over seniority's decisiveness in the assignment process: Nicholas Masters concludes that the committee on committees would favor the member with greater seniority; Charles Clapp maintains that the committee gives greater consideration to the candidate's stand on committee issues and relies on seniority only when all other factors are equal.

Whatever seniority's importance in the average case, seniority is the overriding requirement for the Appropriations and Rules committees. Only

top three committee preferences to him. According to Josephine Wilson, clerk for the House Republican Committee on Committees, 80 per cent of the Republican freshmen in the Ninety-second Congress received at least one of their committee choices and 59.5 per cent of the veteran Republicans who requested committee transfers or additional assignments received one of their choices.[32] Assignments for major committees are just as keenly fought over by Republicans as they are by the Democrats. Jerry Pettis, who now sits on the Ways and Means Committee, ran a three-month campaign for his seat. He estimates that he worked harder to get on the committee than he had campaigned to get to Congress.[33]

After preferences have been announced, endorsements made, and campaigns waged, the Executive Committee finally meets.

> Executive Committee sessions are informal; each member may speak for or against any proposed assignment. And members of the full Committee on Committees who are not on the Executive Committee may participate, making nominations and speaking for particular assignments. Otherwise, the Republicans follow procedures similar to those employed by the Democrats.[34]

Like its Democratic counterpart, the Republican Committee on Committees sends its roster of nominees to its party's caucus for approval. The Republican caucus, like the Democratic caucus, has only recently assumed an active role in assignments. In 1971 it provided for secret ballot on each nomination for ranking minority members. It considers en bloc the remainder of each committee.

Of all Congress' housekeeping chores, committee assignments require the greatest care. A bad appointment may someday give

---

five of the thirty-five Democrats who served on Appropriations in the 92nd Congress joined as freshmen; none of the ten Democrats on Rules at that time won assignment as freshmen.

reign to a bad chairman. If so, Congress has no remedy through its rules and procedures—the code of courtesy and the custom of seniority still hold sway. No reason exists for permitting seniors to sequester power in the committee-assignment process. The ultimate seniors—the chairmen—should certainly not have their present influence, which allows them to bolster their majority on the committee, even if that majority stands foursquare against the floor. In addition, it allows chairmen to rule from the grave: years after the chairmen have left, many of their appointees will remain.

In the Ninety-second Congress, the Senate had 247 seats on seventeen committees. Thus, no matter how arbitrary the Senate's assignment procedures, a competent senator could not be completely shut off from all significant committees, and a single group could not sequester all desirable assignments.

The House, however, had only 669 seats on standing committees for 435 members, which meant that only about half the representatives could hold second committee assignments. In addition, only about one-fourth the House could even have one relatively powerful assignment; the big four committees in the House had only 134 seats. The important committees would be unmanageable if further enlarged, but restricting key assignments to their current number means that more sensitivity and judgment are required in distributing assignments to competent House members.

THE CHAIRMAN'S POWERS

Once these four committees on committees have assigned new members to committees and reassigned members who want transfers,* seniority controls committee advancement from there in most cases. Custom entitles members to retain their assignments as long as they desire, so that committees on committees rarely

---

* Members who are transferred are placed in the lowest seniority (above freshmen members) on the new committee.

remove an incumbent committee member. Since committees-on-committees consider criteria quite separate from expertise, the die is cast that length of service, and not necessarily expertise, make a chairman. The one who longest survives re-election ends up with the prize: a committee chairmanship.

The House Democratic Caucus, though, has revised its rules pertaining to committee-chairman selection in the Ninety-third Congress.

> The Committee on Committees shall recommend to the Caucus nominees for chairman and membership of each committee and such recommendation need not necessarily follow seniority.
>
> The Committee on Committees shall make recommendations to the Caucus, one committee at a time. Upon a demand supported by 10 or more Members, a separate vote shall be had on any committee chairman or any Member of the committee. If any such motion prevails, the committee list of that particular committee shall be considered recommitted to the Committee on Committees.[35]

When this process took place in the Ninety-third Congress, those chairmen already in power by virtue of their seniority won by wide margins.

Since seniority confers the chair, chairmen owe their positions to neither legislators, party leaders, nor committee members. Once they gain the chair, they require no congressional support to retain it. Longevity and re-election are the only prerequisites.

Within the standing rules, committee heads have great discretion to exercise their sway. Whether or not they use their discretion is not the question. That they have so many opportunities to use it is threat enough to keep others in line. The code of courtesy and the reciprocity principle—"I'll do what the chairman wants today so that he'll do what I want tomorrow"—are at work whether or not chairmen invoke their privileges and rights under the rules.

Subcommittees

In both houses, chairmen have the power to control the number of subcommittees their full committee will have.* Since neither house imposes uniform rules on the use of subcommittees, some chairmen remain solidly in control of their committee's activities by having no subcommittees at all. House committees on Ways and Means, Internal Security, and Standards of Official Conduct and the Senate Committee on Aeronautical and Space Sciences do not have subcommittees. For chairmen who want to maximize their powers, the next best thing to no subcommittees is to have subcommittees *without* specified jurisdiction. The House Armed Services Committee, which lists subcommittees by number, is one illustration.

Chairmen may also encourage vague jurisdictions for subcommittees, especially to allow themselves discretion in referring legislation to subcommittee chairmen who will likely do what the powers-that-be want. In the Ninety-second Congress, Chairman John McMillan (D., S.C.) of the House Committee on the District of Columbia referred bills to subcommittee chairmen who supported his antagonistic attitudes toward the federal city. Subcommittee chairman Charles Diggs (D., Mich.), who did not agree with the chairman, did not get his share of bills.

Informal mechanisms frequently develop to resolve controversies regarding subcommittee jurisdiction. In the Senate Committee on Rules and Administration, staff director Gordon F. Harrison says that referral decisions are made in committee meetings. If

* There are limitations on these powers. It is difficult, for example, for a full committee chairman to cross a strong subcommittee chairman. (See Robert P. Griffin, "Rules and Procedures of the Standing Committees," in Mary McInnis, ed., *We Propose: A Modern Congress*, House Republican Task Force on Congressional Reform and Minority Staffing [New York: McGraw-Hill, 1966], pp. 50–52). Also, a few committees, such as the House Committee on Education and Labor, have adopted rules *permanently* establishing certain subcommittees. (See *Rules Adopted by the Committees of Congress*, compiled by the Joint Committee on Congressional Operations, 92nd Congress, October 27, 1971, p. 21.)

there is any objection to a referral decision, the bill is kept by the full committee for consideration. In the Joint Committee on Atomic Energy, staff counsel Gerald G. Fain claims that it is not uncommon for two different subcommittees and the full committee to hold hearings on the same issue, if all are interested in it. Of course, members can challenge referral of legislation if no informal mechanisms are available. But it is not normally worthwhile to expend political capital in the challenge of a single referral decision, according to Ken Adams, legislative assistant to former Representative Abner Mikva (D., Ill.).

The chairman determines the majority-minority ratio on subcommittees—another power. Nowhere is a chairman required to consult with the committee's ranking minority member in doing so.

The chairman also assigns members to the subcommittees. Only by custom does the chairman consult with the ranking minority member in assigning minority members to subcommittees.

In some committees, either by rule or custom, the criterion for assigning members is seniority. The rules of the House Committee on Education and Labor, for instance, provide: "The chairmen of the standing subcommittees shall be the ranking members of the majority party."[36] Interestingly enough, this criterion is sometimes considered a check on the chairman's powers. Otherwise, senior members who might thwart full committee chairmen could be bypassed in favor of obsequious or "dependable" subcommittee chairmen. Only occasionally do chairmen violate seniority in the appointment of subcommittees.

Chairmen can also rein in unruly subcommittees by denying them the subpoena power they need to conduct investigations.[37] And they can create *ad hoc* subcommittees to consider particular bills, when they fear subcommittees already standing will not do what they want done.[38]

To limit chairmen's domination of subcommittees, the Senate adopted Rule XXV, Clause 6(g), which permits a chairman to head only one of his own subcommittees. The House Democratic Caucus similarly restricted its chairmen.[39] Nonetheless, the rules of thirteen House committees and one Senate committee almost destroy this reform's impact by allowing chairmen to sit ex officio as voting subcommittee members.[40] Sometimes chairmen find it in their interest to satisfy members with staff of their choice, or by allowing the subcommittees considerable autonomy. But they are usually sure they have enough votes in the full committee to prevent a subcommittee from getting any disagreeable legislation reported to the floor.[41]

Budget

The chair has power over the committee's budget. This authority is frequently not formalized in the committee's rules, but the power is more or less implicit in the office.[42] Since chairmen control funds for subcommittee investigation, they can always exercise their own discretion concerning the subcommittees' activities.[43]

Committee chairmen also initiate and approve requests for special projects and travel. However, their powers are somewhat circumscribed by the House Administration or Senate Rules and Administration committees. And they must get resolutions for authorizations approved on the chamber floor.

Hearings

It is the chairmen who determine whether or not a bill shall receive a hearing. They set its date; by custom, they select the witnesses. There are three main restrictions on chairmen here. They must give one week's notice through a public announcement in the *Daily Digest* section of the *Congressional Record* that hearings will be held on a certain subject, at a certain place, on a certain date (House Rule XI, 27-f. 1). They must guarantee one day for minority members to call witnesses of their choice, should a majority of the minority request the opportunity (House Rule XI, 27-f. 4). And a majority of the committee's members may go through an involved procedure to call hearings when a chairman refuses to do so. So, to keep control of hearings, chairmen who see that a majority wants a certain hearing or a certain witness will comply.[44]

Calling Meetings and Setting Agenda

In both houses, the chairmen control the agenda of business.[45] They decide which bills will be taken up, which subjects will be considered in committee hearings, and what will be done at any given meeting. Some committees have voluntarily adopted rules limiting the chairman's powers in these areas. The parent house may also curb the chairman's agenda-setting power. It can choose to request that a particular task be performed by a committee, though it rarely does so.[46] It can also affect committee agenda by directing that consideration of a particular piece of legislation must come within a specified time period, if it is to come at all.

Prior to recent reforms, chairmen could avoid considering legislation simply by refusing to call committee meetings. Standing rules now require chairmen to maintain regular meeting days. For example, House Rule XI, 26(a) states:

> Each standing committee . . . shall fix, by written rule adopted by the committee, regular meeting days of the committee, not less frequent than monthly, for the conduct of its business. Each such committee shall meet, for the consideration of any bill or resolution pending before the committee or for the transaction of other committee business, on all regular meeting days fixed by the committee, unless otherwise provided by written rule adopted by the committee.

The rules of four Senate and thirteen House committees, however, explicitly permit their chairmen to cancel regularly scheduled meetings without consultation. At present, the House Committee on Armed Services is one of the few committees which has rules allowing a majority of the members to reverse the chairman's decision to dispense with a regular meeting. But the members must take the positive step of submitting written requests that the meeting be held.[47]

Staff

Chairmen can also unduly influence their committees through their power to hire and fire committee staff. Committee members depend upon the staff for information and expression. Thus, a dissident committee member needing data or desiring to produce an unfavorable report may find no staff available. Even when dissidents are not entirely frozen out, they may receive only grudging cooperation and divided loyalty from staff members who quite pragmatically view the chairman and not the committee as their boss.[48] With the present staff shortages in Congress, subcommittee dissenters have little opportunity for meaningful dispute with the chairman. When they oppose the chairman's policies, they most often use their *personal* staffs.

If the pressure is on to call a meeting on a bill that they do not like, chairmen can schedule a special committee meeting at a time when getting a quorum would be impossible.[49] Or they may bring up a bill on such short notice that members do not know what is going on.* In such cases, a chairman's disposition usually carries.[50]

Parceling Out Debate and Hearing Time

Chairmen can manipulate committees through their power to control debate during meetings. They recognize (or not) members to speak and regulate the time allotted for questioning witnesses at hearings.[51]

Not uncommonly, chairmen allot themselves considerable time to speak and ask questions, dividing up the remainder among the members.[52] The rules of the House provide, "All committees shall provide in their rules of procedure for the application of the

---

* House Rule XI, 26(b), reads: "The chairman of each standing committee may call and convene, as he considers necessary, additional meetings of the committee for the consideration of any bill or resolution pending before the committee for the conduct of other committee business. The committee shall meet for such purpose pursuant to that call of the chairman."

five-minute rule in the interrogation of witnesses until such time as each member of the committee who so desires has had an opportunity to question the witness." (Chairman Wright Patman, House Banking and Currency Committee, for instance, has gotten around this rule by reading a long series of questions that must be answered "for the record," and by lecturing the witnesses while introducing them.)

During committee debates, a chairman may simply refuse to recognize a member who is going to say something that the chairman does not want to hear. At the close of the Ninety-second Congress, Chairman McMillan refused to recognize D.C. Delegate Walter Fauntroy, who planned to bring a home-rule bill to a vote. A newspaper reporter described the scene:

> Following the meeting, the lame duck South Carolina congressman, in a rare conciliatory mood, agreed to answer a few questions from the press. He was asked if home rule had come up. "It didn't come up," he said. Then he noticed Fauntroy standing nearby and he said: "Did you try to bring up your bill, Walter?" Fauntroy said he certainly had. McMillan, smiling ever so faintly, said he hadn't noticed.[53]

Using their powers to limit debate, chairmen can force concessions from their opponents on legislation. When President Eisenhower nominated Simon F. Soboloff for the position of solicitor general, the nomination went before the Senate Committee on the Judiciary for hearings on confirmation. At the same time, the 1956 Civil Rights Act was being considered, and the Judiciary Committee had jurisdiction over it. In a speech in his home state, James O. Eastland, chairman of the Judiciary Committee, later described the tactics he used to stop the Senate version of the civil rights bill:

> I had the committee staff prepare a lengthy brief on Soboloff and in the committee meetings recognized Senator [Olin D.] Johnson (D., S.C.) who spent five weeks of our committee sessions reading it. I told them [reformers] that they could

have him [Mr. Sobeloff] as long as no further civil rights measures were offered and on July 1 we agreed.

As a result, the Senate civil rights bill stayed in committee and died. When the President and Senate majority and minority leaders endorsed the bill, the Senate passed the House version without ever getting its own version out of the Judiciary Committee.[54] During the 1960 committee debate on the civil rights bill, Senator Eastland recognized selected committee members; they used the time to read aloud from Uncle Remus and the Bible.[55]

Miscellaneous Powers

According to William G. Phillips, staff member of the House Committee on Government Operations, on some committees it is common for the chairman to vote first on any issue; other members are thus put on notice about his views. Also, once the committee has reported a measure for floor consideration or issued an investigatory committee report, the chairman can delay its release to the press, thereby blunting the publicity and giving the headlines time to move on to other issues. One method of creating such a delay of a committee report is simply to extend the period granted to members for filing their additional or dissenting views. Those who disagree with the report will naturally cooperate by taking all the time given.[56] Still another major power is the chairman's automatic choice of managing a committee bill on the chamber floor or appointing others to do so. In this way, the chairman controls debate time on the chamber floor, a power which can limit true dissent.

Securely in their positions until death or electoral defeat, chairmen use their powers to maintain their own fiefdoms. As one chairman put it, "All committee chairmen are despots. They can run their committee as they see fit, and they usually do."[57] One member said, "If [a chairman] wants to be a bastard," he can make committee members "feel like first-graders at a seventh-grade party."[58]

Chairmen can throw their weight around because the seniority system insulates them from challenge. Woodrow Wilson's characterization of committee chairmen in 1884 holds some truth today: they are "petty barons," Wilson said, who "may at will exercise an almost despotic sway within their own shires, and sometimes threaten the realm itself."[59] A shrewd staff member observed, "Challenging the power of the chairman is not done because it doesn't pay off. There's no percentage in it. He could make a committee member's life miserable and futile for a long, long time."[60] For one, political alliances are generally short-lived, and chairmen are, under present rules, possessed of remarkable longevity. Committee members defying a chairman on one issue face the prospect of being isolated on others and being frustrated in performing their committee functions. In addition, they must consider the possibility that bills they later submit to his committee may face oblivion.

Only rarely can one house or another summon sufficient power to exert its legislative power against the will of a chairman. William White, long a student of the Senate, has made some observations:

> There are far-separated times when a chairman loses his moral primacy over his issues or reaches with the majority of his committee a conclusion so starkly and hopelessly at variance with the wishes of the Senate generally that he is overruled.
>
> But even then to repudiate his leadership and workmanship is a delicate and queasy task and one not relished by any general Senate majority, however great. If, reluctantly, it is undertaken, the victim is nearly always a *lesser* committee in the tradition of the Senate, say that on Labor. To override, say, the Committee on Foreign Relations or the Committee on Finance involves a parliamentary convulsion scarcely less severe, as the Senate sees it, than that accom-

panying the overturn, say, of a British government. And in fact the one crisis, a Senate decision overturning such a body as the Finance Committee, will hardly occur so frequently as will the other.[61]

Committee rules give potential dissidents no protection. On most committees, rules are haphazard and truncated. One committee may have rules governing subcommittee appointments, while another may have rules on recognition of members. Indeed, the few rules that appear regularly in many committees are those that repudiate floor attempts to limit chairmen's powers—rules allowing chairmen to cancel regular meetings with complete discretion, or rules permitting chairmen to sit ex officio on all subcommittees. In practice, when the rules are silent, the chairman determines procedures *ad hoc*.

Despite recent caucus reforms—like the Democratic provision for the automatic secret-ballot voting on each chairman—the seniority system is still 99 per cent intact. Congress still lacks a mechanism to handle unrepresentative committee chairmen. There is no rule in the House or Senate, or any public law, which systematically declares the rights of committee members in relation to their chairmen. No protection is afforded to the minority, or even to a majority that disagrees with the chairman. Rare are the committees that have rebelled and established rules providing for majority rule in certain areas.*

When it comes to setting an agenda, referring bills to subcommittees, scheduling hearings, and handling the committee budget,

---

* Two rules illustrate what a majority can do at the organizational sessions of their committees, where their rules are adopted. Rule 3 for the Senate Committee on Banking, Housing, and Urban Affairs reads: "A subcommittee of the Committee may be authorized only by the action of a majority of the Committee." The Senate Committee on the District of Columbia's Rule 4 reads: "Unless otherwise determined by a majority of the Committee, written proxies may be used for all Committee business, except that proxies shall not be permitted for the purpose of obtaining a quorum to do business." (*Rules Adopted by the Committees of Congress*, compiled by the Joint Committee on Congressional Operations, 92nd Congress, October 27, 1971.)

a majority often stands by, its voice muted by the congressional custom of deference to chairmen. Junior members are actually persuaded to stand in the wings and wait until they are aged enough to be called to the center of the stage. What is worse, juniors are advised to defer to seniors and not invoke committee rules too heartily; Morris Udall describes this in *The Job of a Congressman*:

> Now there is a problem, I would say, with reference to the use of rules in committee. Let's assume you get to be rather expert in the rules. You look them over and you know them. It is a little like Churchill said: "The difference between number one and number two is . . . that number one has to decide what's right. Number two not only has to decide what's right but whether it's appropriate to say what's right." . . . By that I mean that maybe you will find that somebody isn't proceeding according to the rules [but] the attitude you take toward your colleagues with reference to a strict compliance . . . could be very detrimental [to the member who] got a point of order and exercised it immediately and all that sort of thing. There ought to be an effort not to be super-technical with reference, I would say, to the operation of these committees by new members. Sit back and watch it for a while.[62]

In sum, by surrendering chairman selection to seniority, Congress has lost its check on the chairmen's authority. The next question is how the chairmen's powers affect the electorate.

SENIORITY AND THE ELECTORATE

After thirty years' service in Congress, Arkansas Senator John L. McClellan faced a serious challenge in the June 1972 Democratic primary. His opponent was Representative David Pryor, and to win McClellan emphasized his seniority again and again. He told crowds at every stop in the campaign tour that he had congressional clout that would take a new man another thirty years to develop. McClellan pointed to the local federal buildings, dams, and navigation projects to hammer home the importance of his seniority. These monuments, he explained to voters, came to Arkansas solely because of seniority—his own as well as the state's other senior members of Congress, J. William Fulbright and Wilbur Mills. A vote against him, McClellan warned, "would be a threat to this time-honored system, by which Arkansas and other southern states have gained billions of dollars of federal help."[63] McClellan won the primary and the general election. On returning to Congress in 1973, he was in the powerful and enviable position of surrendering the chair of Government Operations for the leadership of the all-important and powerful Appropriations Committee.

The seniority system stands the American theory of electoral representation on its head. Voters are thrust into the position of returning members of Congress or losing what little seniority they may have gained. The people of a state whose incumbent has retired or died will install someone with little opportunity to be effective on their behalf. Newcomers to Congress may be denied access to committee staff, and their bills may be ignored in committee. They are supposed to listen in silence on the floor during debate, ask questions last at most committee hearings, and defer to their seniors' legislative plans and proposals in lieu of their own.

Meanwhile, without the perquisites seniority bestows, the electorate suffers inferior representation. One legislator's power—through the unwritten, binding custom of seniority—dominates another.

In *Westberry v. Sanders* the Supreme Court held that in apportioning congressional seats within states Article I, Section 2 of the Constitution entitles each voter to an equal voice in the House of Representatives, and Article I, Section 3 guarantees each state equal say in the Senate. The principle at stake in apportionment —equal representation—is therefore violated by the seniority system.

With respect to apportionment, the Court held only that the power of a citizen's vote should not depend on the district in which he or she resides. Clearly at stake was the notion that each voter must have equal say in Congress: "The House of Representatives, the Convention agreed, was to represent the people as individuals, and on a basis of complete equality for each voter." The court concluded: "To say that a voter is worth more in one district than in another would not only run counter to our fundamental ideas of democratic government, it would cast aside the principle of a House of Representatives elected 'by the People.' "[64]

Fair apportionment has proceeded apace since the Court spoke, yet voters still *do not* have an equal say in Congress. Seniority continues to insure that the power of the citizens' votes *does* depend on the district or state in which they reside.

Citizens are long in reaping the value of seniority. Pascagoula, Mississippi, for example, first elected William Colmer in 1932. By 1939 he had sufficient seniority to secure an assignment to the powerful Rules Committee. Not until January 1967 did Colmer become chairman of Rules.[65] Colmer won the brass ring at the age of seventy-seven and gave it up six years later. Then the citizens of Pascagoula had to elect a freshman (Trent Lott), after William Colmer retired from Congress. If Colmer's constituents had abandoned him at any time in those years, they would have lost all the patronage, influence, and power that his seniority conferred.

The waiting time for a chairmanship is the measure of the price that the seniority system exacts. Constituents who send new blood to Congress suffer inferior representation. Voters who retain unsatisfactory incumbents, hoping for the fallout from the seniority cornucopia, suffer less responsive government: the double bind of the seniority system.

Waiting time depends upon the *rate of turnover* in the committees, since members may move up the seniority ladder only as others leave Congress or the committees. The four basic causes of turnover are defeat, death, retirement, and promotion—and less than half leave Congress because of defeat at the polls.

Senate turnover in recent years would cause envy among the best-entrenched nonelected bureaucracy. From 1921 to 1961 the attrition rate regularly soared over 20 per cent per election; turnover in each decade averaged from 19 to 23 per cent (Table 4).

TABLE 4.
Decline in Percentage of First-Term Members
and Increase in Years of Mean Tenure
by Congress, 1921–1971,
U.S. Senate

Congress	Year	First-Term Members	Mean Terms of Service
67	1921	21.9	1.81
68	1923	25.0	1.78
69	1925	19.8	1.76
70	1927	15.6	1.91
71	1929	19.8	2.01
72	1931	22.9	1.96
73	1933	24.0	1.85
74	1935	16.7	2.02
75	1937	18.8	2.01
76	1939	16.7	2.16
77	1941	20.8	2.00
78	1943	13.5	2.11
79	1945	24.0	2.05
80	1947	25.0	1.85
81	1949	28.0	1.79
82	1951	17.8	1.94
83	1953	19.8	1.94
84	1955	21.9	2.01
85	1957	14.6	2.17
86	1959	21.0	2.17
87	1961	13.0	2.19
88	1963	16.0	2.22
89	1965	12.0	2.49
90	1967	8.0	2.54
91	1969	17.0	2.47
92	1971	12.0	2.56

Data compiled from *Congressional Directories* (Washington, D.C.: Government Printing Office).

Since then the rate has remained well below that average, as new blood has flowed into the Senate at a meager rate of 13 per cent per Congress. In 1967 turnover plummeted so low that only nine senators departed.

Even if these figures reflected solely the decline of electoral defeats, they would depict serious political lethargy. The actual explanation, unfortunately, is still worse: re-election defeat accounted for less than half the departures in the Seventy-ninth through Ninety-second Congresses (1945–1972). In those twenty-seven years only 202 senators left office (Table 5). Con-

TABLE 5.

Percentage of Senators Leaving Office, 1947–1971

Year*	Defeated†	Promoted‡	Retired	Died	All Causes
1947	31.25	2.08	5.20	6.25	23.9
1949	34.37	3.13	7.29	6.25	28.1
1951	31.25	2.08	2.08	2.08	16.7
1953	31.25	3.13	3.13	4.17	20.8
1955	25.00	1.04	6.25	6.25	21.9
1957	9.38	2.08	5.21	3.13	13.5
1959	27.00	1.00	4.00	3.00	17.0
1961	6.66	3.00	5.00	3.00	13.0
1963	18.18	0.00	4.00	6.00	16.0
1965	12.12	2.00	3.00	2.00	11.0
1967	15.15	0.00	3.00	1.00	9.0
1969	24.24	0.00	6.00	3.00	17.0
1971	21.21	0.00	4.00	1.00	12.0

* Senators leaving in even-numbered years are included in figures for next odd-numbered year. If a Senator leaving in an even-numbered year was replaced that year, he would be included under All Causes and other columns, thus accounting for any difference between totals in Table 4 and Table 5.

† Includes primary and general election defeat.

‡ Promotion defined as leaving Congress for the purpose of assuming or attempting to assume other public office.

Figures compiled from data in *Members of Congress 1945–1970* (Washington, D.C.: Congressional Quarterly, 1970) and *Biographical Directory of the American Congress 1774–1971* (Washington, D.C.: Government Printing Office, 1971).

siderably less than half—93—were defeated. Calculated per Congress, defeat on the average represented 43.9 per cent of the total turnover, and one year (1961) accounted for only 15.4 per cent. In 1963 more turnover was attributable to death than defeat.

Not only has defeat played an increasingly small part in total turnover rate since World War II, but it is declining absolutely as well. From 1947 through 1953, over 30 per cent of all senators facing re-election were defeated; in 1955, the figure fell to 25 per cent. Since 1955, only one election has seen defeats fall within that range. In the period 1961–1972 only thirty-two senators lost, for an average of 16 per cent, or five senators, per election.*

The result has been an increasingly permanent Senate. Since 1955, average tenure has climbed steadily with but one small reverse (Table 4). By the Ninety-second Congress, the Senate presented a picture of political stagnation. Average senatorial tenure had reached a staggering 2.56 terms (more than fifteen years). Twenty members of that Senate will have served more than twenty years by the end of their terms; thirteen of them commenced service before 1950.

When compared with the House, however, the Senate has glowing electoral health. In the Ninety-second Congress, ninety-four representatives had more than twenty years' service. Three members had tenure ranging from forty to fifty years; another eight arrived in Washington before the bombing of Pearl Harbor.

Since the beginning of the twentieth century, the House has sustained an accelerating trend toward permanent membership. Until 1900, the House frequently convened with new members a majority (Table 6). In thirty-seven of fifty-five congresses freshmen held more than 40 per cent of the seats. After the turn of the century, however, turnover never reached hailing distance of 40

---

* Defeat rates for senators in this section are calculated on a divider of 33, since only one-third of the Senate faces re-election each Congress. All other rates are calculated on a divider of 100—the number of senators in the Senate. To translate defeat percentages into numbers of senators, divide by three.

TABLE 6.
Decline in Percentage of First-Term Members,
U.S. House of Representatives, 1789–1971*

Congress	Year of First Term	Percentage First-Term Members	Congress	Year of First Term	Percentage First-Term Members	Congress	Year of First Term	Percentage First-Term Members
1	1789	100.0	17	1821	45.2	33	1853	60.5
2	1791	46.5	18	1823	43.2	34	1855	57.5
3	1793	56.5	19	1825	39.4	35	1857	40.2
4	1795	38.9	20	1827	33.2	36	1859	45.1
5	1797	43.1	21	1829	41.0	37	1861	53.9
6	1799	36.0	22	1831	38.0	38	1863	58.1
7	1801	42.5	23	1833	53.7	39	1865	44.3
8	1803	46.9	24	1835	40.0	40	1867	46.0
9	1805	39.9	25	1837	48.6	41	1869	49.2
10	1807	36.2	26	1839	46.3	42	1871	46.5
11	1809	35.9	27	1841	37.7	43	1873	52.0
12	1811	38.5	28	1843	66.7	44	1875	58.0
13	1813	52.6	29	1845	49.0	45	1877	46.6
14	1815	42.9	30	1847	50.4	46	1879	42.3
15	1817	59.2	31	1849	53.1	47	1881	31.8
16	1819	40.8	32	1851	53.3	48	1883	51.5

* Chart through 1965 from Nelson Polsby, "The Institutionalization of the House of Representatives," The American Political Science Review (March 1968), p. 146.
Data from 1967–1971 compiled from Congressional Directories.

Congress	Year of First Term	Percentage First-Term Members	Congress	Year of First Term	Percentage First-Term Members	Congress	Year of First Term	Percentage First-Term Members
49	1885	38.0	64	1915	27.2	79	1945	15.8
50	1887	35.6	65	1917	16.0	80	1947	24.1
51	1889	38.1	66	1919	22.7	81	1949	22.3
52	1891	43.8	67	1921	23.6	82	1951	14.9
53	1893	38.1	68	1923	27.1	83	1953	19.5
54	1895	48.6	69	1925	16.3	84	1955	11.7
55	1897	37.9	70	1927	13.3	85	1957	9.9
56	1899	30.1	71	1929	17.7	86	1959	18.2
57	1901	24.4	72	1931	19.0	87	1961	12.6
58	1903	31.3	73	1933	37.2	88	1963	15.2
59	1905	21.0	74	1935	23.4	89	1965	20.9
60	1907	22.5	75	1937	22.7	90	1967	13.8
61	1909	19.9	76	1939	25.5	91	1969	8.7
62	1911	30.5	77	1941	17.0	92	1971	11.0
63	1913	34.4	78	1943	22.9			

* Chart through 1965 from Nelson Polsby, "The Institutionalization of the House of Representatives," *The American Political Science Review* (March 1968), p. 146.
Data from 1967–1971 compiled from *Congressional Directories*.

per cent. Before this, freshmen always composed at least 30 per cent of the House; in the following half-century new members accounted for less than 20 per cent on eight occasions. Then in the twenty years that followed (1951–1971) the rate simply crumbled. The Johnson landslide had only a trickle effect on Congress, carrying away 20.9 per cent of the House. Yet 1965 was the only occasion in two decades that turnover surpassed 20 per cent; other congresses in this period have racked up record-breaking lows. Twice, in 1957 and 1969, turnover accounted for less than 10 per cent.

Even total turnover figures mask the actual political safety of a House seat. In most districts, electoral competition is comatose. From the Seventy-ninth Congress up to the elections for the Ninety-third Congress, 1041 representatives left office (Table 7). Only 45 per cent of these, however, actually left because of electoral defeat. While total turnover has exceeded 20 per cent only twice since 1951, turnover caused by defeat has only twice gone above 10 per cent.

In 1968 electoral vitality waned so low that only thirteen representatives from the Ninetieth Congress suffered defeat. By contrast, sixteen members of that Congress either died in office or retired at the end of their terms. One of these was replaced during the Ninetieth Congress, so in 1969 the Ninety-first Congress welcomed a mere thirty-eight freshmen to their midst. Not only its small size distinguishes the class of 1969, however; its fate in 1971 also demonstrates the degree to which a House seat, once gained, is retained: thirty-three won re-election.* (Two freshmen representatives ran for the Senate; two more lost to the previous incumbent.) Of all the freshmen of 1969 only Allard Lowenstein —running in a brand-new district—actually lost to a new person.

These representatives were not alone in having a walk-through

* Since World War II, in both houses of Congress Republicans and Democrats have shared equal immunity to defeat. Since 1967, however, the Republicans have fared better. (See Appendix 4.)

TABLE 7.

Percentage of Representatives Leaving Office, 1947–1971
Percentage of Representatives Leaving Office

Year*	Defeated†	Promoted‡	Retired	Died	All Causes
1947	10.35	5.06	4.83	2.07	20.0
1949	18.85	4.14	3.68	2.76	29.4
1951	8.51	3.91	4.37	3.45	20.2
1953	7.13	4.60	6.21	2.07	20.0
1955	5.98	3.91	2.07	1.15	13.1
1957	5.06	2.07	3.45	2.30	12.9
1959	9.66	2.53	5.52	2.99	20.7
1961	7.36	2.99	4.14	2.99	17.5
1963	8.28	3.68	3.91	1.84	17.7
1965	11.95	3.45	5.29	1.84	22.5
1967	10.35	3.21	2.76	.92	17.2
1969	2.99	4.60	2.76	.92	10.4
1971	5.06	6.21	1.38	1.84	14.5

* Representatives leaving in even-numbered years included in figures for next highest odd-numbered year. If a representative leaving in an even-numbered year was replaced that year, he would be included in the All Causes and other columns.

† Includes both primary and general election defeat.

‡ Promotion defined as leaving Congress for the purpose of assuming or attempting to assume other public office.

Figures compiled from data in *Members of Congress 1945–1970* (Washington, D.C.: Congressional Quarterly, 1970), and *Biographical Directory of the American Congress 1774–1971* (Washington, D.C.: Government Printing Office, 1971).

at the polls. Among seasoned members seeking re-election to the Ninety-second Congress, 44 representatives ran unopposed. Another 30 garnered over four fifths of the votes, and still another 127 incumbents won by more than two thirds.

The end result was a House whose members' mean tenure in office was 5.94 terms, or 11.88 years—more than double that of the House at the end of the last century. (See Table 8.)

Seniority Today and Tomorrow

Many chairmen, who profited from quicker turnover rates between 1930 and 1960, still climbed spectacularly slowly. Nine

TABLE 8.

Increase in Terms Served by Incumbent Members
of the U.S. House of Representatives, 1789–1971

Congress	Beginning of Term	Mean Terms of Service	Congress	Beginning of Term	Mean Terms of Service	Congress	Beginning of Term	Mean Terms of Service
1	1789	1.00	17	1821	2.23	33	1853	1.69
2	1791	1.54	18	1823	2.29	34	1855	1.81
3	1793	1.64	19	1825	2.42	35	1857	2.04
4	1795	2.00	20	1827	2.68	36	1859	2.02
5	1797	2.03	21	1829	2.55	37	1861	1.83
6	1799	2.23	22	1831	2.59	38	1863	1.75
7	1801	2.25	23	1833	2.15	39	1865	2.00
8	1803	2.14	24	1835	2.23	40	1867	2.12
9	1805	2.36	25	1837	2.13	41	1869	2.04
10	1807	2.54	26	1839	2.17	42	1871	2.11
11	1809	2.71	27	1841	2.30	43	1873	2.07
12	1811	2.83	28	1843	1.76	44	1875	1.92
13	1813	2.31	29	1845	1.90	45	1877	2.11
14	1815	2.48	30	1847	2.00	46	1879	2.21
15	1817	1.93	31	1849	1.92	47	1881	2.56
16	1819	2.15	32	1851	1.84	48	1883	2.22

Chart through 1963 from Nelson Polsby, "The Institutionalization of the House of Representatives," The American Political Science Review (March 1968), p. 146.
Data from 1965 to 1971 compiled from Congressional Directories.

Congress	Beginning of Term	Mean Terms of Service	Congress	Beginning of Term	Mean Terms of Service	Congress	Beginning of Term	Mean Terms of Service
49	1885	2.41	64	1915	3.44	79	1945	4.50
50	1887	2.54	65	1917	3.83	80	1947	4.34
51	1889	2.61	66	1919	3.74	81	1949	4.42
52	1891	2.44	67	1921	3.69	82	1951	4.73
53	1893	2.65	68	1923	3.57	83	1953	4.69
54	1895	2.25	69	1925	3.93	84	1955	5.19
55	1897	2.59	70	1927	4.26	85	1957	5.58
56	1899	2.79	71	1929	4.49	86	1959	5.37
57	1901	3.10	72	1931	4.48	87	1961	5.65
58	1903	3.10	73	1933	3.67	88	1963	5.65
59	1905	3.48	74	1935	3.71	89	1965	5.39
60	1907	3.61	75	1937	3.84	90	1967	5.22
61	1909	3.84	76	1939	3.01	91	1969	5.76
62	1911	3.62	77	1941	4.24	92	1971	5.94
63	1913	3.14	78	1943	4.22			

Chart through 1963 from Nelson Polsby, "The Institutionalization of the House of Representatives," *The American Political Science Review* (March 1968), p. 146. Data from 1965 to 1971 compiled from *Congressional Directories*.

chairmen in the Ninety-second Congress had waited twenty years or more to get their posts. Their service in Congress was, of course, even longer. In the House, each of these chairmen waited twenty-six years to win the brass ring: W. R. Poage (Tex.) of Agriculture; George Mahon (Tex.) of Appropriations; and Edward Hébert (La.) of Armed Services; Wright Patman (Tex.) of Banking and Currency waited thirty-four years; William Colmer (Miss.) of Rules (who retired at the end of the Ninety-second Congress) waited twenty-eight years; John Blatnik (Minn.) of Public Works waited twenty-four years; and Chet Holifield (Calif.) of Government Operations waited twenty-two years. In the Senate, John McClellan (Ark.) of Appropriations waited twenty-three years for the chairmanship; John Sparkman (Ala.) of Banking, Housing, and Urban Affairs waited twenty years.*

With the lethargic turnover of the last decade, current members of Congress must creep by yet pettier pace from rung to rung. If Congress continues to bind itself by the seniority custom, a member might have to be re-elected for thirty years before winning the prize—a committee chairmanship. To predict future waiting times, we constructed a computer simulation based on a continuation of the last decade's turnover rates. We created an imaginary Freshman X, elected to the Ninety-third Congress and immediately assigned to a committee. This freshman never loses or dies in office; indeed he has the profile of all members of Congress who have become heads of committee. The defeat, death, promotion, and retirement rate for each house, for each party, and for each region of the country; the member's vulnerability to these factors at various stages in a congressional career; and the transfer rates of each committee were used to calculate attrition. Using these figures, Freshman X's waiting time for each chairmanship was computed. Waiting times for interim chairmen—current commit-

---

* Some of these members did not sit on the committees they came to chair until several years after they entered Congress. This is often due to the fact that members do not gain a seat on key committees until after they have been in Congress several years, thereby lengthening their wait to become chairman.

tee members who in the simulation succeed to the chair of a committee before Freshman X but after the current chairman— were also computed.[66] (See Appendixes 5 and 6.)

In the Senate, Democratic interim chairmen will need from 13.9 years on the Post Office and Civil Service Committee to 29.3 years on the Labor and Public Welfare Committee to become chairmen. Waiting time for Republican interim chairmen will range from 9.7 years (Agriculture and Forestry) to 34.7 years (Labor and Public Welfare). The first Freshman X Democrat will become a chairman in mid-1994 (Post Office and Civil Service) and the last in late 2009 (Judiciary). Democratic freshmen on ten out of thirteen simulated committees will wait for chairmanships until after the end of the century. Republican freshmen are more fortunate. They will gain the chairs of the Agriculture and Forestry and the Public Works Committees by 1992; only on two committees (Commerce, and Labor and Public Welfare) will they wait until the millennium.

Waiting time in the House will be considerably longer. Democratic interim chairmen will average less than 30 years for only three committees (District of Columbia, Rules, and Ways and Means). The rest will wait from 30 to 37.2 years (Education and Labor). As in the Senate, Republicans will fare better: interim chairmen on thirteen of seventeen committees tested will average less than a 30-year wait, waiting as little as 17.4 years for one and as long as 35.4 years for another (the Education and Labor Committee). Hypothetical freshmen among the House Democrats will have an unconscionably long wait. Only one will become a chairman before 2001; on fifteen of the seventeen simulated committees, they will succeed between 2010 and 2016. Among Republicans, one freshman will succeed before 2001, while ten will fall within the range 2010–2016.

While these results may seem extreme, they are consonant with the existing trend of increasing waiting times. Indeed, none of our projects exceeds extremes already clocked.*

* In the recent past, Carl Hayden served a total of fifty-seven years in the House and Senate; Carl Vinson remained in the House fifty years.

A multitude of factors may influence waiting times on particular committees. The number of rungs as well as the pace affect the time required to make the climb.* The House, for example, has longer waiting times than the Senate overall, and the Democrats move up slower than Republicans in both houses. This difference results in part from smaller committees in the Senate, and fewer Republicans on the committees in both houses.

For voters considering unseating an incumbent, these simulations project a thirty-year price tag on seniority. The Ninety-second Congress included eleven chairmen born before this century began, five of whom were in their eighties.[67] Given the increase in waiting time, eighty-year-old chairmen will become increasingly commonplace, if the seniority custom is maintained in its present state.

A chairman's reign will be cut short by retirement, death, or defeat, and perhaps some will serve less than a year (see Appendixes 7 and 8). Others will remain in office while three or four presidents come and go. A Congress Project simulation of length of a chairman's reign (tenure) revealed no clear pattern, but the lack of predictability works strongly in the chairman's favor. So long as chairmen's tenure remains indefinite, members of Congress, following the code of courtesy and the custom of seniority, will probably not risk opposing their decisions. If dissident members could be sure that a chairman would be out in a fixed time, they would probably form united fronts to check power. Without

---

* It might seem that such major committees as House Rules, Ways and Means, Appropriations; and Senate Appropriations, Armed Services, Finance, and Foreign Relations would have the longest waiting times. As it turned out, these were not the record breakers. For committees such as Rules, a partial explanation lies in its small size. Another fact, however, is the congressional practice of assigning members to these committees only after they have already acquired a fair degree of congressional seniority. This practice results in major committee membership running older than average. While congressional waiting time for these committees runs high, the age of its members produces a shorter committee waiting time. Conversely, such committees as Education and Labor had long waiting times because of the relative youth of their memberships.

that sure knowledge, dissidents will probably continue suppressing their right to act in an uninhibited manner while continuing their frustrating disgruntlement against the chairman's tyranny. This state of affairs minimizes true representative government and is not beneficial to the members' constituencies nor their country.

4

The House Rules Committee and the Senate Rules and Administration Committee

In my opinion, the Rules Committee can propose anything that it wishes provided it is not unconstitutional. From that standpoint, it may be the most powerful committee in the House.
—*Representative H. Allen Smith (R., Calif.),
Ranking Republican on the Rules Committee,
letter to the Congress Project, July 25, 1972*

Over the years, Congress' legislative workload has increased enormously. In the first Congress, only 142 bills were introduced; in the Ninety-second Congress there were 25,354.* Likewise, the number of members of Congress has increased. The first House had 65 members; it has now grown to 435. As the House of Representa-

---

* Some of these bills duplicate each other, but the total number is nevertheless quite remarkable. Only 768 of them were enacted into law.

tives grew, the Rules Committee was given more and more power to control which bills came to the floor for debate and votes. It could pinch off the legislative flow or so restrict it that many bills died on the way to the floor.

By contrast, the Senate is not much larger than the House was in the very first Congress; it now has only 100 members. It tends to operate under the unanimous-consent rule (see Chapter 6), dispensing with rules and operating under informal agreements. Its Rules and Administration Committee does not compare in size, power, or influence to the House's Rules Committee.

BREAKING CONTINUITY: HOUSE RULES COMMITTEE JURISDICTION

Between the standing committees and the House floor in the complex legislative circuit is the Rules Committee. Under House standing rules, its ten majority-party members and five minority members have jurisdiction over the rules and joint rules, the order of business on the House floor, and recess and final adjournments (Rule XI). The House parliamentarian has annotated Rules Committee activities this way:

> Primarily the jurisdiction of this committee is over propositions to make or change the rules, for the creation of committees, and directing them to make investigations. It also reports resolutions relating to the hour of daily meeting and the days on which the House shall sit, and orders relating to the use of the galleries during the electoral count.[1]

Technically, the House Rules Committee is responsible for scheduling an orderly flow of business for all nonprivileged, controversial legislation. It issues a special order, commonly called a "rule" that accompanies legislation to the floor. This rule specifies the time and conditions of floor debate. There are two basic kinds of special orders: open rules (permitting germane amendments) and closed rules (permitting only amendments offered by the committee reporting the bill). The Rules Committee also defines what kind of motions are in order on the floor. For example, it may waive points of order, legitimizing portions of a bill that might otherwise be in violation of House rules. (See Appendix 10 for sample Rules Committee resolutions.)

Before issuing a rule, the Rules Committee may hold hearings at the request of the chairman of the committee reporting the bill. Public witnesses are rarely heard at these hearings, but the chairman, ranking minority member, chief sponsors, and principal opponents usually testify. On the floor, representatives have one hour of debate on the Rules Committee resolution before voting on whether to adopt it or not. The managers of the debate are the majority and minority members of the Rules Committee. Since the rule normally must be accepted before the legislation can be considered, the legislation usually dies if the rule is defeated.

Further power rests in the Rules Committee's opportunity to delay or stop legislation (by not acting on it at all). In this respect, its members sit in judgment on legislation already accepted by standing committees. Another major power—the right to call up legislation that a committee has not yet reported—also belongs to this committee.

A specialist in American national government has summed up the incredible power that this committee wields:

> In short, the Committee on Rules is to a large degree the governing committee of the House. To it the House has largely delegated the power to regulate procedure vested in the House itself by the Constitution. Furthermore, by virtue of its influence in determining the order and the content of floor business, the committee may also function as a "steering" committee, steering the House in whatever direction the exigencies of the hour appear to demand.[2]

Before 1937, the House Rules Committee functioned mainly as the agent of the majority party, helping to facilitate its legislative programs. But that year southern Democrats broke ranks with the majority party over some of President Roosevelt's proposed legislation and formed a coalition with Republicans to dominate the Rules Committee and block or delay many party legislative programs.

One of the strongest leaders of this coalition was Howard W. Smith of Virginia, who became chairman of the Rules Committee in 1955. Smith saw to it that progressive bills favored by the Democratic Party or administration, such as civil rights legislation, never made it to the House floor. "My people did not elect me to Congress to be a traffic cop," said Smith.[3] His main ploy was to leave town so that his committee could not consider legislation in his absence. On one occasion, Smith left the capital to go back to his farm because his barn had burned down. Speaker Sam Rayburn is said to have commented, "I knew that Chairman Smith did not want to hold meetings to consider these administration bills, but I never thought he would resort to arson."

Smith had been an obstructionist too long when, in 1960, he went so far as to scuttle the Federal-Aid-to-Education Conference report. Speaker Rayburn challenged Smith's power by calling for an increase in the membership of the Rules Committee. In a dramatic battle on the House floor, Rayburn won by a three-vote margin. Much was at stake in this vote: Rayburn's own prestige and the balance of power in the House. Two Democrats and one Republican were added to the committee, a move that successfully curbed Smith's despotic power by putting the chairman in the minority of his own committee. The Eighty-eighth Congress permanently increased the committee's size from twelve to fifteen and set the ratio of majority to minority party at ten to five.

The hard-won reform did not curb all of the Rules Committee's powers. The Rules Committee still serves as a scapegoat when members do not want to be held accountable to voters for decisions. Because the committee is not directly responsible to voters, it frequently delays or blocks* bills at the behest of committee

---

* Eight votes are required, if the full committee is present and voting, to report a resolution making the bill privileged for the debate stage. The

chairmen or senior members who never surface to accept responsibility.

Around election time the Rules Committee can be a very convenient scapegoat. In 1970 it buried the Consumer Protection Agency bill that the Government Operations Committee had reported. The bill came to the Rules Committee buoyed up by 130 cosponsors. It established a new federal advocacy agency, and a source close to the Rules Committee explained, "We had caught the business interests napping. They never thought the bill would get out of our committee." But when the measure got to the Rules Committee, business lobbyists were fully awake. Rules Committee members became the center of a massive lobbying effort to stop the bill cold. In addition to receiving an avalanche of mail, Rules Committee members found their 1970 campaign chests increased by substantial business contributions.* Five months after the Consumer Protection Agency bill was reported out of committee, the Rules Committee voted seven to seven, one short to get to the floor.

Richard Bolling is the one Rules Committee member, proponents of the consumer bill believed, who might have helped the bill reach the floor. But he was off on his annual vacation on Saint-Barthélemy in the Caribbean. Aides to Representative Ben Rosenthal (D., N.Y.), who was sponsoring the bill, reached Bolling by telephone the day before the vote. But Bolling said, "I can't leave. . . . It wouldn't do any good anyway."[4] And Bolling was in part right, for members of Congress were caught in an election-

---

procedures for overriding Rules Committee decisions are cumbersome; as a result, they are rarely invoked and even more rarely successful.

* Bankers Political Action Committee (BankPac) alone doled out $2000 to Ranking Republican H. Allen Smith and $1000 each to Ray Madden (D., Ind.); John Young (D., Tex.); Richard Bolling (D., Mo.); William Anderson (D., Tenn.); B. F. Sisk (D., Calif.); Claude Pepper (D., Fla.); John Anderson (R., Ill.); and James Quillen (R., Tenn.). The money was a little late to influence the election but in plenty of time to influence a Rules Committee vote on what some business interests nervously called the "anti-business" consumer bill.

year squeeze. They could not be caught voting against a consumer bill that constituents wanted, nor could they be caught voting for it if the big-money campaign contributors—business interests—opposed it. The Rules Committee was the natural squelcher: it could block the bill, resting on its traditional image of a blocker. The blame could be placed on a committee—an impersonal entity.

Often the Rules Committee uses its power to delay rather than totally halt a piece of legislation. On November 10, 1971, the House Education and Labor Committee reported out a bill increasing the hourly minimum wage and extending coverage to more workers. Chairman William Colmer (D., Miss.) refused a hearing on the bill for five months. He grudgingly gave up his effort to substitute his personal judgment for that of the elected representatives of two hundred million citizens only after great pressure from the House leadership and threats from Democratic members of his committee to override his decision. "I still think it's bad legislation at this time," Chairman Colmer said. "But I have no inclination to prolong this matter unnecessarily."[5] With a rule from the Rules Committee, the bill went to the floor, where a slightly amended version passed by a vote of 330 to 78.

The Rules Committee also breaks the legislative circuit when it uses its authority to discharge bills from committees *before* they have been voted upon.*

Another widely debated power of the Rules Committee is its closed rule and the modified closed rule. The closed rule, which prohibits floor amendments, is often called the "gag" rule because

* While this usurpation of the power of legislative committees has not been used often in the past, it was exercised twice in the 92nd Congress. On August 1, 1972, the Rules Committee voted to discharge the Judiciary Committee from further responsibility for a constitutional amendment barring school busing and sent the bill to the House floor. The amendment had been pending for a year before the Judiciary Committee, which refused to pass it. Earlier in the year, the Rules Committee brought to the floor the West Coast dock strike bill that the Education and Labor Committee had rejected. This action effectively replaced the committee-passed version with a Rules Committee–approved version.

it prevents hundreds of members from seeking changes in a bill on the floor. The modified rule is only slightly less inhibiting. If members know at the Rules Committee stage that they want to amend a bill that is likely to win a closed rule, they may request a modified closed rule that allows their amendments to be offered on the floor. Debate and amendment processes are still limited, because the Rules Committee may decide not to accept the request for a modified rule, and the other members of the House still have no chance to offer amendments to the legislation.

No official count of closed rules is kept, but informal records show that they have been granted to very important legislation. On a Congress Project questionnaire, Congressman Robert Drinan (D., Mass.) noted nine instances between January 1971 and June 1972 where closed or modified closed rules had been invoked.*

A survey of Rules Committee special rules between 1939 and 1960 showed that 87 closed rules and 1128 open rules had been granted. Ways and Means Committee bills are most often protected by the closed rule. Chairman Wilbur Mills convinced a majority that tax and tariff bills (as well as Social Security, welfare, and other Ways and Means legislation) are so complex that floor amendments could damage their integrity and encourage local and regional vote trading. In 1970 Representative Sam Gibbons (D., Fla.) managed to gather enough votes to defeat a closed rule on a Ways and Means trade bill. However, Gibbons' victory was short-lived. Mills announced that he did not have permission from his committee to bring the bill to the floor under anything other than a closed rule. Without a closed rule, Mills warned, the bill would have to go back to the Ways and Means Committee for further action. Implicit in his warning was that the

---

* The interest-equalization tax extension (March 10, 1971), the sugar bill (June 10, 1971), the Revenue Act of 1971 (October 6, 1971), fiscal 1972 appropriations (December 15, 1971), the public-debt limit (February 9, 1972 and March 3, 1971), revenue sharing (June 22, 1972), continuing appropriations (March 18, 1971), and welfare reform (June 22, 1971).

bill would not likely return for a long, long time. The House voted down the Gibbons substitute and accepted Mills's version of the trade bill under the closed rule.

Rules Committee decisions have considerable impact on the substance of House-passed legislation. In granting Wilbur Mills a closed rule waiving points of order on the revenue-sharing bill in June 1972, the Rules Committee sanctioned one committee's encroachment on the jurisdiction of another. The revenue-sharing bill, which distributed about thirty billion dollars, was handled in Mills's committee, much to the chagrin of Appropriations Chairman George Mahon (D., Tex.). In the floor debate on whether or not to adopt the Rules Committee's special rule, Chairman Mahon asserted:

> Mr. Speaker, it is utterly incredible that one committee of the House . . . should attempt to seize the authorizing authority of the legislative committees and ruthlessly—yes, ruthlessly—grab the appropriating jurisdiction of all 435 members of the House, and at the same time be asking for a closed rule, in effect telling the 435 members of the House, "You are not to be trusted."[6]

The battle of the titans—Mills and Mahon—ended with a majority vote to accept the Rules Committee's decision. Here again, members were reluctant to upset the closed-rule tradition or contradict the fifteen-member panel. The Rules Committee was left free to exercise its power to issue rules in a way that sets national policy.

Many members have raged against the limitations of the closed rule, calling it "a legislative abomination entirely contrary . . . to the most basic principles of a representative government,"[7] and pointing out that it "blocks a true expression of congressional feeling in many important issues and puts enormous power in the hands of a few committee chairmen and members of the Rules Committee."[8] Opponents of the closed rule also object to the notion that they cannot be trusted to amend legislation; they suggest that it is a defiance of their right and duty and that it "insults not only Members of Congress but also the constituents who have elected them."[9]

In March 1973 there was sufficient objection to the closed rule for the House Democratic Caucus to initiate and pass a closed-rule restriction which requires a layover of four legislative days before a closed rule can be sought or granted. If during that time fifty Democratic members serve written notice that they wish to offer a particular amendment, a caucus must be called to decide whether the Democratic members of the Rules Committee should be instructed to make the amendment in order. But even if the signatures are obtained, senior members like Mills can work their will by requesting no amendments. Congressional courtesy dictates that senior members not be defied.

CIRCUIT REPAIRS

Members of the House do have access to rules and mechanisms for dealing with a Rules Committee that refuses to report a bill with a rule or refuses to hold hearings on a bill.

Calendar Wednesday is one such rule. As outlined in House Rule XXIV, on most Wednesdays committee chairmen may take turns calling up for consideration on the floor any bills already on the house or union calendars, but not yet reported favorably by the Rules Committee. But the procedure is subject to formal limitations that make it virtually impossible to use. It does not apply, for example, to controversial measures or privileged bills. Furthermore, committees are called in alphabetical order; general debate is limited to two hours; and action on a bill must be completed in one Wednesday. These requirements are an open invitation for the opposition to use dilatory maneuvers, such as repeated quorum calls, yea and nay votes, and moves for adjournment. For these reasons, each week, in session after session, the majority leader rises and asks unanimous consent that calendar Wednesday be dispensed with that week.

The alternate procedure for circumventing the Rules Committee is the discharge petition. First written in 1910, the procedure was amended several times, taking its present form in 1935. Under Rule XXVII, Clause 4, a member may file a motion to discharge the Rules Committee from further consideration of any bill kept in its domain for at least seven days. The motion is filed with the clerk of the House, where it stays until it acquires the signatures of 218 members of the House. At that time, the motion is referred to the Calendar of Motions to Discharge Committees. After seven days, any member who has signed the motion may call it up on either the second or fourth Monday of each month.

The discharge procedure is neither politically nor procedurally practical. House Rules Committee files reveal that between 1937 and 1960, more than two hundred discharge petitions were filed, but only twenty-two received enough signatures to go on the discharge calendar. Fourteen of these were passed by the House, but only two—the Fair Labor Standards Act of 1938 and the Federal Pay Raise Act of 1960—became law. The weaknesses of the discharge procedure are attributable, in part, to House members' unwillingness to violate the code of courtesy, which counts a committee chairman's prerogatives to be inviolate.

On rare occasion, a member might try to get around the Rules Committee by the device known as suspension of the rules. To get a bill placed on the suspension calendar, a congressman must offer a motion to suspend the rules that meets rather rigid requirements: two-thirds vote, only forty minutes of debate or no debate under some circumstances, and no amendments from the floor. However, a bill that can obtain the vote of two thirds of the membership with less than one hour of debate is unlikely to be controversial enough to be held up in the Rules Committee.

To date, the only effective means of forcing the Rules Committee to release a resolution authorizing immediate consideration of a bill has been the 21-day rule. Under this regulation, the chairman of a standing committee may demand recognition to call up a reported bill which has been before the Rules Committee for more than three weeks but has not been granted a rule to get to the floor. The 21-day rule has been in force during only two congresses: eight measures were brought to the floor of the House in the Eighty-first Congress, and seven of them passed; the rule was again used eight times during the Eighty-ninth Congress.

After each of these two trial uses of the 21-day rule, members voted to delete it from the standing rules of the House. Two basic arguments were cited against it. First, some argued that it placed too much power in the hands of the speaker, for only he had the authority to recognize a member who wanted to call up a reported bill under the 21-day rule. Since a speaker can refuse to recognize or ignore a member seeking recognition, the rule might lie dormant. (Rules Committee member Richard Bolling has told of a time when he was acting chairman and "just looked straight ahead" to avoid seeing a member who stood to be recognized. "Duplicate that a thousand times and you get a picture of a small fraction of the power of the chair." Some argued that the rule had been misused. According to Spark Matsunaga (D., Hawaii), all committees began demanding the 21-day rule at the same time as a bill was reported to the Rules Committee, trying to get around full consideration in the Rules Committee, when the real intent of the rule was to prevent intentional delay.

At the opening of the Ninety-second Congress, there was another attempt to revive the 21-day rule. In floor debate, Richard Bolling asked:

> Why is it that the American people should be kidded? Why should not the majority party have the right to exercise its responsibility to bring to the floor of the House and have debated and voted up or down the legislation it favors? That is all the 21-day rule will assure.[10]

Rules Committee Chairman Colmer countered that the Rules Committee served an important function—protecting members who had introduced or sponsored bills they never really wanted to see enacted:

I would say that the Committee on Rules serves as a buffer for the Speaker, the leadership, and the membership of this House as well as the republic.

Oh, how many times, how many times have I been implored and other members of this Committee on Rules been implored, "Please, for God's sake, do not report that controversial bill out; it would defeat me for re-election.[11]

Members of the Ninety-second Congress voted down the 21-day rule, burying yet another means by which they could be held accountable to the public for their legislative activities. At the opening of the Ninety-third Congress, members did not broach the issue when they adopted rules reforms. Apparently, a majority of members want the Rules Committee to be quite powerful at the interchange between committee and floor debate. They seem to want the possibility of short circuits to keep themselves clear of blame. Meanwhile, debate on the floor is sometimes no more than dressing, and the public sees little of what goes on behind the scenes—in Rules Committee hearings and negotiations.

BY CONTRAST

The Rules Committee's Senate counterpart, the Rules and Administration Committee, has less to do with rules, mainly because the Senate puts less emphasis on rules. It has five majority and four minority members, and does not wield the same kind of power as the House Rules Committee. Its wide jurisdiction includes authorizations of payment for congressional administration (such as the Library of Congress, congressional staff salaries, and members' authorized trips abroad on congressional business), and it also handles "matters relating to the election of the President, Vice President, or Members of Congress; corrupt practices; contested elections; credentials and qualifications; Federal elections generally; [and] Presidential succession." Far down on the Rule XXV list of this committee's duties are parliamentary rules. This assignment appears in a string of other duties, such as "floor and gallery rules; Senate Restaurant; administration of the Senate Office Buildings and of the Senate wing of the Capitol; assignments of office space and services to the Senate." As if these duties were not varied enough, the Senate Rules and Administration Committee has also been delegated jurisdiction over matters relating to the printing and correction of the *Congressional Record*.

Committee business tends to focus on administration rather than rules. (The House Administration Committee is its counterpart in this respect.) According to Gordon F. Harrison, staff director, the Senate Committee on Rules and Administration performs a policing function—overseeing and regulating congressional administration. In addition to regular budgets, the Senate Rules Committee handles special requests for consultants (regular or part time; retainer or not) and contract studies by consulting firms, and also takes care of procedures for borrowing agency personnel.

Harrison claims that the Senate Rules and Administration Committee focuses mainly on the rules, as in the legislative reorganization hearings and bill, and on election laws. But his own activities and the committee's output indicate otherwise. Harrison maintains elaborate, indexed files on *committee rules* and remains an expert on rules for the administration of the Senate wing of the Capitol. However, after serving as staff director for eighteen years, he depends, according to his own assessment, upon the Senate parliamentarian, Floyd Riddick, for information about Senate floor rules.

In addition, the Senate Rules and Administration Committee has been far less active than the House Rules Committee in analyzing and recommending reforms. In 1965, its Standing Rules Subcommittee was appropriated $60,000 for studying the Senate's standing rules. The study was to stand in the place of any examination by the Joint Committee on the Organization of Congress, whose recommendations for *House* rules reforms ultimately became an integral part of the 1970 Legislative Reorganization

Act. But little came out of the appropriation. In fact, the Senate rules last underwent a major reform in 1884. In the Ninetieth Congress, the Subcommittee on Standing Rules of the Senate spent only $47,491 of the $134,000 that it was authorized to use for investigations. According to professional staff member John P. Coder, the $60,000 in 1965 and the $47,497 went toward staff salaries, with one report as the major work product. (The subcommittee received no funds for "investigations" in the Ninety-first or Ninety-second Congresses.)

Neither the House Rules Committee nor the Senate Rules and Administration Committee has put enough emphasis on reforming the parliamentary rules and procedures of their chambers. They have especially failed to look at ways to invoke sanctions against those members who abuse, manipulate, or ignore the rules in the legislative arena. When a committee is told to report to the full chamber by a certain time, and the report is never forthcoming, what should the members do to ensure that the rule is invoked? When the parliamentarian is ordered to publish the precedents and provided over $80,000 to do so, what should members do if the precedents never come out? When there are abuses of rules about using proxies, publishing committee votes, or printing conference reports with a three-day layover before final votes, what rights, what recourse do members have? So far, the answer in each case has been to hold more hearings, vote on more bills with provisions to re-require what has already been stipulated in the rules, and then wait again for the outcome.

Next, even though House Rules Committee members were largely responsible for the Legislative Reorganization Act of 1970 —what scholars have called the most important legislative reforms in twenty-five years—they have protected their own powers to halt legislation rather than finding new approaches to scheduling legislative business. B. F. Sisk (D., Calif.), for example, has said that the Rules Committee merely "runs the store," implying that it is not as important or powerful as it once was. But he believes that "anarchy" would result if the Rules Committee did not maintain its current privileges. In 1971 Sisk introduced the amendment to abolish the 21-day rule. In explanation later, he said, "The 21-day rule obviates the whole process of the Rules Committee and I don't think the powers of the Rules Committee should be taken away; it's as simple as that."

The House Rules Committee should be looking for alternative ways to solve the problem of scheduling hundreds of bills for floor action. A committee of fifteen is not the answer alone. Its hearings and all votes should be open, and its members should provide detailed analyses of their decisions to accompany the resolutions going with bills to the floor. The public should be invited to testify, so that chairmen cannot scuttle bills behind the scenes in closed Rules Committee hearings; so that members cannot use the committee as a scapegoat to remain unaccountable to constituents for the "failure" of a bill; and so that the closed rule and the waiver of rules will be severely challenged before the Rules Committee's special order is issued. The committee's goal should be to give full, fair, and open hearing to the legislation it considers.

5

Unanimous-Consent Agreements: Almost Anything Goes

Unanimous consent is a formal rule to allow members to dispense with certain rules if there is a consensus to do so. If they don't want to hear the reading of the Senate *Journal*,* unanimous consent can do the job. If everyone agrees to refer a certain House bill to a committee that has no established jurisdiction over it,

---

* By order of Article I, Section 5 of the Constitution, the House and Senate must keep an official record of proceedings, in a *Journal*. Unlike the *Congressional Record*, it does not include verbatim reports of the debates but only the actions taken in each chamber. According to Senate Rule III, "The Presiding Officer having taken the chair, and a quorum being present, the *Journal* of the preceding day shall be read, and any mistake made in the entries corrected. The reading of the *Journal* shall not be suspended unless by unanimous consent."

unanimous consent arranges it. However, despite the fact that a single objector could stop it, a unanimous-consent mechanism is commonly used not just to oil the groaning wheels of Congress but also to sneak controversial legislation through or to delay legislation, sometimes to the point of crippling it.

IN THE SENATE

Unanimous-consent agreements in the Senate date back to the mid-nineteenth century, when senators discovered that many disputes could be resolved by informal agreements. Members developed a technique to bind the whole Senate to informal agreements without having to resort to the cumbersome and time-consuming task of making a motion, getting a second, and voting. With a unanimous-consent rule, a senator could simply ask if there was any objection. When nobody objected, the agreement would become binding.

Senate Standing Rule XL now reads: "Any rule may be suspended without notice by unanimous consent of the Senate, except as otherwise provided in Clause 1, Rule XII [on yea-nay votes]." Walter Kravitz, a government specialist, has estimated that, under this rule, unanimous consent is used to ignore about 90 per cent of the rules. Unanimous consent is required for such diverse requests as assigning bills to more than one committee, clearing the chambers for a vote, rescinding quorum calls, waiving the reading of an amendment (some are twenty-five to forty pages long), allowing modification of an amendment, and recognizing someone out of order during a debate. It has been suggested by close observers that since the whole Senate functions by unanimous consent and informal agreement, few senators need to know the rules.

Unanimous consent is not a simple procedure; it can have a profound effect on legislation. Its most significant Senate use, next to scheduling bills, is in setting the conditions for floor debate and the amending processes—such as setting the hour for considering a bill, limiting the time among the senators, and determining the time at which a vote will be taken. Because there are no provisions in the Senate standing rules for time limitations, unanimous consent to limit debate must be granted by the entire membership. Once granted, the agreement operates as the law of the Senate and is enforced by the presiding officer. To be permitted to speak under a unanimous-consent time limitation, a senator must request time from the floor manager and then be recognized by the presiding officer. In addition, many of the agreements set limitations concerning the number and germaneness of amendments, whether or not amendments are to be allowed at all or if only a committee may present them.[1]

Members have to work out unanimous-consent agreements before they are called for formally on the floor to avoid objection without skulduggery. This process of negotiation falls to the majority leader and the whip. They consult with proponents and opponents of the legislation and are usually successful in working out compromises.*

In seeking unanimous-consent agreements, Senate leaders have the unwritten rules on their side. The strictly observed tenet of senatorial courtesy dictates that senators not object to the unanimous-consent agreements worked out by the leaders, except in extreme circumstances: "except on highly controversial matters it is generally accepted Senate etiquette to agree to those self-imposed limitations."[2]

Although they may not object often, many senators disapprove of the unanimous-consent device to schedule Senate business. Senator J. William Fulbright (D., Ark.) once issued a strong statement against unanimous-consent agreements, especially for the power they place in the hands of a few. He cited the allocation

---

* Of all the people—about a third of the senators and their staff personnel—interviewed in July 1972 by Congress Project workers, not one would cite a single instance in which the Senate leadership blatantly ignored the views of any senator in advance unanimous-consent negotiations.

of debate time as one example of the way that unanimous-consent agreements muzzle senators:

> I find that, by making long-time unanimous-consent agreements, with few Senators present at the time, one or two Senators can control the time. Any Senator ought to be free to come in, under reasonable circumstances and talk about one of the most important subjects we must face. . . . I suppose I could make a unanimous-consent request that from now until the end of this session, all the time be divided between me and the Senator from Mississippi, and, if everyone agreed, there would be nothing anyone could do about it.[3]

A Congress Project survey of unanimous-consent agreements requested during floor consideration of five major bills reveals how "courteous" senators are in shifting from formal, written, long-standing rules to informal agreements. The Project tabulated the number and purpose of each unanimous-consent request printed in the *Congressional Record*. During the debate and vote on the civil-rights bill of 1968, 142 requests for unanimous consent were granted. Of these, 54 were to rescind a quorum call, 24 were to waive reading of an amendment, and 10 were to allow modification of an amendment. The 121 requests for unanimous consent during floor debate on the controversial 1971 Lockheed loan bill included 36 requests that material be inserted into the *Congressional Record*, 29 for rescinding quorum calls, and 9 for yielding the floor. The other requests covered 28 separate types of activity, related primarily to changing times and yielding times. (The complete tabulation of every use of unanimous consent on the selected bills may be found in Appendix 11.)

Any senator refusing to cooperate with these unanimous-consent requests could have held legislation up. As the chief counsel of the Senate Commerce Committee, Mike Pertschuk, says, "Anyone can object and mess the whole thing up." The success of unanimous-consent agreements teaches us that members can be courteous to a fault—bargaining their promise not to object for something else that they need or want. It also teaches that not many senators are even in floor attendance to be able to object.

There have certainly been times, however, when members have exercised their right to object. During the SST controversy in 1971, for instance, Senator William Proxmire (D., Wis.) and others promoting a filibuster* refused to agree to unanimous-consent requests for limiting debate time on the Department of Transportation appropriations bill, which included the SST money. And in 1971, Frank Cook, an assistant to Senator Mark O. Hatfield (R., Ore.), explained, opponents of the McGovern-Hatfield Amendment had to keep an objector on the floor at all times to stop those unanimous-consent agreements designed to push the legislation through easily. On another occasion, in 1972, Senate leaders Mike Mansfield (D., Mont.) and Robert C. Byrd (D., W.Va.) sternly urged their colleagues to adopt a unanimous-consent agreement limiting consideration of the Office of Economic Opportunity bill. The leaders finally got unanimous consent after threatening that they would not soon schedule the Debt Limitation Bill for floor consideration; since some of those who opposed the OEO bill supported the debt-limitation bills, the threat worked. (Secretary for the Senate Majority Charles Ferris has explained that to achieve unanimous-consent time limits, Senate leaders often use this device of alternately scheduling bills between ideological sides.)

While unanimous consent generally works, a double-edged question surrounds its use. Why should the Senate need unanimous-consent requests? Senate parliamentarian Floyd Riddick believes that unanimous consent allows for flexibility or "elasticity." But one could also argue that the Senate's written

---

* A filibuster is a delaying tactic used by a minority to prevent a vote on a bill. The Senate's unlimited debate rules allow room for this tactic. But parliamentary maneuvering, such as repeatedly demanding quorum calls (especially in the House), may also be used as a form of filibuster.

rules would work inadequately without this major eraser, this way of rubbing them out at numerous points in the legislative process. Invoking all the current standing rules might mean endless delays to accomplish such routine matters as inserting material into the *Congressional Record* or reading the *Journal*. The second, and perhaps more crucial half of the question is why should any truly important decisions on the Senate floor be subject to veto by one objector? Majority rule is more appropriate for legislative decisions in a democracy. As Senator Fulbright declared, "I think the Senate must consider that there has to be a limit as to how far we use this device to overcome or withhold the application of other rules in the Senate."[4]

IN THE HOUSE

Members of the House began to use the unanimous-consent mechanism by about 1832, when they felt the pressure of too much legislative business and the need for a fixed order for floor consideration. According to House precedents for Rule XXIV, Clause 1, as annotated by House Parliamentarian Lewis Deschler,

> A request for unanimous consent to consider a bill is in effect a request to suspend the order of business temporarily. Therefore any member, and the speaker is, of course, included, may object, or demand the 'regular order.' The Speaker, however, usually signified the objection by declining to put the request of the member, thus saving the time of the House.

The House also has a consent calendar under Rule XIII, Clause 4, adopted in 1909. Bills on the house or union calendars may be transferred to this calendar for consideration on the first and third Mondays of each month,* if there are no objections to them. The House has institutionalized an official objectors' com-

---

* It is only on these two days that the speaker may entertain motions to suspend the rules: "No rule shall be suspended except by a vote of two-thirds of the members voting, a quorum being present; nor shall the speaker

mittee to be a watchdog on the consent calendar. All representatives, of course, have the right to object to the placement of a bill on this calendar. However, since they do not have time to examine every bill that comes up, the objectors' committee is counted upon to make sure that controversial measures do not slip onto the calendar. In 1965, the House consent calendar committee adopted these rules: it would object to a bill that

· Involves an aggregate expenditure of more than a million dollars.

· Changes national or international policy of the United States.

· Affects the districts of a majority of members of the House of Representatives.

· Has not been cleared by the Bureau of the Budget, the government departments affected by it, and neither the chairman of the committee that reported the bill nor its sponsor appears to justify this deficiency.[5]

Almost any legislative action may be accomplished through the use of unanimous consent, which has the effect of suspending the formal rules of the House. Members may ask for unanimous consent to bring up a bill for immediate consideration, even though it has not been scheduled for the floor. They may ask unanimous consent to close debate on an amendment or a bill, to speak out of turn, or to win additional debate time not yielded to them. Behind its widespread acceptance is that strongest rule of all: the code of courtesy. One representative has said,

> We do so many things by unanimous consent here that it sort of dulls the blade. If rules and correct procedure were to be followed throughout the deliberations, the whole operation could bog down in a minute. There is a sort of *fraternal feeling* on matters of procedure to the extent that parliamentary tactics are not resorted to.[6]

---

entertain a motion to suspend the rules except on the first and third Mondays of each month" (Rule XXVII).

Even though unanimous consent is frequently employed, it should not be taken as an uncontroversial or unimportant tool. Members may use it at those times in the day when few representatives are on the floor, perhaps having decided that the risk of offending others—by requesting a unanimous-consent agreement when hardly anyone is around to object—is worthwhile; or perhaps recognizing that a unanimous-consent request can be disposed of when only a few members are on the floor. Representative Bella Abzug (D., N.Y.) tried to use unanimous consent to revive her House Resolution 595, seeking information about United States involvement in South Vietnamese elections. She tells of arriving on the floor just minutes after the House convened (indeed well before the time business generally begins), only to find that an opponent, Representative Thomas (Doc) Morgan (D., Pa.) had made a motion to table her resolution. Morgan's motion was accepted by voice vote. Next, Abzug asked for unanimous consent "to vacate the procedure under which House Resolution 595 was laid on the table." She tried to make this request in a quiet voice so that no one would object, but as she tells it, "Carl Albert's too clever for that. He asked me to please step into the well, where there's a microphone, and repeat myself." Someone did object immediately, and Abzug lost her bid for information. After the episode, she stormed up to the House leaders, Speaker Carl Albert and Majority Leader Hale Boggs, and said,

> Okay, fellows, you broke the rules of your own club; if that's how you play, I can play that way too. I'm not going to give unanimous consent to anything anymore—you guys are going to have to vote on everything in this House.[7]

Objections to unanimous-consent requests may be used as tactics to cripple House activity. According to a House Democratic Study Group report, a member may

> 1. Object to adoption of the journal, move the journal be read, demand the roll call vote on the motion.

2. After each quorum call, object to dispensing with further proceedings under the call.

3. Object to any request that the reading of the resolution be dispensed with, and if a motion is made to dispense with the reading, demand the yeas and nays.

4. Object to any requests for dispensing with the reading of a bill. If a motion is made, tellers with clerks can be demanded.

5. Object to unanimous consent request by any member to speak additional minutes.

6. Object to unanimous consent request of any member to speak on a nongermane matter.

7. Object to unanimous consent request to end or close debates and demand a teller vote on a subsequent motion.[8]

The power to object is the ability to paralyze the House. Alternatively, a clever use of unanimous consent can help a generally senior member sneak measures past colleagues with little notice. (A junior member taking such liberty would be considered brazen and discourteous; a senior member is successful because questioning a chairman breaks the code of courtesy.) Members' bills often get through Congress with little floor debate this way.

In another misuse of unanimous consent, a member can have his remarks placed in the *Congressional Record* before the vote on a piece of legislation, even though he may have actually spoken the words *after* passage of the bill or may have merely submitted them for publication, never speaking them at all. Through this maneuver, the member's words become part of the legislative history of a bill, and judges and attorneys may rely on it in interpretation of the legislation. A member may have a personal reason for speaking only after the passage of the bill. The words may give an interpretation that other members would find so unreasonable that they would rather have seen the bill defeated.

Unanimous consent agreements have a special impact on floor activities—debates and votes. Their essential ingredient, courteous compromise, is used to limit the time spent in debating issues and to control conflict among members on the floor. The result of such action is twofold: at times, members debating on the floor have a tendency to replace advocacy with artful rhetoric; legislative business is facilitated by these agreements to dispense with the rules, but often at the expense of congressional analysis and deep deliberation. On the other hand, unanimous consent has the advantage of saving the members' time, and thereby allowing more, not less, time for debate and analysis; it eliminates the need for unnecessary rereading of bills and debates which can just as easily be placed in the *Congressional Record* for use at a later date.

Like any other rule, unanimous consent can be used either to improve the legislative process or to deter it. It is the responsibility of members of Congress to properly utilize unanimous consent.

6

Floor Debating
and Voting:
Rules for Tuesday-
Thursday Clubs

*What this Senate is degenerating into—and [I] use the word
advisedly—is a 3-day-a-week body. We are all becoming members
of the Tuesday to Thursday club, inclusive. And I think we are
marking, by our own actions here, the apathy and the malaise
which are affecting this Republic today.*
    —*Senate Majority Leader Mike Mansfield, February 9, 1972*

It is often taken for granted that Congress' significant legislative
activity occurs in committee sessions. But at some point, a bill
may have the fortune of reaching the chamber floor for public
debate and votes. It is on the floor, contrary to prevailing notions,
that a good deal of significant, though often abstruse, legislative

wheeling and dealing—through the rules and procedures—reshapes bills. It is here that the amending process revamps committee bills, sometimes in minor ways (when more could be done), sometimes in major ways (when less drastic surgery would have been better). It is here that members decide whether or not to challenge the decisions of the "powers that be"—the House Rules Committee's resolutions, the parliamentarian's rulings, or the Senate leader's scheduling of bills. And it is here that members have the duty to represent their constituents' interests as well as the nation's, *by participating* in an informed fashion in the decision-making process.

SPEAKING FOR POSTERITY

House Debates

Since the first Congress, in 1789, there have been so many representatives vying for attention that the House has had rules to limit debate:

· No member may speak more than once to the same question without leave of the House, unless he be the mover, proposer, or introducer of the matter pending (Rule XIV, Clause 6).

· A member has to be recognized by the chair before taking the floor to engage in debate (Rule XIV, Clause 1).

· Debate could be cut off and the matter brought to a vote if a quorum was present to move for the previous question and adopt it by a majority (Rule XVIII).

In the 1840s, two more rules were added:

· No member shall occupy more than one hour in debate on any question in the House or in committee [of the Whole] (Rule XIV, Clause 2).

· When general debate is closed by order of the House, any member shall be allowed five minutes to explain any amendment he may offer, after which the member who shall first obtain the floor shall be allowed to speak five minutes in opposition to it (Rule XXIII, Clause 5).

Such rules were necessary, for members would rattle on and on, without really contributing to consideration of a bill. Indeed, early in the nineteenth century, a representative paused in his long speech to address Speaker Clay: "You, sir, speak for the present generation, but I speak for posterity." Clay replied, "Yes, and you seem resolved to speak until the arrival of your audience."[1]

By the 1880s, the last two limitations on debate were added:

· Under suspension of the rules, debate is limited to forty minutes (Rule XXVIII, Clause 3), the time being split between those in favor of the proposition and those opposed.

· The Committee on Rules may, by special order, report limits on general debate, which, if accepted by the House, are invoked (Rule XXIII, Clause 5).

These rules have maintained the *status quo*, order out of conflict. As Speaker Joseph G. Cannon (R., Ill.) warned early in this century:

> It is a fine thing to declaim about the right of the individual member and the tyranny of the order which keeps him down, but it would be a trifle inconvenient to the country to permit him to range in his native freedom unfettered by a rule, for, notwithstanding the noble provisions of our Constitution, we might be left without any lawful or orderly government.[2]

Some questions in the 1970s are whether the rules are so manipulated, so obscure, so hidden in files and behind glass doors, that they are serving to maintain order and dullness at the same time; whether the members' use of the rules is hindering debate and stifling the search for creative solutions to the country's problems; and whether the members' ignorance of their own rules and procedures is substituting the decisions of a few who know the rules for the responsibility of all to represent constituencies.

Today the rules—both written and code—stress a common quality, courtesy. Congressional decorum calls for agreement instead of debate. Members tend to liken debate to conflict to be avoided at all costs.

> One's overwhelming first impressions of a member of Congress is the aura of friendliness that surrounds the life of a congressman. No wonder that "few die and none resign." Almost everyone is unfailingly polite and courteous. Window washers, clerks, senators—it cuts all ways. We live in a cocoon of good feeling.[3]

Advocacy cannot long survive in such a never-never land. Not only are personal names of members of Congress avoided in debate on the floor, but the Senate is called "the other body" to play down the conflict between the houses. Hostility in debate is sublimated with stylized language, a language which often skims over the real argument at hand.

The code of courtesy extends so far through the written and unwritten rules that very important decisions are deferred to the leaders' will. For example, during floor debate members have the right to appeal a speaker's decision on a point of order. But an appeal to the chair is sometimes interpreted as a personal attack on the integrity of both the speaker and the parliamentarian, even though the decision may be wrong according to parliamentary practices, procedures, and rules.

In addition to the limitations on debate that stylized courtesy brings, chronic absenteeism also takes its toll on floor debate and, ultimately, on the legislation that Congress enacts. Taking over the speakership in 1971, Carl Albert tried to overcome years of tradition—by which members were not asked to attend Friday floor sessions except in emergencies—and declared a five-day week, in place of the Tuesday-through-Thursday informal schedule. His plan was ignored. Reformers in the past had argued for a

Friday work session, but they did not always attend themselves. With a majority of members unwilling to get in gear and attend debate, House business is slow to get off the ground. According to *Congressional Quarterly*, the House met only forty-three times in the first three months of the Ninety-third Congress (1973) for a minuscule total of eighty-eight hours. The legislative business taken care of during these hours included fifteen relatively old, minor, noncontroversial bills, cleared but not completed in the previous session.

Just as the number of committee, leadership, and parliamentarian decisions have increased, the individual member's opportunities to express opposition and disagreement have been sharply reduced.[4] But it is the individual member who can exercise the right of true advocacy and the responsibility of floor attendance. Further abdication through low attendance and capitulation to the code of courtesy at the expense of advocacy only serve to let power slip into the hands of a few. Members' failure to debate can no longer be excused with the words "nothing happens on the floor," for attendance would make something happen on the floor and would hold members accountable for their decisions at the same time.

Senate Debates

Delegates to the 1787 Constitutional convention pictured the Senate as a council of wise men, chosen for longer terms, older than their House counterparts, with only one third standing for election at the same time. The senators' right to extended debate was established to afford the opportunity for full public hearing for all geographical and political viewpoints.

Today, Senate rules insuring full debate, when invoked, also allow ample opportunity for delay and lack of focus. For example, Senate debate does not have to be germane. It can leap from subject to subject; it does not continue with one subject until it has been disposed of. There is thus often little continuity and much delay in the completion of pending business.

A 1961 study by Senator Joseph Clark's staff revealed that one third of the time on the Senate floor was consumed in nongermane discussion.[5] In 1964 the Senate amended Rule VIII, Clause 3 to require that all debate for three hours following the morning hour must be germane to the specific question then pending before the Senate. But there is a major exception: "except as determined to the contrary by unanimous consent or on motion without debate." The new attempt at achieving germane debate was greeted with "hoots of derision and attempted sabotage," according to Senator Clark.[6] So, by 1967, Lewis Froman has written, the germaneness rule was "honored more in breach than in practice."[7] When Senator Robert Byrd (D., W.Va.) took up the position of majority whip,* he generally tightened up floor procedures. But Dan Leach, Assistant Secretary to the Senate Majority, says the members still frequently fail to heed the germaneness rule.

Given the discontinuity of Senate debate, senators are not as prepared as they might otherwise be to debate issues that come up. Their lack of preparation serves to delay debate just as their failure to follow the germaneness of debate rule does. For example, on August 3, 1972, the Nixon-Brezhnev treaty limiting the nuclear arms race was scheduled for consideration. However, senators were not ready to debate it. Majority Leader Mike Mansfield (D., Mont.) expressed his frustration:

> I do not intend, in view of the fact that no one is ready to say anything, to call a recess. We will just have to stand here, twiddling our thumbs, and wait for expiration of our time limitation, unless those who wish to offer amendments or understandings, or those who wished to speak on this most important treaty, will come to the floor and undertake the responsibilities which are theirs and which are the Senate's collectively.[8]

*Byrd, who won the post of whip in a race against Edward Kennedy (D., Mass.) in 1971, said after his 31-to-24 victory: "My role will be that of a legislative tactician. I view the office of Whip as one which expedites the flow of legislative business. I want to facilitate a condition in which every Senator can exercise his will." *Congressional Quarterly Weekly Report*, XXIX, January 22, 1971, p. 180.

Senator Henry Jackson (D., Wash.) explained why he could not be prepared to speak for another two hours. And Senator Gordon Allott (R., Colo.) suggested a plan to fill the time:

> Mr. President, I have some remarks prepared which I do not intend to give verbally but to have printed in the *Record* on the treaty and the interim agreement. If it would be of any assistance, I would be very happy to proceed at this time. If I give the entire matter, it would probably take as much as two hours.[9]

In these circumstances, quorum calls are usually requested to fill the gaps of time between legislative matters. On a typical day, there may be as many as twenty-five short quorum calls, none going the full length of the roll of senators. When the senators are finally ready to proceed to the next matter, the quorum call is rescinded by unanimous consent. During the consideration of the Open Housing Act of 1968, for instance, there were fifty-four quorum calls, all rescinded by unanimous consent before completion of the roll of senators. (Each call delays business anywhere from one to twenty minutes.)

A standard ingredient in the Senate's deliberation and delay is the filibuster, the "talkathon" or the privilege of unlimited talk. Using the filibuster, a determined minority, or even a single senator, can hold the floor, delaying the majority's decision. Through the filibuster, they halt all other Senate business until the majority capitulates—either by throwing out the offending measure or by amending it to the minority's satisfaction. Only a two-thirds majority can vote to end the filibuster, which is often more a delaying tool than an informing mechanism.

Time pressure is at the heart of the filibuster's effectiveness in forcing a compromise. Senators maintain busy schedules, both on and off the chamber floor, so that any tactic which halts Senate business and uses a great deal of time is a potentially effective lever to force compromises from those who become anxious to move on to other business. The longer the filibuster lasts, and the more the pressures to conduct other Senate business on the floor mount, the more leverage the minority gains. In fact, the mere threat of a filibuster can be effective to extort concessions before members reach the Senate floor.

It is difficult under Senate rules to stop a filibuster. Rule XXII (adopted in 1917) provides that debate on a measure may be closed by a two-thirds vote of those senators present and voting. If two thirds of the senators pass the cloture motion, all senators are thereafter allowed only one hour to speak. Also, no further amendments may be presented after the cloture motion is passed; only amendments that the presiding officer determines are germane to the bill may be considered for a vote; all points of order must be decided without debate; and a final vote must be taken on the second calendar day thereafter.

Filibusters have been instrumental in delaying and defeating many kinds of Senate bills. They played a significant role in delaying statehood for Oregon, Oklahoma, Arizona, and New Mexico. In 1890 a filibuster delayed the "force bill" that called for federal supervision of elections, and in 1915 a filibuster blocked Senate passage of President Wilson's request to arm merchant-marine ships.* In the 1950s and 1960s, the filibuster was most frequently used by southern senators to block civil-rights legislation. Clarence Mitchell, NAACP Washington bureau director, lists five civil-rights measures that were significantly delayed, modified, or even defeated by a filibuster in recent years: the 1957 civil-rights law, the 1960 voter-enrollment plan, the 1962 proposals to extend voting rights to all persons with a sixth-grade education, the 1964 voting rights and literacy tests, and the 1968 federal guarantees of open housing.[10]

In the 1970s the very senators who sympathized with the reform movement to limit the filibuster used the filibuster tool

---

* It was the outrage of the public and the President at this frustration of majority will that brought the Senate to enact the cloture rule to provide some means to restrict an "irresponsible" minority.

themselves. As their southern colleague James Allen (D., Ala.) reminded them in floor debate,

> It is interesting to note in the closing days of the Ninety-first Congress that those who were resorting to the use of extended debate or filibuster were Senators who favor making it easier to cut off debate. I refer to the distinguished Senator from Wisconsin [Mr. Proxmire], who by engaging in extended debate on the SST conference report, was able to defeat the full funding of the SST project.* The distinguished Senator from New York [Mr. Javits] and, I believe, the distinguished Senator from Minnesota [Mr. Mondale] were threatening use of extended debate with respect to the import quota legislation. The import quota legislation was not passed by Congress. The full-funding of the SST was not authorized.[11]

By 1972 the filibuster was used to delay, defeat, or modify consumer-protection and women's-rights legislation. The Democratic leadership shelved the consumer-protection bill providing for the establishment of an independent consumer-advocacy agency after three votes to end a filibuster had failed. The demise of the bill was seen as a major victory for corporations that believed an agency representing consumer interests would cause undue government monitoring of their weakly regulated activities.[12]

Southern and business-oriented senators joined together to force a weakening of the enforcement powers of the Equal Employment Opportunity Commission (EEOC). For five weeks on the Senate floor, Senators Sam Ervin, Jr. (D., N.C.) and James Allen (D., Ala.) discussed their preference for court enforcement

---

* After the SST filibuster, Senators Alan Cranston (D., Calif.), Frank Church (D., Idaho), and Charles McC. Mathias (R., Md.) announced their support for the *two-thirds cloture* rule to cut off debate and stop a filibuster instead of the reform measure calling for a *simple majority* vote, which would be easier to achieve. These and other senators who formerly opposed the filibuster realized that there might come other times when they would need the filibuster and benefit from the stricter rule (two-thirds cloture) before debate could be limited.

rather than agency cease-and-desist powers. After two attempts to end the filibuster had failed, the majority passed an amendment substituting the weaker court-enforcement procedure; before the filibuster, they had twice rejected the amendment.

Since the cloture rule went into effect in 1917, only sixty-one votes on cloture motions have been taken. (See Appendix 12.) A mere ten have gained the necessary two-thirds to shut off debate. If the Senate could have shut off debate by a simple majority vote, there would have been only sixteen and not fifty-one successful filibusters. And, as Senator Frank Church (D., Idaho) has pointed out, "the record cannot disclose the many times that cloture has not even been attempted, due to the foreknowledge that the attempt would be futile."[13]

The Senate, however, has consistently voted to maintain the two-thirds cloture rule. The issue has been raised at the opening of each new session since 1959, and each attempt to lower the number of senators needed to invoke cloture has been defeated. The votes (listed in Appendix 13) clearly indicate that the majority of senators do not favor a change from two-thirds to a simple majority rule.

Ironically, at these opening-session debates on the cloture rule, proponents of the filibuster threaten to filibuster any change in the cloture rule, questioning whether a simple majority of the senators should have the right to amend the Senate rules at the opening of a session. Unlike the House, where the rules are readopted at the beginning of each new congress, the Senate has been considered a continuous body whose rules stay in existence from one congress to the next. Filibuster supporters contend that changes in Senate rules could be talked to death, unless two thirds of the membership is willing to invoke cloture under Rule XXII. If, on the other hand, the Senate is not counted as a continuing body, it could adopt new rules each session, cutting off debate on the new rules by a majority vote. On January 26, 1971, Vice-President Spiro T. Agnew ruled that a two-thirds majority was required to cut off the prevailing filibuster on the rules change; he thereby scuttled any cloture-motion reform for the Ninety-second Congress.[14]

At these ritualistic, early-session attempts to change the cloture rule, the arguments about the filibuster focus on whether or not the rights of a strong minority could be protected under any reforms in the current rules. During the 1971 debates on Rule XXII, Senator Ernest Hollings (D., S.C.) asserted that the filibuster, as a delaying tactic, was the guardian of minority rights.[15] Senator John Stennis (D., Miss.) expressed his belief that the filibuster was the only tool left to halt the foolish and politically expeditious actions of the majority:

> This is the last place, this is the last forum, this is the last spot in our parliamentary system where a halt can be called and thorough examination made. . . . When we destroy that procedure [filibuster], there is no other.[16]

Opponents of the filibuster agree that minority opinion must be protected, but they contend that members holding a minority opinion should not be in a position to veto majority legislation. Former Senator Joseph Clark wrote that paranoia about majority tyranny has created minority tyranny through the filibuster procedure and its protective Rule XXII; that this minority veto has frustrated the essential basis of democracy—majority rule. With the filibuster, American government specialist George Galloway said, the minority can prevent legislation or extract personal, local, or sectional concessions "at the expense of the general welfare."

While maintaining their right to unlimited debate, supporters of the filibuster who know the rules well have used them, sometimes peppered with senatorial courtesy in *denying* unlimited debate to their opponents. Senator James Allen, for example, has been an active opponent in the fight to amend the cloture rule, but on occasion he has stepped in to stop full and free discussion by his colleagues. It was Allen who gained the floor during a March 1972 filibuster of the Post Card Registration Act and moved to table the bill, an action that forcibly put an end to the discussion.

It was also Allen who raised a procedural technicality to deny Senators Mike Gravel (D., Alaska) and J. William Fulbright (D., Ark.) the floor during their attempted filibuster of defense funds for Cambodia. He applied Rule XIX, Clause 1, which says, "No Senator shall speak more than twice upon any one question in debate on the same day without leave of the Senate." (To maintain a filibuster, the minority needs to win adjournment each day or have enough members who can speak long enough to keep from breaking this rule.) Use of the rule rests on the distinction between a legislative day and a calendar day. Adjournment ends a legislative day; recess merely ends a calendar day. If a senator speaks twice on a question on one calendar day, and the Senate *adjourns*, he or she may speak twice on an issue again the next day. But if the Senate only *recessed*, a senator may not speak on that question again until adjournment.

On the evening of December 15, 1970, Gravel and Fulbright spoke against the Cambodian funds. After Fulbright had spoken twice, Senator Robert Byrd moved to recess and the motion carried. The following day, the Senate continued where it had left off the day before, and Gravel was recognized to speak against the Cambodian funds. After a few hours, Fulbright took the floor and continued to speak against the Cambodian appropriations. Senator Allen raised the point of order that Fulbright had already spoken twice on that question on this *legislative* day. The presiding officer, Senator Stennis (D., Miss.), upheld the point of order under Rule XIX, and the Fulbright-Gravel forces lost the floor.

Presiding Officer Stennis then recognized Allen, who yielded the floor only for business other than the Cambodian discussion. After Allen persisted in holding the floor to the exclusion of the Cambodia issue, Gravel agreed to vote on the matter that afternoon. Accepting his defeat, Gravel commented, "I would only like to state that this Senator and the Senator from Arkansas should be getting lessons on parliamentary procedure from the distinguished Senator from Alabama." Senator Allen had used the rules to take the floor from his opponents and then played on the Senate's high regard for courtesy through a unanimous-consent request to end the attempted filibuster.

RUNNING FOR COVER: VOTING

Once the rules have been used to channel debate into a rather courteous, even humdrum, series of sparsely attended lectures, then the voting process begins. These two processes alternate throughout the day, throughout the weeks, to engage the curious and bore the uninformed.

Members are more visible and accountable for their decisions during the voting process than at other times in their legislative activities. They may thus opt to avoid the voting process altogether, but they run the risk of breaking the rules. Senate Rule XII provides that senators may force a member to state his or her reasons for declining to vote when present on the floor. The presiding officer may ask the Senate, "Shall the Senator, for the reasons assigned by him, be excused from voting?" The senators decide whether their colleague should be excused without debate and before the final vote results are announced. Under House Rule VIII, members are required to vote "unless [they have] a direct personal or pecuniary interest in the event of such question." But according to parliamentarian Deschler's annotation in the House *Manual*, "It has been found impracticable to enforce the provision."

Nor may members hide from their constituents by changing their votes. Both houses have rules that prohibit a change in a floor vote after a final result has been announced, unless there has been a mistake in recording a vote. Following Jefferson's *Manual* (Section XLI) and House precedents, a member *may* change a vote, if the chair has not announced the final result of a vote. Likewise, a member who voted "present" may change to "yea" or "nay." Deschler's annotation of Rule XV, Clause 1 ("On Calls of the Roll and House") reads: "But a vote given by a member may not be withdrawn without leave of the House." By Senate Rule XII, senators must have the consent of the Senate (unanimous consent) to change or withdraw their votes. A Senate vote change is rare, except where there has been a mistake in listing the vote. Both the House and Senate rules provide that vote changes cannot be dispensed with by unanimous-consent agreement.

Without trying to change a vote or failing to cast a vote, members can keep their constituencies from knowing what their decisions have been. The voting process—whether in committee, on the floor, or in conference—provides members with several cloud covers to remain less visible and less accountable to the electorate.

Basic Kinds of Votes

1. *Proxy voting (in committee only).* A proxy empowers one committee member to vote for an absent member who has delegated the right. Not all committees use this method of voting. When used regularly, proxies are a sign of lazy legislating, for they signify that the members have made up their minds without listening to all viewpoints in committee debate and that they agree all too readily with the person holding their proxy.

The most common justification for proxies is that members are too busy to attend all committee meetings*—indeed, they are sometimes supposed to attend more than one meeting at the same time. And there is the argument that constituencies must be represented on all votes. As Representative William Steiger (R., Wisc.) put it, "If the majority of the members of a committee

---

* At the organization meeting of the Senate Foreign Relations Committee in January 1972—a time when the committee lays out its strategy for the coming session and approves its budget ($375,000 this time)—only two of the fifteen members attended. At public hearing in the same week to determine the fate of a treaty banning nuclear weapons on the seabeds, two senators were present. Some of the absentees were off giving speeches (James B. Pearson, Frank Church), campaigning (Edmund S. Muskie), or attending other committee meetings (Stuart Symington and Claiborne Pell). John W. Finney, "Study in Absenteeism: The Senate Committee's Week," *New York Times,* January 30, 1972.

want something, their will should prevail regardless of whether they are all present at a particular meeting."

But the question remains, why are proxies not allowed in floor votes, if they are supposedly so democratic? The answer lies, in part, in the members' duty to consider legislation in full debate—in committee and on the floor—instead of blindly following a leader or letting a trusted colleague vote for them. The final report by the Joint Commiteee on the Organization of Congress makes the point this way:

> Although proxies may serve a useful purpose by allowing members to go on record when conflicting demands on their time make it difficult for them to be present for a committee vote, the evils of the practice outweigh their advantage. The use of proxies discourages committee attendance. It frequently permits the chairman or ranking minority member to control a bill in the face of major "live" opposition. You cannot argue with a proxy: a proxy cannot consider an offered amendment; a proxy cannot compromise. No one suggests that proxy voting should be considered on floor votes—yet a member's vote in a closely divided committee may be far more significant than the vote of a member on the floor on the same bill. It is time to abandon a practice leading to legislation in which many committee members play no responsible role.[17]

This recommendation was not followed, but Congress adopted some new proxy rules in the 1970 Legislative Reorganization Act. Senate rules now permit committees to prohibit proxy voting; they also require that all proxy votes be made only when "the absent committee member has been informed of the matter on which he is being recorded and has affirmatively requested that he be so recorded."[18] The House rules are somewhat more strict: "No vote by any member of any committee with respect to any measure or matter may be cast by proxy unless such a committee, by written rule adopted by the committee, permits voting by proxy and requires that the proxy authorization shall be in writing, shall designate the person who is to execute the proxy authorization, and shall be limited to a specific measure or matter and any amendments or motions pertaining thereto."[19]

Although these rules do not eliminate proxy voting, they curb some of the abuses. The chairman of a committee, for example, may not reach freely into the "barrel of proxies"[20] to come up with the votes to win his point. He must actually have proxies to vote rather than simply the knowledge that an absent member would be unlikely to buck his will after the fact. And the member donating a proxy must be specific about what measures are being supported, instead of blindly depending upon someone else's decision.

On balance, proxy voting, even with the rules reforms, does more harm than good. In the words of the 1965 Joint Committee on Congressional Organization, "It is time to abandon a practice leading to legislation in which many committee members play no responsible role."[21]

2. *Unrecorded, voice votes.* This kind of vote leaves a member unaccountable for his or her stand. In the Senate, a majority of votes are unrecorded.[22] And once a Senate voice vote has been taken, it is then too late to request a recorded roll-call vote.[23] One illustration serves to show the dangers of this procedure: working under a unanimous-consent agreement, only a handful of members are needed to pass legislation. According to the Associated Press, only six senators were present for a *voice vote* on an amendment by Senator Sam Ervin (D., N.C.) on February 22, 1972. The amendment passed: it exempted all employees of churches and religious institutions from the ban on job discrimination on account of religion.[24]

3. *Record-teller votes (on amendments).* Before passage of the Legislative Reorganization Act of 1970, members of Congress were able to hide their votes by walking up an aisle between two tellers, on one side of the question or the other, who counted their number but did not take down their names. This unrecorded teller vote originated years ago in the English Parliament—out of ne-

cessity: members wanted to vote with their backs to the King's spies, who came to learn how they voted on major questions. The British abandoned the system in the 1830s, when the King was less powerful, but the American Congress clung to the rule until 1970. The House now has a *recorded* teller vote: members walk up an aisle and drop a signed card in a box.

A Democratic Study Group analysis of the first year of the record-teller vote* showed that an average of 375 members (86 per cent) voted on record-teller votes, a slightly higher average than the 365 (84 per cent) who voted on roll calls and 351 (81 per cent) on quorum calls. But only 30 per cent of the votes on amendments were record-teller votes.[25]

In 1972, however, Speaker Carl Albert had to squelch a movement that threatened to make it more difficult to get a record-teller vote by requiring forty or more, instead of twenty, members to agree to it. Part of the impetus for the movement, according to one political analyst, is the members' desire to keep out of public view. The teller vote on the SST amendment, for example,

> gave members no way to hide from a record vote on the issue. Under the old rules, many a member would have looked at the conflicting pressures and decided that prudence dictated that he stay off the floor and let those chiefly concerned have their way. But new rules did not allow anyone to duck.[26]

4. *Yea-and-nay or roll-call votes (usually on final passage of a key or controversial bill).* Roll-call votes are recorded for the public in the *Congressional Record,* and those who miss the vote are listed "Not Voting."

In 1973 the House of Representatives began to use an electronic voting system to replace the thirty-five-minute-long roll call and quorum call. The new system gives almost instant results. The House may save as much as seventy-five hours a year with this one change. Members vote at one of the forty-nine voting

---

* A teller vote may be demanded by one-fifth of a quorum.

stations in the chamber. They insert a permanent card that acts like a key, unlocking the name, and then vote (green for yea, red for nay, and amber for present).

A roll-call vote may be used as an approximate index to members' attendance on the floor, although it does not indicate how much of the debate, if any, members heard before voting.

Senate floor decisions—votes—are seriously marred by chronic absenteeism. Many times the Senate must operate without a quorum, because its attendance is so low. (Through unanimous consent, the quorum rule can be dispensed with.) On the first day of the 1972 session of Congress, only 56 of the 100 senators were on hand to open the chamber for legislative business. By February 9, 1972, Majority Leader Mansfield berated the members for an abysmal attendance record:

> We [the Senate leadership] cannot force you if you do not
> want to face up [to] your responsibilities, but you are doing
> a distinct disservice to the Senate and to the people whom
> you have the honor to represent.[27]

5. *Pairing (on roll-call votes).* If a member is on the floor but does not want to be held accountable for affecting the course of legislation, he or she may pair with another on the opposing side of the issue. A "live pair" occurs when a member withholds a vote and pairs with an absent member on the opposing side of a question. A "simple pair" is formed when two absent members on opposing sides pair. And a "general pair" occurs when members plan to be away for several days and leave instructions that they be opposites on all matters that come up.

Occasionally, a senator's pair may have the same effect as a vote, though it would appear otherwise. For example, on a close vote for which the support side can muster only a one-vote majority, a live pair would create a tie vote, and the measure would fail to pass. On July 23, 1964, such a case arose when (1) Senator Winston Prouty's (R., Vt.) amendment on an administration antipoverty bill carried 45 to 44. Senator Jacob Javits (D.,

N.Y.) moved to reconsider the vote. Senator Prouty moved to table the motion to reconsider, and a roll-call vote was requested. A senator who opposed the amendment but had missed the first vote appeared on the floor, and (2) the motion to table was defeated by a 45-to-45 tie vote. Another senator appeared, and (3) the motion to reconsider carried 46 to 45. The new vote (4) on the Prouty amendment failed 45 to 46.

On all four votes, Senator Herbert S. Walters (D., Tenn.) had a live pair with the absent Senator Edward Kennedy (D., Mass.). In each case, Senator Walters announced that he would have voted for the Prouty amendment, and Senator Kennedy would have voted against it. Had Walters voted alone on the second and third votes—the motion to table and the motion to reconsider— the Prouty amendment would have passed.[28] Thus, Walters' "nonvote" permitted federal administrators, under the aegis of the 1964 antipoverty bill, to work out plans for states who failed to draw up their own. Walters helped determine the fate of a significant states'-rights issue, but appeared to his Tennessee constituents to have withheld his vote.

More Cloud Covers

The Constitution makes the Congress directly responsible to the people, unlike the judicial branch, for example. But Congress' rules have been used to hide substantive decisions behind procedural votes; members have used the rules to abdicate their responsibility to represent the people.

The House leadership's ability to avoid or put off any direct vote on the Vietnam war over about a ten-year period serves as one major illustration. For years, the key vote on the Vietnam war, Representative Thomas M. Rees (D., Calif.) pointed out, was put in the form of procedural questions. As Rees put it, in session after session the vote on the war came in something like a previous-question motion that decided whether a closed rule could be amended. "How can one go to his constituents and say, 'I voted against this closed rule, which shows my opposition to

the war'?" Rees asked. "And similarly," Rees said, "how can anyone be successfully attacked for not voting for (or against) a
closed rule? It just isn't a clear-cut case of position taking."

In one case, Representative Michael Harrington (D., Mass.),
according to his staff associate Christine Sullivan, managed to get
fifty signatures to call a meeting of the Democratic caucus to vote
on the Senate-passed Mansfield Amendment against the war. On
the day before the caucus meeting, when only five or six members
were on the House floor, the House leadership asked for unanimous consent to direct the House to convene the next day at ten
o'clock instead of the usual meeting time at noon. The caucus
would thus not be able to meet, and a recorded and clear-cut vote
on the war issue was avoided.

Another way to take a stand that constituents might not approve is to make a motion to table. If accepted, it sets a proposition aside so that a member can bring it up at a later time.
However, it may also serve as a way to scuttle a motion, for it
requires a suspension of rules to be brought up again. As Lewis
Froman put it, "A tabling motion is a common procedure for
glossing over a vote, to make it appear other than a defeat in the
matter."[29] In 1972, according to P. J. Mode, Chief Counsel of
the Subcommittee on Constitutional Amendments, Senator
George Aiken (R., Vt.) was caught in a temporary bind by the
Democrats' proposal to increase social security benefits by 20 per
cent. The Republican administration opposed the 20-per-cent increase as inflationary. On the other hand, to vote against the
increase would appear to go against the needs and interests of
constituents. Senator Aiken found the answer. He proposed a 30-
per-cent increase in benefits. Democrats then were faced with the
dilemma: either to accept a very high increase, or to vote against
the needs of constituents, or to table the motion. They tabled the
motion. The Republicans were free to vote against a 20-per-cent
increase because they had introduced a 30-per-cent increase.[30]
They could herald their attempt to provide an increase and at the
same time stay in the party fold by objecting to the Democrats'
proposal.

A motion to commit can also be used to defeat legislation without seeming to do so. It can be explained as a step taken to give the bill further study, while the actual result is the same as a negative vote. Only opponents of the measure can make the motion to send the bill back to committee (from which it rarely emerges again).

By far the most common technique for significantly affecting the content of a bill, without constituents' being fully aware of it, is voting in support of weakening amendments. The final vote on a bill is often the least significant vote of all, in comparison with the votes on amendments to the measure. A committee-reported bill is likely to pass on the floor, so the real question is the form and strength of the bill determined by the fate of proposed amendments. Members of Congress may vote to *weaken* a bill at every stage, but vote *for* it in the final vote, the one that their constituents see listed in their newspapers or members' newsletters. Or a member may work diligently to prevent weakening amendments but vote against final passage of the bill, knowing that it will pass. Members who do not want to answer to their constituents for their actual point of view may take either course, banking on the importance of the amendments to a committee bill.

In the preface to his *Manual of Parliamentary Practice*, Thomas Jefferson foresaw that the rules of Congress should be the protectors of order and civility. But they had a purpose—to free each member to participate in the legislative process and to let the majority work its will. Today, the concepts of order and civility have become a goal in themselves. Disingenuous debating and voting have become widespread. Add to these twists of purpose in the rules the chronic absenteeism that plagues Congress and you have a body where a majority may be handing its rights and powers over by default to a small, less representative, but very active set of individuals.

7

Runs Silent, Runs Deep: The Conference Committees

As a practical proposition, we have legislation, then, not by the voice of the members of the Senate, not by members of the House of Representatives, but we have legislation by the voice of five or six men.
—*Senator George W. Norris (R., Neb.),*
Address at Lincoln, Nebraska, February 22, 1934

Conference committees remain a mystery to Americans inside and outside Congress. Few know that the fate of most key legislation is settled in ironclad secrecy. About 10 per cent of our legislation each year must be deliberated in conference.[1] A bill must pass both houses with exactly the same wording and important legislation rarely meets this criterion without negotiations between the houses.* Emissaries from the respective committees of the House and Senate meet at a conference table in secret sessions to formulate a bill to be presented in identical language in both houses. These representatives, called managers or conferees, present their compromise to their respective houses in the form of a conference report. Once both houses vote to accept the report, the bill goes to the president for signature. And there is great pressure to accept the compromise made in conference in order to get some version of a measure enacted.

THE SETTING

The Massachusetts Bay Colony in 1645 was the site of the first American conference. Conferences soon spread to other legislatures throughout the colonies and found general acceptance as a meeting ground for bicameral government even before the first United States Congress. And on the first day of Congress, April 7, 1789, the House and Senate appointed committees to meet together and prepare rules on conferences.[2]

In his *Manual of Parliamentary Practice*, Thomas Jefferson relied entirely on the example set by the English Parliament† for

---

* Appropriations and revenue bills take up the bulk of conference time and haggling. For appropriations bills, in particular, conferences are the decisive legislative stage, since the president hardly ever vetoes an appropriations bill. See Richard F. Fenno, Jr., *The Power of the Purse: Appropriations in Congress* (Boston: Little, Brown, 1966), p. 616.

† Conferences first developed as a necessary adjunct to English bicameralism. In the fourteenth century, after the knights and burgesses decided to meet separately from the nobles and clergy, the two houses needed some form of communication. Under Edward III, the House of Lords developed a custom of sending a delegation to confer with the entire House of Commons. Later in the century, selected members from both houses conferred separately and reported back to their own houses. With the development of the cabinet system in the eighteenth century, conferences became quite unimportant in English government. From 1851 on, the House of Commons received messages from the House of Lords about points of disagreement, with no convening of a conference unless it was especially desired. Conferences are now a thing of the past in England, although the technical

his discussion of conferences. Jefferson opted for "free" conferences, open to members' statements of position and bargaining, as opposed to "simple" conferences, where each delegation simply presented its house's position.

During the nineteenth century, the American conference committee evolved into an institution of trusted power. In the years before the Civil War, the House and Senate repeatedly deadlocked in disagreement. Party leaders believed it would be easier to reach agreement in a small group, and they used conferences not only for compromising on specific bills, but also for settling other quarrels.[3] The increasing load of legislation in the nineteenth century also encouraged greater dependence on the conference for efficient legislating.

Conference style has not changed much since 1852, by which time "the customs of presenting identical reports from the committees of conference in both houses, of granting high privilege to these conference reports, of voting upon the conference report as a whole and permitting no amendment of it, of keeping secret the discussions carried on in the meetings of the conference committee, had become established in American parliamentary practice."[4]

But there is one significant modern innovation that served to embroil the two houses in a major dispute—a dispute that reared its head every time the House and Senate disagreed over major legislation and tried to negotiate in conference. The culprits were the "nongermaneness" clauses added to House rules in the Legislative Reorganization Act of 1970 and revised effective January 1973.

In the House, germaneness has long been a point of resentment against the Senate. Representatives have repeatedly complained about the way the Senate could attach a nongermane amendment to a House bill and get it accepted in conference. Members of House committees with jurisdiction over the nongermane addition

machinery for them still exists. See Ada McCown, *The Congressional Conference Committee* (New York: Columbia University Press, 1927), pp. 23 and 33.

would not have had an opportunity to scrutinize it; nor would members on the House floor have had a chance to vote on it. House members could not express their sentiments on the amendment separately from the rest of the conference report, since a report could only be voted on as a whole to ensure that the bill remained identical for the two houses.

Members of the House had watched their bills become transformed by the Senate until they were virtually unrecognizable to the original sponsor.

Until the 1970 changes in House rules, the Senate, anticipating House opposition to its amendments, could move to insist on its version and request a conference without returning the bill. This course of action was usually adopted for the simple purpose of saving time: the Senate could appoint its conferees without waiting for the House to request a conference.

Members of the House used the Legislative Reorganization Act of 1970 as a vehicle to correct this problem with three changes in their standing rules: Clause 1 of Rule XX was revised so that a member of the House could demand a separate vote on any nongermane Senate amendment; Clause 3 of the same standing rule was altered to specify that House conferees could not accept nongermane Senate amendments unless they got specific permission from the House; and, under Rule XXVIII, Clause 3, conference committees were prohibited from adding nongermane amendments to a conference report when neither version of the bill had contained them.

These clauses in the Legislative Reorganization Act markedly changed the old House rules and precedents that the conference could consider all Senate amendments.* Yet the Senate was ig-

---

* For many years preceding the 1970 act, representatives saw the Senate's ability to attach nongermane clauses as an insult to the prestige of the House. Representative Paul C. Jones' (D., Mo.) speech was typical of the rivalry: "For many years this House has permitted the Senate to emasculate legislation originally in this body by the addition of amendments which would be rejected in this body on a point of order that the amendments were not germane. We have sacrificed our dignity, we have acknowledged

norant of their import until the House tried to eliminate some Senate amendments.

On June 8, 1971, Senator John Sherman Cooper (R., Ky.) came back from conference with news of that strange animal, Clause 3 of Standing House Rule XXVIII, the new nongermaneness rule. Cooper reported that the House, on advice of their parliamentarian, would not allow the Senate conferees to make any modifications to Title I of the Public Works Act, which the House had attached to the Appalachian Regional Development Program. Cooper was amazed and angry at this departure from the traditional practice of negotiating all Senate amendments to a bill. He had never heard of the rule, and it was obvious from the response to his explanation that most of his colleagues had never heard of it either.

Cooper urged the Senate to vote down the conference report, so that it would avoid setting a precedent for House jurisdiction over certain Senate amendments.[5] Senator John Tower (R., Tex.) agreed: "The Senate must in all good conscience reject this conference report so that our conference can return to the House and inform them that we will not accept this secondary role. . . . If we give in on this matter, the duality of our legislative system will come into question."[6] Senator Howard Baker, Jr. (R., Tenn.) was equally adamant on the "inflexible" rule of germaneness: "I doubt that the parliamentarian's interpretation outlawing all nongermane Senate amendments was intended when we passed the Legislative Reorganization Act of 1970, but . . . we are being held hostage to that interpretation."[7]

At the time, not enough senators saw the House rules changes as a threat to their own power; they accepted the conference report by a vote of 45 to 33.

Still another quirk developed in the controversy over how to

---

our inferiority, we have refused to recognize the inequity of the situation, and we have attempted to justify our action by the specious argument that all of this is necessary to maintain comity between the two branches of Congress." *Congressional Record*, February 10, 1965, p. H2445.

maintain the delicate balance between House and Senate rights to amend legislation. By the House parliamentarian's interpretation of Section 126 of the Legislative Reorganization Act, nongermane amendments could be taken as amendments in the nature of a substitute. In this way, representatives would lose their right to vote on separate nongermane amendments, because if they voted down an amendment, the whole conference report was voted down. According to this ruling, if the House voted down a nongermane amendment, no law could be enacted until the bill ran the whole legislative gamut again. The House could not go on to the next amendment in the conference report, and send the amendments still in disagreement back to conference for further negotiations.

On October 13, 1972, almost a year after the House-Senate friction began, Representative B. F. Sisk (D., Calif.), who guided the Legislative Reorganization Act through the House floor, introduced a new set of rules to clear up the confusion over the 1970 reforms.

> I think we all understood the basic purpose of section 126, the nongermaneness rule. It was to give the House an opportunity to have a separate debate and a separate vote on Senate nongermane provisions attached to House-pased measures. Unfortunately, the way in which that section was written did not take into account the special parliamentary problems raised by amendments in the nature of a substitute.[8]

The House that day passed H. Res. 1153, effective January 1973, to allow the House to vote on each of the nongermane parts of the Senate report separately—without jeopardizing the whole conference report.

The seldom-told story of conferences reveals the power struggles to maintain the integrity of one house against another. But more than that it exposes the manipulation of rules and traditions for the power of a few at the expense of a cowed majority. The following conference episodes reflect many stages of development —where the House was at the mercy of Senate nongermane amendments to negotiate any bill at all; where the Senate was at the mercy of the House; where the House was at the mercy of a few powerful, senior conferees who did not condone any votes on nongermane amendments contained in conference reports; and, most of all, of conferees at the mercy of their own leaders and lobbyists from the executive branch as well as business and labor.

GETTING A CONFERENCE IN MOTION

To be appointed to a conference committee . . . is a grant of legislative power in one of its least adulterated forms.
—*Daniel Berman,* In Congress Assembled
(Boston: Little, Brown and Co.), 1966, p. 304

The first stage in the conference sequence is calling a conference and assigning conferees to negotiate there—a crucial stage. When bills are in disagreement, they cannot become law; so without a conference, the bills would die. And the conferees are the negotiators for their respective houses; if they fail to represent the majority's will they can crush the bill or so change it that it is unrecognizable.

Calling a Conference

Both houses must agree to a conference before it can convene. If neither house calls a conference, and neither "recedes" (or backs down) on the points of disagreement, the bill fails. (See *House Manual,* section 521, precedents.) Because the house that requests the conference acts last on the conference report, which can be a strategic disadvantage, there may be a reluctance to be the first to make the call. And since conference reports tend to fall within the last two months of a session, pressure for negotiation and solution are strong. Once one house accepts the conference report, the other, in the last days of the sessions, has to settle for the up-and-down vote on the entire report. The whole report or points of disagreement in it could not be recommitted to conference, for the first house to pass the report would automatically discharge its conferees—and the end of the session would be looming ahead. If the report were not accepted, the bill would expire at the end of the session.

For one house to refuse to go to conference to negotiate points of disagreement is a bargaining tactic. The refusal either scuttles a bill or forces the other house to change its mind without a conference. Until 1965, the House Rules Committee was in a position to refuse to send bills to conference. After a rules change, the majority of the House could send a bill to conference without the interference of the Rules Committee. On the floor, a representative of the committee with jurisdiction over the bill must be recognized by the speaker and then make a motion disagreeing with the Senate amendments and requesting a conference. Or a member may request unanimous consent from colleagues to make such a motion. A member rarely has difficulty obtaining a conference at this stage. As a former legislative aide to Representative Don Riegle pointed out, a member can always ask unanimous consent to request a conference at twelve-fifteen, right after the House convenes at noon but before more than a handful of representatives are on the floor. The code of courtesy, however, would suggest that the proper way for a member to proceed is to visit all possible objectors to insure that the motion for unanimous consent will not be blocked on the floor.

Managers

Once both houses have decided to go to conference, they must each appoint the conferees—"managers" is the formal title—to present their side. The number of conferees varies from a minimum of three on a side to as many as twenty (to negotiate long, complex bills). According to the rules of both houses, the presiding officer in the Senate and the speaker of the House appoint the conferees.* In practice, however, these leaders merely parrot the committee chairmen's choices. As a result, conferees are not necessarily chosen on the basis of demonstrated ability in diplomacy (the criterion used in the eighteenth and early nineteenth century) but rather on their trustworthiness to follow the chairman's inclinations. So, today seniority is the major criterion for selecting conferees. One day in 1959, Senator William Proxmire (D., Wis.) took a look at who held the "immense power" of serving as conferees. Twenty-six of the sixty-four Democratic senators on that day had been assigned to conferences. An elite group of eleven senators held thirty-three of the forty-nine conference positions. These eleven were all of high seniority, and seven, he noted, were from southern states. The seniority system had helped exclude thirty-eight Democratic senators from any conference position at all.[9]

Even though chairmen have the informal power to choose the most knowledgeable committee members on the bill, only rarely have they selected an expert from another such committee to

---

* In the House's early history, the speaker customarily appointed the conference committee members. This custom was formalized in Rule X, Clause 2 (1890): "The Speaker shall appoint all select and conference committees which shall be ordered by the House from time to time." This standing rule has been buried under the weight of nineteenth-century customs: by 1848 committees had an influence on who became conference managers, and by the early 1850s the appointment of high-ranking committee members to conference became a trend. The speaker has not exercised his express power to appoint conferees since July 8, 1947, when Speaker Joseph W. Martin, Jr., of Massachusetts surprised the House by replacing a committee chairman's choice with another member.

In the Senate, according to parliamentarians Watkins and Riddick, there is a division between the theory and the practice of appointing conferees: "The conferees in theory are appointed by the presiding officer but in fact are designated by friends of the measure, who are in sympathy with the prevailing view of the Senate and with consideration for the usual party ratio. And the Senate, on motion, may elect its conferees as it sees fit. A second method of selecting conferees, Senate election, has also been ignored; Rule XXIV, Clause 1 reads: "All other committees (including conferences) shall be appointed by ballot, unless otherwise ordered and a plurality of votes shall appoint."

represent a bill at a conference.* And there are occasions when the rule of seniority is successfully broken and a junior committee member with expertise on a particular bill wins appointment as a conferee.

Unrepresentative Conferees

The prevalence of seniority-heavy members on conference committees sometimes weights conferees against the bill that they are supposed to negotiate. Big committee powers, especially chairmen, tend to oppose any floor amendment that they consider inimical to their original committee bill. So they may take the opportunity to select conferees who will back their desire to oppose or gut a controversial section in conference, even though a majority has passed it on the floor.

A House Republican policy manual instructs committee staff that there is little hope of getting the prevailing view of the House represented when the chairman is on the minority side of the issue:

> Suppose that the Minority has won a floor fight and the House has agreed to a conference. What can the Minority do to protect itself in conference? In theory, it should not have to do anything, for conferees are supposed to be chosen to represent the attitude of the House. They often are not. . . .
>
> Although in apparent violation of the fundamental concept that conferees should represent the attitude of the

---

* The chairman of the House Education and Labor Committee, Adam Clayton Powell (D., N.Y.), broke the unwritten rule of seniority in 1965 when he appointed a junior member, Representative Charles Goodell (D., N.Y.), as a conferee on an anti-povery measure (H.R. 9293). Goodell had not been a member of the subcommittee that considered the bill. The committee's ranking minority member, William Ayres (R., Ohio), protested: "This is most unethical, most unorthodox, and most unusual." With effusive apologies for the insult to Ayres' rank, minority leader Gerald Ford requested that the House replace Goodell with Ayres, who should have been appointed "by tradition and otherwise." Ford's request was carried out.[10]

House, it is common practice in this assumed situation for
the Speaker to consult with the Chairman, a man whose
attitude was not the prevailing one, to determine what conferees to appoint.[11]

A committee chairman's power to bargain very little for provisions that he does not really support can affect preconference
debate and floor votes. Farsighted members sometimes make an
effort to win the committee chairman to their side before they
introduce amendments on the floor. Amendments that pass after
such negotiations are in a more favorable position to last through
a conference, for the chairman would likely be backing them.

With such expressed bias on various provisions in bills going to
conference, conferees appointed on the basis of seniority may not
fully represent the expressed will of their respective houses. Since
before the time of Jefferson, a principle of conferences was that
conferees should represent the prevailing view of their house.
Jefferson's *Manual* quotes an English parliamentarian explaining
why a bill should be managed by those sympathetic to it: "The
child is not to be put to a nurse that cares not for it." But to
this day bills are entrusted to conferees that care not for them.

The English parliamentary ethic of declining to serve on a
conference committee when in disagreement with the controversial parts of the bill under consideration is not widely practiced
today in Congress. However, there have been several cases,
mostly in the late 1800s and early 1900s, when members of
Congress have willingly stepped down from appointments to conferences on the grounds that they did not support their house's
position.

In the main, conferees who object to the prevailing position of
their chamber do not immediately and willingly step down. So
challengers must take other steps. According to present rules on
conferences, the only way that a member can challenge the choice
of a conferee is by casting aspersions on his or her character,
negotiating behind the scenes, instructing conferees, or blocking a
conference.

In 1959 Senator Joseph Clark (D., Pa.) argued, "If a Senator wishes to protest that the practice as stated in the manuals [that conferees represent the prevailing view of the Senate] is not being adhered to, he must publicly or privately challenge the conferees who have been designated and ask one or more to step aside."[12] But, he noted, this procedure was seldom followed because "Friends of the measure have found themselves in the embarrassing position of appearing to challenge the integrity of senior senators."[13]

In the face of this congressional folkway—don't publicly challenge members with seniority—negotiations with conferees take place behind the scenes. During consideration of the Submerged Lands Act in 1952, Senator Russell Long (D., La.) protested against three of the five conferees that the Senate had approved. As grounds for this motion, Long said that they had voted against the majority position. After negotiations out of public view, the three senators who had opposed the substitute amendment asked to be excused from service on the conference committee. Long accepted appointment to the conference and withdrew his protest.

If, following negotiations, the objectors are still not convinced that the majority opinion will be represented by the conferees and the conferees refuse to step down, the conference can be avoided altogether. The House Education and Labor Committee's fair-labor-standards bill of 1972, for example, never got to conference, for a majority of the House did not trust Chairman Carl Perkins (D., Ky.) and his conferees to fully represent the House position in the matter. On the House floor, a substitute to the committee's bill, introduced by John Erlenborn (R., Ill.) had passed, much to the dismay of the committee. Six out of ten of the conferees Perkins selected opposed the Erlenborn substitute— among them John Dent (D., Pa.), sponsor of the original House bill and chairman of the subcommittees that had considered it. But then Perkins had to try to get the bill to conference. First, Erlenborn objected to Perkins' request for unanimous consent to go to conference. A later vote lost by a 198-to-190 margin. Since he was not about to go outside the jurisdiction of his committee to appoint conferees, Perkins had to engage in informal, off-the-floor negotiations with the Erlenborn forces. When he believed that enough concessions had been made, he asked for another vote to go to conference. On the floor, Erlenborn quoted from Jefferson's *Manual:*

> In selection of the managers, the two large political parties are usually represented, and also care is taken that there shall be a representative of the two opinions which almost always exist on the subjects of importance. Of course, the majority party and the prevailing opinion have the majority of managers.

Erlenborn wanted the conferees to agree to support particular provisions on major issues in the House-passed bill. But Dent remained adamant that he had a right to agree with the Senate version "wherein the views of the House in comparison with the views of the Senate are inferior," granting that where the House views "are in favor of and do good for the people covered by the bill, I will uphold it." A majority of the House was not satisfied. Perkins' motion was rejected once again, 188 to 196. Congress adjourned that session without passing a minimum-wage raise.

Instructing Conferees

When conferees publicly state their opposition to bills but refuse to step down from their special assignments, then members of Congress must decide whether to issue precautionary binding instructions.

It is rare for either house to instruct its conferees before they have attended at least one conference meeting on a piece of legislation. The House instructs its managers more frequently than the Senate, but, according to Parliamentarian Lewis Deschler's annotation of the House rules, "The propriety of doing so at a first conference is open to serious doubt." Most members share this doubt. The House took only five votes on motions to instruct in 1971,* and rejected every single one. The Senate has departed from an early precedent that managers not be instructed only a few times.

Members of Congress are reluctant to instruct conferees for two basic reasons. First, since Jefferson's praise of free conferences, the conference has been the ultimate bargaining session; to instruct would be to limit the power of conferees to negotiate. Second, it is a breach of congressional etiquette to tell fellow members what they know they must do; according to the Republican Policy Committee's 1971 instruction manual, preconference instruction of conferees would be "an affront to one's colleagues," unless it is made before the conferees have been appointed.[14] This unwritten rule was expressed by Representative John Dent in March 1972: "I fought on this floor, in every instance since I have been a Member, against any binding of the powers and the rights of conferees."[15]

Usually if conferees fail to come to an agreement with the other house, they return to their colleagues for "instructions" on how to resolve the conflict. But the chamber is not the active instructor in this case. Instead, the conferees will inform their respective houses that they want permission to "recede"—the catchword for conceding—on a certain amendment. The house passively notes formal permission (technically "instructions") for the conferees to do as they themselves have suggested.

Under House precedent, only one motion to instruct can be voted on.[16] Once the House has considered and voted on one such motion, any other attempt is out of order. The rush for

* The motions to instruct included: "1. To accept a Senate amendment adding money for education programs to the education appropriations bill. 2. To accept the Mansfield Amendment for total U.S. troop withdrawal from Vietnam. A motion to table [kill the instruction motion] was adopted twice by the House in 1971. 3. To accept the Senate amendment barring uses of funds appropriated for the Subversive Activities Control Board. 4. Not to accept any nongermane Senate amendments of the defense procurement bill." *Congressional Quarterly Almanac* (1972), p. 395.

gaining the speaker's recognition to make the motion is often hectic, and the speaker's decision can profoundly influence the kind of legislation ultimately negotiated in conference.

This procedure serves as a device to avoid instructions from one's opponents at the same time that it warns chairmen and their conferees that they are not fully trusted to represent their colleagues. Given the elaborate code of courtesy, especially with its mandatory respect for members with high seniority, a motion to instruct serves as a slap at the conferees' prestige.

But even with instructions, conferees may still go on and do what they want at the conference. There are no sanctions against disregarding instructions in conference, except the majority's decision not to accept the conference report on the floor—though this seldom, if ever occurs.

Going into the conference, then, are a few members of Congress who have been selected by the chairman with jurisdiction over the bill to be negotiated. They have been selected because of their points of view and allegiance—not to the majority of their chamber but to the chairman. They rarely act under specific instructions from their chamber and often do not fully support the bill. They go armed with the power to negotiate without being held publicly accountable for their words or votes since conference-committee meetings, unlike standing-committee meetings, are governed by no rules, and are therefore almost always closed. The conferees are free to act in their own interests instead of the majority's. In short, they have little to lose, except in the rare instances when their conference report is not accepted by the majority voting on the floor. In the main, they are protected by the incredibly binding force of the congressional code of courtesy, which hinders challenges to their integrity or actions and cows the majority into accepting their conference appointments and the work they entail.

RITUALS IN CONFERENCES BETWEEN
THE HOUSES

*In the privacy of the conference, mutual concessions may be
made [involving] provisions which would never pass if considered openly in the House or Senate. The conference committee has much power of independent action, but it is not held
responsible.*

—Ada McCown, The Congressional
Conference Committee, *p. 311*

Often called the third house of Congress, the conference committee can wield even more power than the Senate and House of
Representatives combined. Since legislation cannot be enacted
into law unless both houses exactly agree, the responsibility of
conference negotiators is enormous. *Whatever* they agree to must
be accepted in whole by both houses or *nothing* is passed.

Technically, conference committees may negotiate only *differences* between the houses.* But as long ago as 1790 a conference
committee overstepped these limits by changing items already
agreed upon. A conference in that year ignored identical House
and Senate appropriations for ambassadors' pay by *increasing* the
amount by $10,000.

Congress has also tied its own hands by granting extraordinary
powers to a handful of conferees who are under no formal obliga-
tion to publicize their votes or discussions. One major gift of
power to conferees came in 1862 when both houses adopted the
practice of passing new bills as "substitutes" to bills already
headed to conference, thereby throwing the job of fashioning new
legislation from two entirely different bills into the conferees'
hands.† Although House and Senate rules expressly forbid the

* According to Jefferson's *Manual*, "The Commons resolved that it is un-
parliamentary to strike out at a conference, anything in a bill which hath
been agreed and passed by both Houses."
† As early as the 1860s Speaker Schuyler Colfax maintained that the substance of legislation was being formed not by the House and Senate but by
the conference committees.

conferees to write new legislation, conferees in several instances have changed a House or Senate bill so dramatically that they essentially legislated it in conference.

In addition to uses of conference power mandated by Congress are conference rituals where no congressional rules set boundaries. It is through rituals that the bulk of conference operations take place. Through them, members have made daring changes in House- and Senate-passed bills.

Ritual 1: Place of Conference Meeting

In 1962, House Appropriations conferees precipitated a four-month impasse between the House and Senate by refusing to walk over to the Senate building for a conference. Balking at a hundred-year custom that allowed Senate conferees to preside over conferences in Senate chambers, the House conferees wanted a more suitable place for negotiations. Senator Carl Hayden, chairman of the Senate Appropriations Committee, finally proposed the most acceptable solution to end the battle: he found a room in the center of the Capitol building. A table could be placed strategically so that representatives could sit on the House side of the Capitol and the senators could face them from their own territory.[17] Appropriations conferences take place in the center of the Capitol until this day.

Ritual 2: Choosing a Conference Chairman

There is no written rule on how to select conference-committee chairmen, so each pair of committees has developed its own rituals. In Agriculture conferences, the Senate chairman will say to the House committee chairman, "Bob, I want you to be chairman." "No, Senator," the representative will answer, "I want you to be chairman." "All right, I'll be chairman this time," the senator concedes. Chairmanship of Appropriations conferences is decided by a flip of a coin or sometimes by rotation. At the chairman's side (if the House is presiding at Appropriations conferences) is the subcommittee chairman, so that House consultations can take place in whispers as the subcommittee chairman helps manage the bill and lead conferees to decisions on it.

Ritual 3: Follow the Leader

Conferees ritualistically stick behind the powerful chairmen who appointed them. Representative Otis Pike (D., N.Y.) described his first conference on the Armed Services Committee in a way that reveals the power of this third ritual. In sumptuous surroundings, the Senate and House conference chairmen did most of the battle with onlookers getting more and more bored by the minute. The conference room was situated fairly deep in the Senate wing of the Capitol. Conferees were seated around a long table covered with felt in a room whose vault-like cabinets stretched to the ceiling. In front of each chair was a glass of water, a pad, and a colored pencil—one end blue, the other red. Pike occupied his time by keeping score of which chairman "won" a point: "Whenever our team scored a point I made a mark with a blue end of the pencil; whenever their team scored a point I made a mark with the red end of the pencil." Pike summed up his impression of the conference in this definition for his constituents: "A conference is two gentlemen from Georgia talking, arguing, laughing, and whispering in each other's ears."[18]

Ritual 4: Secret Agenda

At the start of each conference comes the ritual of making out a nonpublic agenda to list the differences—either chronologically or in order of importance—in the two versions of a bill. The fourteen-week conference* on the higher-education bill, which ended in May 1972, had to solve more than 383 differences between the houses. According to Education and Labor Committee Chairman Perkins, the conferees sat down with a 423-page House bill and a 754-page Senate bill. Each day the conference would prepare an

---

* The conference met twenty-one times, usually convening in the early afternoon and continuing well into the evening hours. The last session lasted fifteen straight hours and let out at five-thirty in the morning.

agenda of the subjects to be negotiated. At the end of each session, the staff would prepare a listing of the agreements reached and summarize the discussions on the points of difference.

Ritual 5: Hidden Persuaders

In addition to preparing agenda, staff members have another area where they can be influential: they are responsible for the style of the amendments and for insuring that differing votes between the houses are carefully identified by amendment number. Legislative counsel for both houses are usually present during the conference sessions and may work intensively together.

Ritual 6: The Parliamentarian Again

Another conference ritual is checking with the House parliamentarian on germaneness questions, to ascertain which agreements fall within the authority of the conference. This constant reference to the parliamentarian coupled with most members' uncertainty about the new rules makes the parliamentarian another important influence on the conference's outcome.

Ritual 7: Very Secret Horse-Trading

"You start a conference like diplomats," one senator told the writer. "There's a lot of hand-shaking and backslapping. If you have a bad conference, a real ugly one, you end it just before there is a general fight."[19]

The horse-trading does not proceed at a terribly subtle level. Trade-offs are typical bargaining tools in reaching a conference agreement: "We'll give you points 1, 2, and 3, and you give up points 4, 5, and 6." Often the most stubborn, boisterous party wins out on the basis of sheer stolidness. The determined conferees must be more willing to spend time waiting for the opposition to come around, even walking out on the conference to make it clear that they are serious.

Interestingly enough, this kind of horse-trading goes under the title of "diplomacy." The custom of equating bargaining between the houses with diplomacy began in the nineteenth century. In 1837, a House conferee reported to his colleagues what a Senate manager had said in a conference. John Quincy Adams rose and asked if it was "in order" to reveal what had occurred in conference. No reply is recorded, but the parliamentary inquiry in itself shows that secrecy is expected.[20] By the 1850s, writes Ada Mc-Cown, the assumption was firmly established that "conferees were diplomatic agents of the two houses and must be surrounded with the traditional secrecy attending diplomacy."[21] To this day, an aura of diplomacy envelops conference sessions, so that the public and their congressional representatives have few glimpses of the actual bargaining going on behind the doors. There are no official records of conference discussions.

There is no standing rule of either house of Congress that stipulates that conferences must be held out of the public eye.* But secrecy has long been an unwritten requirement; indeed, it has been based on such a strong precedent that it would take the force of a standing rule to open conferences to the public. According to *Hinds' Precedents*, "Conferences are usually held . . . with closed doors, although in rare instances Members and others have been admitted to make arguments."

Two justifications for hiding conference activities from Congress and the people have been invoked frequently: conferees can bargain with more candor, and secrecy minimizes pressure from

---

* The first conference on legislation in the United States Congress was open to all members of the House and Senate. The point of disagreement—should the United States discriminate on import rates in favor of nations with which it held treaties—was so interesting that members strayed in and out of their chambers to watch the conferees bargain. The conference became so popular that the Senate adjourned and the House did not bother to carry on business at all that day. (See Ada McCown, *The Congressional Conference Committee*, p. 42).

The next open conference was also the last. In 1911, Senator Robert M. LaFollette (R., Wis.), acting as the presiding manager, opened a conference on tariffs to the press. In line with Progressive Party policies, he pushed for publicity of caucus and committee meetings. But the practice of open conference sessions was never again adopted, even by LaFollette.

lobbyists with a vested interest in the outcome. But evidence points another way: bargaining in secret conference meetings has not always been frank, and the lobbyists from government and industry have had access to sessions that the public and other members of Congress have not had.

Ritual 8: Executive Lobbying

In recent times, and especially during the Nixon administration, every conference has proceeded under the watchful eye of the executive branch. The group is smaller, and the conferees are thus more susceptible than the assembled houses to presidential persuasion, flattery, and threat in these closed-door maneuvers. As forms of lobbying, the president or his spokesmen write letters to conferees; some administration personnel show up at conference meetings; and the president freely threatens to use his veto unless conferees compromise.

While the public is kept out of conference meetings and has access to no records of the negotiations, executive-branch personnel are allowed to "testify" or give their points of view at many of these secret meetings. The thin wire between providing information and lobbying for the president's position is not always maintained by administration personnel who are allowed to come into the conference room.

In addition to sending administration officials to conference meetings, presidents have another strong tactical tool—the threat of a veto. President Nixon did not hesitate to make his veto and executive power felt in conference: conferees were willing to draft and redraft bills, tailoring them to the President's wishes in the hope of avoiding a veto.*

* Nixon's threat of a veto became such a burden that one conference adopted amendments to make it politically embarrassing for the President to veto their bill. The Public Works conferees on the federal water-pollution control bill (S. 2770) in 1972 accepted amendments offered by Representative William H. Harsha (R., Ohio) specifying that the authorization was "not to exceed" eighteen billion dollars over the next three years and that "all" sums authorized need not be committed, though they must be

A president can pressure the conference into accepting his modifications of a conference report at the price of a signature, but the conferees can fight back by refusing to release a report he sorely wants.*

Ritual 9: Some of the People All of the Time—Other Lobbyists

Every lobbyist knows that the ranking members of the committee handling their pet bill will inevitably head the conference. In that case, it is not always necessary for the lobbyist to pressure the conference specifically—they can do it for months before a bill goes to conference and, once it is in conference, stop intensive lobbying and merely await the outcome.

Lobbyists sometimes participate in preconference negotiations so intensely that their meetings with members take on aspects of a conference between the House and Senate.

Ritual 10: Pretend to Fight and Win

House and Senate members expect their conferees to fight and win. The public ethic is that conferees should defend the chamber's bill no matter what personal views they hold. But conferees

---

allocated. With these amendments, Senator Edmund S. Muskie (D., Me.) explained on the Senate floor, it would be clear that the only reason Nixon was vetoing the bill was that he disliked the strict enforcement of pollution standards, not that the program was uneconomical.

* This happened with the military-draft extension bill (H.R. 6531) in 1971. The draft expired June 30, 1971, but the conference remained deadlocked until July 30. The President wanted the Mansfield Amendment (demanding troop withdrawal frm Indochina within nine months) dropped from the bill. He also wanted the draft extended; otherwise he would be in the embarrassing position of drafting five million previously deferred men, many of whom would be over the age of thirty-five and married. To lure the President's approval of the Mansfield Amendment, the Senate conferees used the stall tactic at the same time they made the draft issue bait. With the President's countertactic of heavy administration lobbying, the question became a matter of which side would hold out longer. Since Mansfield was opposed to the draft anyway, he could afford to wait until Nixon accepted a compromise.[22] The conference report reflected a compromise: extending the draft and declaring a sense of Congress that the

from both houses sometimes come to an agreement or a disagreement so quickly that proponents of the legislation under consideration cannot believe any bargaining occurred at all or that the conferees really had the bill's contents at heart.* And when conferees return with a conference report, they invariably claim victory for their side. They defend their mutually agreed-upon report from critics with the argument that it was necessary to compromise. For this reason, it is often difficult to figure out how intransigent the other side really was or how the conferee is exaggerating in order to win support for a negotiated compromise.

Examples of comradely conferences flourish: managers give and take in such a way that each of them gains. The verbal attacks that members declaim in chamber speeches about the intransigence of conferees in the other house are, in this context, merely justification for horse-trading. They conveniently make it appear to colleagues and constituents that someone else is to blame for their failure to "win" on all, or even some, issues.

A major tactic for this ritual is to get one's amendments through the other chamber instead of one's own. The House Ways and Means Committee uses this technique when it wants to introduce special-interest legislation that it expects the House to vote down. Its members, it seemed, could hardly wait to rush over to the Senate and have their bills offered as amendments in 1964

United States should end its military activities in Indochina "at the earliest possible date."[23]

Administration lobbying did not stop with the writing of the conference report. A few days before the Senate voted on it (September 21), every senator received a personal letter from the White House signed by the three military service chiefs. It warned that further delay in extending the draft "might jeopardize beyond redemption the prospects of achieving an all-volunteer force by July 1, 1973." The Senate passed the report 55 to 31.

* The swiftness of many conference discussions once prompted former Senator Eugene J. McCarthy (D., Minn.) to comment wryly, "At least when we go to conference, we ought to walk slowly on the way . . . and very slowly on the way back, so at least one hour would elapse from the time we sent conferees to negotiate for settlement and the time they came back to the Senate to tell us they could not do anything against the firm stand of the House of Representatives."

when the Senate was considering H.R. 7502, a bill providing special income-tax treatment for disaster losses. "It reminds me of a candy store that's burned down," a staff man quipped: "All the little kids are running over to the Senate to get the candy while the door's open." Once in conference, the House conferees can graciously accept the Senate amendments. This cooperation has been dubbed a "love-affair conference."[24]

There have been other occasions when members of the House committees which are supposed to initiate revenue and appropriations bills have not objected to Senate amendments—times when legislation the committee members favor would fail in a House vote. They want to go to conference and accept the amendments, despite the fact that the representatives have not hashed them out in committee or on the floor.

At the same time, the Senate Finance Committee, counterpart of the House Ways and Means Committee, appreciates the opportunity to "lose" some of its amendments in conference. They make gains by the mere offer of amendments; they can tell constituents that their interests have been guarded as much as possible, but the House conferees have taken the candy away from them. In Finance Committee sessions, senators considering an excise-tax bill (H.R. 11376) in 1960 willingly voted for their colleagues' special-interest amendments in return for the same favor toward their own measures. According to Chairman Russell Long himself, the tax-cutting spree, removing taxes on special interests to the grand sum of five hundred million dollars, was politically motivated.[25] But in conference the Senate conferees dropped almost all of their measures. The excise-tax bill emerged from conference in the same form as the House bill and became law without the Senate's massive tax benefits for selected special interests.

This ritual, then, requires a variety of face-savers to blunt criticism. Conferees who have to recede (or do so willingly) on important amendments turn around and propose hearings, initiate special staff studies, or make vague promises about the other chamber's probable support next time. However, the minimal time they sometimes take to negotiate can give them away.

Ritual 11: Deadlock

To "win" a conference, one side may hold it in deadlock until the other side becomes anxious enough to compromise. This type of action has been used in conferences, and though it can be successful, it can produce bitterness.

When rituals are supported by vaguely worded rules and go untested and unchallenged, then the secret legislating of a few takes precedence over the educated debating and voting of the majority. Today, so little is known inside and outside Congress about the details of conference bargaining that it is evident that many legislators are comfortable with rituals in place of public accountability, ignorance in place of understanding, and secret trade-offs in place of public deliberation. Where in the Constitution is such a third branch of Congress ever sanctioned? Where in Congress' own rules does it say that conference meetings should hold sway over law-making?

IN THE END: THE CONFERENCE REPORT

Some grim amusement can be drawn from the loud hurly-burly which accompanies a bill through its initiating stages, the countless hours of haggling in committee, on the Floor—for a comma or an adjective; and then to observe the whole business disappear, swallowed up in a Conference Report.
—*Representative Clem Miller, Newsletter, August 15, 1961*

Secret conference discussions may take anywhere from minutes to months, depending on how fast the points of disagreement can be resolved. Each group votes separately on each point of disagreement—a majority from each house decides the position for that house. All conferees do not vote together on the issues.

After they have come to agreement, the conferees issue a joint "conference report." This document will become, word for word, the law of the land if it is approved by both houses and the president. According to conference rules, a majority of the House and Senate conferees, voting separately, must agree to sign the conference report. A minority which disagrees with the report may refuse to sign it. But under present rules, the minority may *not* issue a minority report or supplemental view, and a conferee cannot formally demand the attention of his fellow members the way one can raise objections in a standing committee's minority report.

In the House, conference reports have been privileged since 1850 (although not by formal rule until 1880)—that is, they may interrupt any other floor legislation except calendar Wednesday business (House *Manual*, Section 909). Since 1848 conference reports have been adopted under the "previous question" procedure. (The motion for the previous question, a debate-limiting device, is not in order in the Senate.) To prevent hostile members from trying to stop the report on a second vote, one member moves to reconsider and another immediately moves to lay that motion on the table. Since only one motion to reconsider is allowed on conference-report votes, the maneuver is effective.

Even when conference-committee rules are fairly explicit, members willfully break or manipulate them, as if oblivious to their intent or callous to their protections. A look at some of the conference-report rules and their uses illustrates the point.

The Three-Day Rule

Conferees must have the conference report printed in the *Congressional Record* three days before it is debated and voted upon (House Rule XXVIII, Clause 2). But members have given themselves several ways to get around this rule. First, under House rules, conference reports do not have to lay over three days if they come to the floor during the last six days of a session. When a conference chairman wants to jam through a conference report, he brings it to the floor in the hectic days before holidays or ends of sessions.* Also, if no conferee objects to a unanimous consent request when made in committee, the three-day rule may be waived. Amazing as it seems, there is no minimum number of conferees necessary for a quorum to vote on a unanimous-consent request. A conference chairman and one or two other conferees alone could vote to dispense with the printing of a report.

Explanatory Statements

The Legislative Reorganization Act of 1970 states that conference reports must be accompanied by an explanatory statement prepared by the conferees. The statement must "be sufficiently detailed and explicit to inform the Senate (or House) as to the effect which the amendments of propositions contained in such reports will have upon the measure to which those amendments or propositions relate." However, despite the safeguard of clarity in the rules, a confusing form encases the conference report when it comes to the floor. Members must often struggle to unravel what the conferees have done to their bills.

The rules do not require the conferees to follow the same guidelines of comprehensibility when they write a report as the members of standing committees do. Both House and Senate rules require that standing-committee reports making changes in existing laws must show clearly what changes are proposed.† Another method common to standing-committee reports, parallel columns, could be used to show the differences between the individual House and Senate clauses. Conference reports, however, do not use these logical forms that clearly indicate what has been changed. Without any guidelines on how to prepare a conference report, a member can cleverly bury any differences from House- or Senate-passed versions in "blind" amendments and obscure language. (See Appendix 14.)

---

* In the last six days of the 92nd Congress, the Senate passed twenty-seven conference reports; the House, sixteen. Seventeen went to the White House for signature.
† House Rule XIII, Section 3, and Senate Rule XXIX, Section 4.

Will the Real Minority Step Forward?

Before 1970, all debate time on conference reports was controlled by committee chairmen. Dissenters sometimes had difficulty getting recognition to speak. The Legislative Reorganization Act of 1970 sought to redress this problem by providing that debate should be divided equally between rival political parties. Neither House nor Senate reform, however, recognized that the majority and minority sides on a point of controversy may have nothing to do with party affiliation. And since there is no requirement that conference-committee reports include minority or supplemental views, members voting on the floor may have no knowledge of strong dissent within the conference. If the majority on a particular issue is controlling both halves of the debate time, and does not want the opposition to undermine the conference report, the minority view does not emerge.

Cannon's *Procedures* recognizes that opposing parties and opponents in argument may not always be the same.* But reformists' attempts to make the rules quite explicit in protecting the expression of minority opinions on issues have so far not met with success. The Legislative Reorganization Act of 1970 did not follow up on any suggestions to allow for the expression of a minority position if it does not follow party lines.

Waive Rules

One way to "break the rules" is to ask the House Rules Committee to "waive" them. On request from a member of Congress, the Rules Committee may consider granting a rule waiving points of order against a conference report. If such a ruling is granted and accepted by a majority of House members, a report becomes all but

---

* According to Cannon's *Procedures:* "A division of debate between those "for and against" a proposition does not necessarily provide for such division between the majority and minority parties of the House, but between those actually favoring and opposing the measure [VII, 766] and recognition is alternated according to differences on pending questions rather than on account of political differences [II, 1444; VII, 1010]," p. 153.

impervious to accusations of procedural violations. Further, the decision to grant or withhold this privilege may be quite arbitrary, dependent on nothing more than the sentiments of the committee members. The special rule waiving points of order has become increasingly popular since the addition of the House "germaneness" rules in 1970 (modified effective 1973). The germaneness provisions have allowed for a point of order to be made against a report on each amendment considered nongermane. That portion accused of nongermaneness is then immediately subject to forty minutes of debate followed by a vote to determine its acceptability.

New Matter Inserted

In 1917, House and Senate members gave their stamp of approval to a report only to discover that the conferees had added special provisions exempting senators, representatives, and all government employees from taxes on their salaries. None of the provisions had been in the original bills. This scandal aroused national indignation.

The next year, the Senate added a clause to a standing rule forbidding additions and deletions extraneous to the original bill.* If the conference report contains such illegalities, it is subject to a point of order.[26] The House has a similar rule (Rule XXVIII, Clause 3.†)

During the 1860s, Congress seized upon the point of order as a procedure to fight illegitimate additions to conference reports. By

---

* Senate Rule XXXVII, Clause 2, states: "Conferees shall not insert in their reports matter not committed to them by either House, nor shall they strike from the bill matter agreed to by both Houses. If new matter is inserted in the report, or if matter which was agreed to by both Houses is stricken from the bill, a point of order may be made against the report, and if the point of order is sustained, the report shall be committed to the committee of conference."

† According to the House precedents, "the managers of a conference must confine themselves to the differences committed to them and may not include subjects not within the disagreements even though germane to a question in issue. . . . In the House of Representatives the Speaker may rule out a conference report if it can be shown that the managers have exceeded their authority," but the speaker hardly ever does so.

the 1880s, the point of order was an important weapon to use against conference reports. Nearly a hundred years later, it is practically useless, for speakers of the House have consistently overruled points of order in landmark precedents.

If a point of order is sustained, the conference report must be recommitted to conference. The original conferees reconsider the report if the other house has not yet approved the conference results. If one of the houses has accepted the report and the other rejects it, a bill has no conference to go to; it has been dissolved. The report reverts to the same status it had before the conference.

Even when a point of order is sustained, members can find ways to get around the barricade. For example, a bill's manager may move to substitute the language of the conference report as an amendment to one house's version of the bill, which makes the adoption of the conference report unnecessary.

Not fearing points of order, conferees continue to add to legislation. And despite criticisms from inside and outside Congress, members continue to pass reports that have violated their conference rules.

Appropriations Conference Reports

If rules are violated in appropriations conference reports, chances are that the conferees can get away with whatever changes they make as a result. Appropriations reports usually pass the House with a minimum of controversy. Richard Fenno's study of major appropriations bills between 1947 and 1962 found that the House took a half hour or less than the Senate to discuss and vote on two-thirds of the conference reports. The same study found that only 7 per cent of these reports in the sample were subject to a motion to recommit.* Until the Nixon administration, the president rarely vetoed appropriations measures. Between 1952 and

---

* In the Committee of the Whole, where there are no roll-call votes, the minority traditionally has the right to make a motion to recommit. This motion is usually made just before the vote on the question of passing a bill and serves as a record of the minority's position. If a *simple* motion to recommit is adopted, the bill usually dies, for all previous committee deliber-

1968, only three appropriations bills were vetoed out of a total of 232 vetoed bills. In the Ninety-second Congress, President Nixon vetoed two appropriations proposals out of twenty-one vetoed bills.

In all bills involving appropriations of money, conferees must choose a figure somewhere *between* that put forth in the House bill and that of the Senate bill. However, conferees sometimes disregard the limits set by Congress' rules—and still get the bill approved on the floor.

The rules on conference reports are twisted out of shape. And some of them are so vague as to allow discretion on the part of the conferees, the parliamentarian, and the speaker or presiding officer. Furthermore, true debate on the conference reports rarely takes place. Without much discussion or analysis, conference reports get ramrodded through Congress, especially in the closing days of a session, and get signed into law. Some of them contain glaring evidence of legislating by a handful of conferees.

Members assail conference procedures only in moments of controversy, when conference defects become most clear. Otherwise, they remain content to rattle off a few criticisms and then vote in favor of a conference report bearing unmistakable signs that the conferees took great liberties with the rules.

After legislation she had supported was ruined in a conference report, one member voted against the report and called for reforms:

> We talk about congressional reform—why has the confer-
> ence committee, this step in the legislative process—escaped

ations, Rules Committee action, and floor debate and amendments are null and void; the bill must then start the legislative circuit all over again. A motion to recommit *with* instructions serves as an amending mechanism. If this kind of motion to recommit is adopted, the chairman of the committee with jurisdiction over the bill usually stands and reports the "instructions" in the form of an amendment. The House proceeds to vote on the amendments and then the bill as a whole.

all scrutiny by those who would reform? Many other items pale into insignificance compared to this crucial part in drafting legislation and making laws for 200 million people.[27]

Yet there is little visible movement to reform conferences. Legislating behind the scenes, by a few hand-picked conferees who usually have a lot of seniority or feel responsible to their chairmen, goes on unhampered. Conference reports still contain vague, obscure language that hides the true changes made in House- and Senate-passed legislation. They are still introduced for votes at the last minute. They still rather automatically become the law of the land.

KING OF CONFERENCE MANIPULATIONS, WILBUR MILLS

Back in 1950 and 1951 Mills was a member of a number of conferences. He was usually the guy who would come up with the compromises that would settle the differences. He was the "Henry Clay of the conference," the "Great Compromiser."
—*Tom Stanton, Tax Reform Research Group, July 1972*

Wilbur Mills (D., Ark.), powerful chairman of the House Ways and Means Committee since 1959, has long been master of the conferences on revenue matters. The door of the Ways and Means Conference Room, H-208, bears his name. Except when the Senate Finance Committee and the House Ways and Means Committee gather for conferences, the room is Mills's own private territory, where, on a typical work day, he even eats his lunch.[28]

His geographical domain is symbolic of the political power that Mills wields over the conferees from both houses. The conference is only the final extension of Mills' power in the committee room. His pre-eminence has never been challenged by the Senate in the way that the House Appropriations Committee chairman's power was disputed in 1963. Mills presides over the conference on his home ground, and, as a tax expert, he has immense advantage over Senate Finance Committee members, who have many more committee assignments and therefore less time to become experts.

In the Ways and Means Committee, Mills drafts bills with an eye toward the conference. An anonymous Ways and Means member described Mills' process of shaping legislation for future bargaining:

> Mills will say, "Maybe we can live with 10 percent but if we send it over they'll make it 15 and we'll have to live with 12. So let's make it eight." You say O.K. and go along.[29]

Mills' foresight is not uncanny. As a former representative put it, "It is a rare House chairman who does not pilot his bill through the House without keeping at least one eye on the conference which will almost certainly result, for rarely does an important bill exactly conform to the companion bill in the Senate."[30] Since Mills has a propensity for asking the Rules Committee for a closed rule* when he reports committee bills, members of Congress are even more bound than usual by the decisions made in committee and cultivated by a single representative—Mills.

When he was only a junior on Ways and Means, Mills had a remarkable ability in a sphere usually reserved for the most senior veterans of Congress—compromise. Mills' skill has become legendary, and he is now famous for guiding the conference discussion to an "everybody agreed?" conclusion.

Since conferences are held in secret, glimpses of Mills' skills as a conference tactician are rare. But strong signs of his ability to compromise and to get what he wants can be observed before and after conferences.[31]

More than once, long before the scheduling of a conference, Mills has used the tactic of getting senators to introduce amend-

---

* This rule prohibits members on the floor from making any amendments to the committee bill. It is subject to the approval of the Rules Committee and the members on the floor. It has usually been granted to revenue-raising bills, which come out of Mills' committee, and is a source of growing controversy.

ments that he wants to discuss at conference. He bypasses his own committee and the full House this way. With his consummate skills as compromiser, manipulator, and maneuverer, and with his undisputed expertise in tax policy, Wilbur Mills has managed to move his legislation through the House, or through the Senate on those rare occasions when his committee or the House wouldn't follow him quickly enough. But in the case of his overriding desire to boost social security payments by 20 per cent, Mills grasped at too much power. He won what he wanted, but the outcome would have been different if others used the rules as skillfully as Mills.

In the first public step in his maneuvering, on June 30, 1972, Mills managed to secure a conference on the public-debt limitation bill (H.R. 15390). Before agreeing to a conference, his colleagues, who were not sure why a conference should be held, asked a few questions. Mills acted as though he himself knew very little about what was going on. A surprised John Byrnes (Wis.), ranking Republican on the Ways and Means Committee, inquired, "I assume [the Senate] must have amended the title?"

> MILLS: I am not certain. I want to go to conference to find out what they have done.
> BYRNES: We do not even know what they have done in the other body and we are going to the conference?
> MILLS: I never do know altogether what they have done in the Senate when I ask for a conference with the Senate. I find out when I get to conference that things have happened that I do not know about.[32]

Chairman Mills could not even answer an inquiry as to how many amendments the Senate bill carried: "I am not certain. I am not certain because I just found out that the Senate had passed the bill only a few minutes ago, and it has just come to us." One thing was obvious. Mills was not following normal rules and procedures: he did not follow the usual practice of disagreeing to a Senate bill and then proposing a conference.

That very same day Mills returned to the House with a conference report on the debt-limitation bill, the second public phase of his maneuver. The report included his legislation for a 20-percent social security increase, which the Senate Finance Committee had adopted when it was clear that Mills wouldn't be able to get the measure through his own committee. It had been deadlocked in Ways and Means since February 23.

This June 30 was the last day Congress would convene before its summer recess; the House would not be meeting again until July 17. Since Mills wanted to pass a conference report on the public-debt limitation before the recess, he had to find a way around three conference-report rules: the three-day layover, the publication of the report in the *Congressional Record* before the vote, and the circulation of explanatory statements to members on the floor. He found that way—his third public maneuver: he introduced the report on the floor "in disagreement."* This move surprised the committee's ranking minority member, John Byrnes, who wondered what the "disagreement" with the Senate had been; a majority of conferees, he explained to the House, had voted *to go along* with the Senate version of a 20-per-cent increase in social security. But Mills answered that the Senate amendments to which the House managers had agreed were nongermane. Technically, then, the conferees had taken an improper step, since the 1970 Reorganization Act specifically forbids House managers to accept nongermane material without House

* According to the *Congressional Quarterly*, Mills was one of the first members to disregard the 1970 Legislative Reorganization Act. In 1971, in connection with social security amendments to the debt-ceiling bill, he asked for a waiver of the three-day layover rule by unanimous consent. So, parts of this June maneuver were not new.

On October 13, 1972, the House finally got around to tightening up loopholes in the 1970 act by voting on the Rules Committee's H. Res. 1153. After explaining a proposed rule that reports in disagreement be subject to the same layover rule as other conference reports and must be printed in the *Congressional Record* (effective January 1973), B. F. Sisk (D., Calif.) specifically cited Mills' June 1972 tactic and said, "Section 2 of this resolution is designed to prevent this situation from recurring." *Congressional Record*, October 13, 1972, p. H9880.

approval. The agreement in conference, Mills informed Byrnes, had been an "informal action." As with Appropriations bills, he said, the House would have to vote to accept the amendments individually.[33]

Fourth, Mills gave the clerk eleven pages of fine print—the first amendment in the conference report—to deliver orally. Unless members had memorized the original House and Senate bills, they were not likely to know what they were hearing, as this sample illustrates:

> Sec. 203. (a) Section 215 (a) of the Social Security Act (as amended by section 201 (c) of this Act) is further amended—
> (1) by striking out "paragraph (2)" in the matter preceding subparagraph (A) of paragraph (1) and inserting in lieu thereof "paragraphs (2) and (3). . . ."[34]

Byrnes asked for and was granted unanimous consent to dispense with the further reading of other amendments because he recognized the inanity in reading such meaningless terminology when the members had no copy for reference. Faced with a vote before a deadline on a conference report they had never seen, some representatives protested. Durward G. Hall (R., Mo.) made a point of order against the conference report on the grounds that the use of the "disagreement" tactic was a "travesty" upon the rights and privileges of each individually elected member of Congress. Hall charged that the conference report could be considered in disagreement only if you read into "the fine print of the rules of the House." The procedure had been drawn out of these rules by a "circuitous route in a tenuous mind," Hall continued. The speaker overruled Hall's point of order, however. John Rhodes (D., Ariz.), who had been trying unsuccessfully to get a copy of the report, inquired, "Do not the rules of the House provide that each member should be provided with a copy of the amendment to be offered like this so that amendments could be perfected and submitted at the appropriate time?" The speaker replied, "The chair knows no such rule."

Mills had on his side not only his own cleverness, plus the support of both the parliamentarian and the speaker, but also time. By delaying until just before the recess and by reporting the conference in disagreement so that no copies were available to members, Mills had confidence that his legislation would be approved. Byrnes realized that, no matter how rushed the Mills approach had been, few in the House wanted to be responsible for halting the machinery of the government (the effect of voting against the debt ceiling) just because they disagreed with one or two amendments or with the method of their sudden appearance. He revealed how Mills held the Congress in his pocket:

> Think of what is being attempted here today—holding the entire operation of the Government hostage to an increase in Social Security taxes. We insist on tying a Social Security increase to legislation that is absolutely essential to the operation of Government and then we immediately cut and run, because the motion or resolution to recess this Congress and get out of town will be the next order of business.[35]

Byrnes proposed a substitute which did not include the social security increase but when Mills asked the House "to vote down the substitute and agree to the Senate amendment," his side won by a vote of 253 to 83. Mills's motion that the House recede and concur in the Senate's 20-per-cent hike won by a vote of 302 to 35. Mills thereby successfully bypassed several congressional rules and his own committee's consideration of the measure.

On many occasions, Mills's maneuvers have proved effective. Despite the 1970 rules reforms designed to protect members from just these kinds of abuses, a majority often bows, in the last-minute rush, to expediency—and the King of Conference Manipulations, Wilbur Mills. Not until October 1972 did the majority have second thoughts and close off some of the loopholes that Mills had finagled open.

By precedent alone, conference committee meetings are held behind closed doors. By the code of courtesy, conferees, the senior members of Congress, are given leeway to break the written conference rules, with no sanctions being imposed. The speaker of the House may rule out a conference report if someone on the floor demonstrates that the managers have exceeded their authority (Hinds' and Cannon's precedents, V, 6409-6416; VIII, 3256; and elsewhere). But rare are the times that a majority stands on the rules to challenge abuses of conference rules. Instead, they are cajoled into voting on conference reports they have not read or analyzed.

Members have many tools at their disposal to stop this onslaught on democratic procedure. They must instigate counterattacks on the system of assigning conferees to conferences which replaces those who are experts in the matters to be negotiated with those who have high seniority. Members of Congress can launch some successful counterattacks by using the *ad hoc* tactics and fundamental reforms discussed in the concluding chapter of this book.

8

Exchanging
Tools

The harsh fact is that the present rules and methods of operation of the Senate and of the House are stacked against the people of the United States. They penalize those who seek action in the national interest in a time of world crisis. They reward those who cling to an outmoded status quo which threatens our very survival.

—Senator Joseph Clark, speech July 1, 1960

The rules and procedures governing Congress' operations fill up many volumes: the Constitution, Jefferson's *Manual*, the forty-four standing rules in each house; the eleven volumes of House precedents to 1936; the secret scrapbooks of more recent precedents of the House and Senate parliamentarians, and many others. Far from being mere guideposts to legislative behavior and action, Congress' rules and procedures are tools by which legislators can achieve what citizens ask for and need. But members of

Congress cannot be responsive to the needs of the American people if they refuse either to invoke the rules that they have or to discard the ones that no longer serve the public interest.

Under the Constitution, Congress has the power to make war impose taxes, and provide for the public health, safety, and welfare. To do this, it allocates over 300 billion taxpayer dollars a year. But secrecy, archaic rules, absenteeism, and other outgrowths of the legislators' weak or improper implementation of their own rules have seriously weakened Congress' power to find creative legislative solutions to America's problems or to supervise the programs and plans that it has already enacted.

As long as these tools are used effectively by only a handful of members, abused by others with no sanctions imposed, and ignored by the vast majority (who say that the pressure of a heavy workload is too cumbersome to allow for deep study of the rules), then Congress will only grow weaker in the face of executive-branch challenges.

Rules don't enforce themselves. And members are notorious for waiving their rights under the rules. Most rules can simply be ignored unless someone calls attention to them, and the one who does point them out becomes the enforcer.

Rules mean power, even for the junior member, and the leadership knows this. As a result, the leaders of Congress commonly attempt to prevent members from invoking the rules. A common weapon is the personal affront. Committee chairmen or members with high seniority take grave offense if a nonestablishment member questions their authority by making a point of order (procedurally seeking to enforce the rules). To prevent the rank and file from exercising the power it has under the rules, the leadership thus places negative sanctions, such as less favorable committee or subcommittee assignments, on parliamentary challenges.

In recent years Congressional leaders have faced several major challenges to their power. But two are notable for their potential to increase *knowledge* about the rules. First, the side benefit of the 1970 Legislative Reorganization Act, according to a former minority counsel to the Rules Committee, Bob Hynes, is that a great many members who had not previously taken procedural matters seriously are now learning the rules. The number of those who know the rules has doubled since the act was signed into law, and members who are at least interested in rules and precedents have sextupled, Hynes declared. Second, the instructions in this 1970 act for the House parliamentarian to codify the precedents could lead to further erosion of the leaders' power. According to William G. Phillips and Norm Cornish of the House Government Operations Subcommittee on Freedom of Information, a compilation of the precedents would erode the power of the leadership, which wants to run the show.

By further changing the rules so that they can be used more easily and by setting the stage for the possibility of rank-and-file control without an outright rebellion, members would be more likely to use the rules to make them a workable legislative tool in the pursuit of the public interest.

Since the first Congress, at least four hundred substantive changes or amendments have been made in the House rules.[1] The House Rules Committee has undertaken large-scale revisions of the rules on many occasions, most notably in 1811, 1822, 1837, 1860, 1890, 1911, 1931, 1946, and 1970.[2] Since the Senate rules were first adopted in 1789, they have been subjected to four general revisions: in 1806, 1820, 1868, and 1884. Minor, piecemeal changes in Senate rules have been made, but there has been no general revision since 1884. Except in committee rules and the appropriations process, the two major legislative reorganization acts of 1946 and 1970 did not affect Senate rules substantially. Both acts specifically prohibited changes in Senate rules, practices, procedures, and precedents.

The rules have improved through all these changes, especially in allowing the public more and more to exercise its *right*, not its *privilege*, to observe an open, deliberative governing body. In the first three Senates, debates were kept secret and the public was not allowed to observe proceedings. "The reason for this aloofness from the public, apparently, was a belief that the Senate represented the states rather than the general population. . . . It was several years [after the Fourth Congress opened its doors to the public], however, before the Senate debates were recorded as fully as those of the House."[3]

But the realities of changing Congress' rules are that those who maintain power through the rules are not likely to let them be changed quickly or easily, if at all. Perhaps the late Senator Everett M. Dirksen best exemplified the mentality of the entrenched power structure when "he responded to one proposal for change with 'ha, ha, ha, and I might add: ho, ho, ho.' "[4]

It apparently takes a tide of public pressure, in addition to members' impatience over delay in substantive legislative issues, for enough members to stand up and be counted on the side of one rules reform or another. For this reason it is likely that the next major reform will change conference rules. Today it is in conference meetings that two constituencies are ignored—the public and the members of Congress who are not conferees. With no public record of what is said and how conferees voted, frustration is rising as legislation returns in the form of a conference report with *additions* and *changes* not called for by a majority of either house. But courageous members of Congress do speak out against felt iniquities. Representative Edith Green (D., Ore.), for example, found that the conferees had seriously weakened a bill she had authored and a majority of the House had once accepted:

> If representative government and if democracy means anything perhaps we should look on this particular step in the legislative process [the conference meeting]. It is behind closed doors; no record of proceeding is kept. Yet this also is public business and the public has as much right to know who voted in what way—as the public has a right to know who voted in which way on a recorded teller vote in the House. In fact very often votes in the conference committee are far more critical than are House teller votes.[5]

Thomas Jefferson wrote in the preface to his *Manual of Parliamentary Practice:*

> It is much more material that there should be a rule to go by
> than what that rule is; that there be a uniformity of proceed-
> ing in business not subject to the caprice of the Speaker or
> captiousness of the members. It is very material that order,
> decency, and regularity be preserved in a dignified body.

This sentiment is understandable for a fledgling government. But the system has had many decades to evolve and reshape itself since these words were written, and it is now "much more material" that the rules be fair and that they be used. It is more important that they not place dignity and courtesy above advocacy and analysis. Nonetheless, even today, members have buried themselves in a thicket of parliamentary entanglements to camouflage their decisions and remain unaccountable to constituents.

Members of Congress owe it to their own legislative efforts—and most of all, to the citizens of the United States—to challenge the system by *using* its rules, not for delay but for complete debate. Instead of bowing to the unwritten code of courtesy—or, indeed, the unacknowledged system of trade-offs—members should seek some new rules that will allow them to act as equals rather than disfranchised supplicants, and to win on the merits of their arguments, not the thinness of their compromises. The recommendations that follow are intended to provide a framework for these much-needed new rules.

9

Conclusions

The following suggested reforms involve two major mechanical changes in the operations of Congress:

· Closed-circuit television should be placed in the office of all representatives and senators to broadcast floor proceedings, and

· Computer terminals should be available in strategic places in the Capitol to facilitate immediate data retrieval concerning legislative scheduling, parliamentary rulings, and so on. (Standard call formats could be devised to make the process simple to use.)

PARLIAMENTARIANS

1. The rulings of the parliamentarians should be immediately codified and made public. The precedents should be cross-indexed for easy reference by members and the public. They should be computerized for instantaneous recall. Computer terminals for members' use should be located on the floor of both chambers and in designated Senate and House office buildings.

207

2. The parliamentarians should henceforth be required to keep the precedents up to date each day and to publish indexed updating reports quarterly.

3. The parliamentarians' salary should be docked for each day of noncompliance in publishing the precedents.

4. Where the parliamentarian receives a request for an informal ruling before a point of order or other question is raised on the floor, and where he issues an opinion, he should print the opinion in the *Congressional Record* the same day. If there is not enough time, he should circulate mimeographed copies to members' offices.

5. The *Daily Digest* in the *Congressional Record* should contain a special section summarizing any rulings or points of order made on the floor.

6. Seminars on the rules for members of Congress and their staffs should be offered in the months between November and January of each new Congress, even before oaths of office have been taken.

7. The parliamentarian, instead of being appointed by the speaker and becoming his policy maker, should be elected by the caucus at the beginning of each Congress, so he will be responsive to the majority.

COMMITTEE ASSIGNMENTS

1. Beginning in the Ninety-fourth Congress, committee assignments are made by the members of the party caucus steering committee, half of whom are elected by the caucus and the other half appointed by the speaker. Every member should have a guaranteed right of first refusal of his committee assignment, with immediate reassignment to another committee after declining to serve on the first.

2. No senator should be permitted to sit on more than two major committees and four subcommittees.

3. There should be automatic rotation of committee assign-

ments. Every two years, one-third of a committee would be automatically reassigned to another committee. No member would be on the same committee more than six consecutive years.

SENIORITY

Congress is the only national legislature in the world that honors seniority.[1] Seniority's chief virtue, proponents argue, is that it is automatic. It avoids the logrolling, back-scratching, and divisiveness endemic to an elective system, they say, and it insulates chairmen from presidential influence and pressure. And besides, they add, as bad as seniority may be, no better system exists.[2]

Republican and Democratic caucus reforms in the Ninety-second and Ninety-third Congresses have moved in the direction of separate votes on chairmen, but these are *votes of confidence*, not competitions. Although the new procedure—an automatic secret ballot on each chairman's nomination—did not produce any changes in the Ninety-third Congress, it resulted in the removal of three House chairmen in the Ninety-fourth. It is still unclear what effect it will have in the long run. The role of outside interest groups in preparing evaluations of the chairmen could be critical. At the time of the caucus vote, chairmen can call in political debts. They are further aided by the absence of competitors and the challengers' fear of political reprisals.

Some reformers, notably former Senator Joseph Clark (D., Pa.), envision the caucus vote as a potent disciplinary weapon in the hands of strong party leaders.[3] The caucus could oust chairmen who failed to cooperate with stated party aims or with a president of the same party. But this reform could have the effect of *increasing* the chairman's powers *without* getting rid of seniority. Chairmen's actions would bear the imprimatur of party leadership and possibly of the executive, so that challengers would face reprisals not only from an angered chairman but from a whole political party as well. Seniors would continue to be favored in chairmanship assignments, since party leaders would probably select members with proven political durability and accumulated political debts. And voters would still face a difficult choice in elections: should they vote for a representative who more nearly conforms to their points of view or for a representative who is in a powerful position to meet their needs?

Direct reform of the seniority tradition is not the solution to the dilemma of power in the hands of a few committee chairmen, entrenched in their positions by virtue of their tenacious grip on the electorate. The solution is fluidity-insecurity in committee assignments. With a fluid committee membership, seniority would not likely govern the selection of chairmen because the hold Congressional leaders (senior members) exercise over junior members' careers would be weakened. Automatic rotation of committee assignments would introduce an insecurity factor; thus members could feel more comfortable about bucking the seniority tradition rather than rubber-stamping the selection of senior committee chairmen out of fear of retribution in the form of unwanted committee assignments. Assuming automatic rotation of committee assignments, election within the majority caucus of each committee would be an appropriate method for nominating chairmen.

DECENTRALIZING THE CHAIRMAN'S POWERS

1. *Subcommittee Establishment.* The caucus rule adopted in the Ninety-third Congress, giving the committee caucus, not the chairman, control over creating and abolishing subcommittees should be enforced. All committee rules should define their permanent subcommittees' jurisdictions. The rules should state that no new subcommittees, even *ad hoc* ones, can be added without the approval of the majority committee caucus.

2. *Subcommittee Composition.* The rules should define the ratio of majority to minority members on all subcommittees to reflect their numbers in the chamber as a whole. Members should be assigned to subcommittees first by preference, and second, where too many want the same assignment, by lot. Subcommittee

chairman should be elected by the majority caucus, as required in the Ninety-fourth Congress.

3. *Referral of Bills.* Subcommittee jurisdictions should be as closely defined in committee rules as possible—to minimize the full committee chairman's discretion in referring bills.

4. *Committee Staff.* Most committees must have more professional staff with expertise in technical areas relevant to the committee's work. Recruitment of experts could be facilitated if the two employment agencies currently operated by the Joint Committee on Congressional Operations devoted more time and attention to the recruitment and referral of professional people, as well as clerical help. The augmented staff should be divided, with about half assigned exclusively to legislative responsibilities while the other half is devoted entirely to oversight activities. This allocation of resources to oversight, perhaps under the supervision of a vice-chairman for oversight activities in each subcommittee, would make feasible an annual oversight hearing on each of the agencies within the jurisdiction of the committee.

Committees in general suffer from the lack of adequate staff, but the minority party in particular has felt that inadequacy directly. It is no secret that most committee staffs are partisan, reflecting the views of the chairman and the majority members of the committee, while coopting the power of the minority to the point of total ineffectiveness. When the minority party in Congress is not the party in the White House, lack of an effective minority party can result in a serious erosion of the governmental system of checks and balances.

In order to insure that the minority party is able to act as an effective force in the legislative process, minority committee staffing should be increased to at least one-third of the total committee staff. Minority members should be guaranteed by rule a one-third proportionate share of any permanent staff authorization, as provided by the Ninety-fourth Congress.

5. *Calling Meetings.* A regular meeting time, now required by committee rules, should not be broken, unless one-fifth of

the committee membership submits a written consent to do so. A petition specifying time and place of a special meeting, signed by a majority of the committee, should be sufficient procedure to call a meeting. Notice should be given to the office of all other committee members. If a chairman calls a special meeting, under the current procedure, he should be required to give three days' notice. To allow for emergency meetings, an exception clause could require the signature of a majority of committee members before a special meeting could be called in less than three days.

6. *Calling Witnesses to Hearings.* Each committee member should be guaranteed the opportunity to choose at least one witness for each committee hearing. In this way, all "minorities," not just a political party minority (now authorized one day to call their witnesses), would be able to participate in the witness-selection process.

7. *Floor Management.* If a measure is reported out against the chairman's will or without the chairman's vote, a supporter elected by the committee's majority caucus who in good faith favors the bill should be the floor manager.

RULES COMMITTEE

1. Rules Committee members should be elected by their respective party caucus or conference. The ratio of party members on the committee should be proportionate to the number of party members in the chamber.

2. After the House Rules Committee has had twenty-one days to act on a bill, it should be required to report the bill to the floor upon the request of a committee's majority vote. The bill would be debated under the standard rule allowing a half hour of debate on each side of the issue.

FLOOR RULES AND PROCEDURES

Scheduling

There should be digests published daily and weekly of the latest scheduling of bills. There should be a phone service that gives an instant response to a member's query about the up-to-date status of a bill in the scheduling process, and the same information should be available through the computer terminals.

1. With such ready information, chairmen (or committee majorities) should schedule committee meetings that would not conflict with other congressional business.

2. Furthermore, days should be set aside for floor business only. In this way, committee sessions would not be interrupted on their meeting days.

3. Both Democratic and Republican caucuses (conferences) should have the ability to order all party members on specific committees to report a specific bill to the floor of the House or Senate upon majority vote. Because members are assigned to committees by their parties, they should be held accountable to their party caucus for getting bills to the floor if the caucus so directs. Each party body should form a special discipline committee to impose a series of party sanctions on members who disobey party directives at the committee level. Sanctions could include: denial of special delegation positions, denial of party positions, removal from committee seniority, loss of party campaign funds, loss of chairmanship, and dismissal from the party.

4. The clerk of the House and the secretary of the Senate should compile and publish in the *Congressional Record* daily attendance lists of committee and floor activities.

Debate and Voting

1. All committee and caucus votes should be made public and published in the *Congressional Record* if they are recorded or roll-

call votes, except for caucus votes on party or leadership positions.

2. A cloture motion to end a filibuster in the Senate should require a three-fifths vote.

CONFERENCES

Choosing Conferees

The 1970 Legislative Reorganization Act was silent on the questions of unrepresentative conferees, conference secrecy, and congressional seniority in general. It did not incorporate reform proposals by former Senators Joseph Clark, Fred Harris (D., Okla.), and others to ensure more representative conferees. In 1959, Senator Clark introduced a proposed change in Senate Rule XXIV, adding this new clause:

> A majority of the Senate members of a committee on conference shall have indicated by their votes their sympathy with the bill as passed and their concurrence in the prevailing opinion of the Senate on the matters of disagreement with the House of Representatives which occasion the appointment of the committee.[4]

However, committee chairmen and others in congressional leadership generally considered the resolution to be a threat to their power to select conferees. Clark's measure failed to pass in 1959, 1961, and 1967.

In 1972 the chairman of the Ad Hoc Committee on Senate Reform, Fred Harris, presented a resolution before the Senate Democratic caucus stating that chairmen would submit a proposed list of conferees first to the majority leader. The leader would have the job of forwarding the list to the presiding officer for final appointment. If the majority leader decided that the group was not representative of the Senate position, he could appoint new, sympathetic conferees. The Democratic caucus

passed Harris' recommendation, but it eliminated the enforcement power originally delegated to the majority leader.*

Conferees should be chosen by party leadership, not solely
according to the preference of committee chairmen. The slate
should be subject to the approval by a majority vote of the party
caucus if requested. A majority of the conferees must have voted in
good faith for the version approved by the body. These procedures
would not only help insure that conferees would represent the
dominant opinion of the House but also involve the rank-and-file
members more fully in the conference process. At present, former
Senator Albert Gore (D., Tenn.) has written, the less powerful
members in both houses "feel that matters are out of their hands
after initial floor action on a bill has been completed."[5]

Meetings

Conference committees should hold their meetings in public, as
required by the House and Senate in the Ninety-fourth Congress
(unless the meeting is closed by a majority vote). The only basis for
closing a conference, however, should be that it is dealing with
matters of national security, with a narrowly defined use of this
term, which should not offer protection every time executives or
legislators want an excuse to carry on their business secretly. Conferences should be governed by the same rules currently controlling
committees. All roll-call votes taken by conferees should be public

---

* "The committee chairmen in the nominating of members of Committees
of Conference shall make certain, insofar as practicable, that at least a
majority of the proposed conferees shall have indicated their support for
the bill in question as passed by the Senate, and their support for the
prevailing opinion of the Senate on the principal matters of disagreement
with the House of Representatives which occasioned the appointment of
the committee and need not, as Senate precedent already permits, be
limited to nominating committee members to Conference." *Congressional
Record*, April 19, 1972, p. H4342.

Clearly, the resolution keeps the power of appointment in the committee
chairmen's hands and relies on their good graces to choose a sympathetic
conference. The weak "insofar as practicable" gives the committee head a
loophole without sanction.

information, published in the *Congressional Record*. Daily transcripts of conference proceedings should also be published in the *Record*. Open meetings would reduce some of the pressure now exerted by the executive branch and special interest lobbyists behind closed doors.

Conference Reports

1. Conference reports should not go beyond the terms set by House- and Senate-passed legislation. Existing restrictions should be enforced.

2. Conference reports should be in the form of commitee reports, with changed words crossed out so that members can tell what has been eliminated from a chamber-passed bill or with double columns showing the conference bill "before" and "after." Currently the reports are confusing and breed confusion in floor discussions and voting. Members should demand that this stage in the legislative process not be buried in an elite code.

3. All loopholes in the three-day layover rule should be stopped up. The six-day rule, allowing conference reports to be brought to the floor for a vote without any layover at the end of the session, should be abolished.

4. Consideration of a conference report on the House or Senate floor should be prohibited if every member of each body has not received a copy of the report and adjoining explanatory statement. Fulfillment of this requirement by a printed report in the *Congressional Record* should be permitted *only* in the closing days of a session.

5. Conferees who disagree with the majority on any part of the conference report should be able to incorporate their views in the form of "minority" views in the final report. This reform, which already applies to regular committee reports, would tell the members on the floor what the pros and cons on an issue are.

7. Minority views should be given one-third of the floor debate time on the conference report. This reform would encourage advocacy and sharpen the issues before all members of Congress.

Debate time would thus be divided among the two sides of senior conferees, who often agree, and provide time for the real minority, whose views have hitherto not been provided for in the conference report itself and have rarely been heard in the floor debate on the conference report.

REFORM SESSIONS

There should be an automatic special session, every six years for four months, to examine the question of congressional reform.

CONGRESSIONAL GENERAL COUNSEL

To perform as an effective overseer of executive branch activities, Congress must have the capability to challenge illegal activities by those charged with executing the laws. Increasingly members of Congress have turned to the courts when the executive has failed to enforce the laws as Congress wrote them. This ability to litigate should be institutionalized in an Office of Congressional Counsel charged with responsibility for defending Congress when its authority is challenged and, at the request of a committee or a group of members, suing when others usurp its reserved powers or ignore its will.

CITIZEN ACCESS TO CONGRESSIONAL INFORMATION

1. The roll-call committee votes now required to be available to the public at the committee offices should be printed every quarter in the *Congressional Record*, with a statement of the pros and cons for each vote. Subcommittee and conference committee roll-call votes which are not now public should be subject to the same rule. Records of attendance at subcommittee, committee, and conference committee meetings should also be published.

2. The Joint Committee on Congressional Operations should

publish quarterly a listing, with a reliable index, of all committee reports and hearings published by the committees, so the public and congressional offices can locate congressional publications without delay.

3. The committees should be required to publish their committee calendars quarterly, and the Joint Committee on Congressional Operations should publish a booklet of all the calendars every six months.

4. The *Digest of Bills* prepared by the Library of Congress' Congressional Research Service for members only should be available free of charge or at cost to the public.

5. An Office of Congressional Information should be established to answer routine public inquiries about the status of bills, hearing schedules, witness lists, voting records, bill listings, and other questions that currently clog committees' and members' offices. This office should also set up a large reading room for the public with all pertinent documents about congressional activities (*Congressional Record*, bill listings, committee calendars, committee reports and hearings, *Congressional Quarterly*, *National Journal*, etc.) and assist in the creation of similar reading rooms across the country in depository libraries.

6. Committees should be required to assure that all points of view on controversial subjects are represented in hearings and should be authorized to pay travel expenses when necessary to assure that such views are presented.

7. The Government Printing Office should be prohibited from continuing its routine practice of shredding old congressional documents or other books. It should be required instead to distribute them free of charge.

Appendices

Leadership Changes, 1955–1972

	Opportunities	Changes	Vacancies (death or retirement of the party leader)	Battles (more than one candidate actively seeks votes)	Challenges (battles involving an incumbent leader)	Upsets (successful challenges)
House of Representatives						
Democrats	27	6	6	4	3	0
Republicans	27	6	3	7	5	3
Senate						
Democrats	18	6	4	3	2	2
Republicans	18	6	6	4	1	0

APPENDIX 2.

Transfers of House Committee Assignments,
80th–89th Congresses (1949–1968)

Standing Committee	Number of transfers to	Number of transfers from (low numbers indicate committees members consider most desirable, influential)
Agriculture	22	18
Appropriations	85	2
Armed Services	26	6
Banking and Currency	15	33
District of Columbia	2	13
Education and Labor	18	15
Foreign Affairs	34	5
Government Operations	8	33
House Administration	5	29
Interior and Insular Affairs	4	31
Interstate and Foreign Commerce	32	17
Judiciary	19	12
Merchant Marine and Fisheries	4	35
Post Office and Civil Service	2	40
Public Works	13	28
Rules	33	1
Science and Astronautics (created in 1959)	6	7
Veterans' Affairs	2	46
Ways and Means	47	0

SOURCE: Udall and Tacheron, *The Job of a Congressman* (Indianapolis: Bobbs-Merrill, 2nd ed., 1970), p. 163.

APPENDIX 3.

Growth in House Committee Size (1947–1971)

Committee	80th Congress 1947	92nd Congress 1971
Agriculture	29	36
Appropriations	43	55
Armed Services	35	41
Banking and Currency	27	37
District of Columbia	26	25
Education and Labor	25	38
Foreign Affairs	25	38
Government Operations	25	39
House Administration	25	25
Interior and Insular Affairs	27	39
Internal Security	9	9
Interstate and Foreign Commerce	27	43
Judiciary	27	38
Merchant Marine and Fisheries	25	37
Post Office and Civil Service	27	26
Public Works	27	37
Rules	12	15
Science	25	29
Veterans' Affairs	27	26
Ways and Means	25	25

SOURCE: 1947 and 1972 *Congressional Directories*

APPENDIX 4.

Percentage of Senators Leaving Office by Reason and by Party
(1947–1971)

Year*	Defeated†		Promoted‡		Retired		Died	
	(D)	(R)	(D)	(R)	(D)	(R)	(D)	(R)
1947	25.00	6.25	1.04	1.04	3.13	2.08	5.20	1.04
1949	6.25	28.13	2.08	1.04	3.13	4.17	3.13	3.13
1951	25.00	6.25	2.08	0.00	1.04	1.04	0.00	2.08
1953	15.63	15.63	1.04	2.08	2.08	1.04	2.08	2.08
1955	9.38	15.63	1.04	0.00	1.04	5.21	4.18	2.08
1957	3.13	6.25	2.08	0.00	4.17	1.04	2.08	1.04
1959	0.00	27.27	0.00	1.00	0.00	4.00	2.00	1.00
1961	6.66	0.00	3.00	0.00	3.00	2.00	2.00	1.00
1963	6.66	12.12	0.00	0.00	2.00	2.00	3.00	3.00
1965	3.33	9.99	1.00	1.00	3.00	0.00	2.00	0.00
1967	15.15	0.00	0.00	0.00	1.00	2.00	1.00	0.00
1969	18.18	6.66	0.00	0.00	3.00	3.00	2.00	1.00
1971	12.12	9.99	0.00	0.00	3.00	1.00	1.00	0.00

* Senators leaving in even-numbered years included in figures for next highest odd-numbered year.
† Includes both primary and election defeat. Divider of 33 used to calculate percentages. Divider of 100 (or 98) used for other columns.
‡ Promotion defined as leaving Congress for the purpose of assuming or attempting to assume other public office at any level of government.

Figures compiled from data in *Members of Congress 1945–1970* (Washington: Congressional Quarterly Service, 1970) and *Biographical Directory of the American Congress 1774–1971* (Washington: Government Printing Office, 1971).

Percentage of Representatives Leaving Office by Reason and by Party
(1947–1971)

Year*	Defeated†		Promoted‡		Retired		Died	
	(D)	(R)	(D)	(R)	(D)	(R)	(D)	(R)
1947	8.97	1.38	3.45	1.61	2.53	2.53	.46	1.38
1949	2.07	16.78	1.84	2.30	2.30	1.38	1.84	.92
1951	7.59	.92	2.30	1.61	1.61	2.76	1.84	1.61
1953	4.60	2.53	2.76	1.84	3.68	2.53	1.38	.69
1955	1.84	4.14	1.84	2.07	1.15	.92	.92	.23
1957	2.99	2.07	1.15	.92	.69	2.76	1.61	.69
1959	1.38	8.28	1.15	1.38	.69	4.83	1.38	1.61
1961	5.98	1.38	2.53	.46	1.61	2.99	1.38	.46
1963	5.29	2.99	2.30	1.38	1.61	2.30	1.38	.46
1965	2.99	8.97	1.84	1.61	2.99	2.30	.92	.92
1967	9.66	.69	1.61	1.61	2.30	.46	.46	.46
1969	2.30	.69	1.15	3.45	2.53	.23	.69	.23
1971	2.53	2.53	1.15	5.06	.69	.69	.92	.92

* Representatives leaving in even-numbered years included in figures for next highest odd-numbered year.
† Includes both primary and election defeat. Divider of 435 used to calculate percentages.
‡ Promotion defined as leaving Congress for the purpose of assuming or attempting to assume other public office at any level of government.

Figures compiled from data in *Members of Congress 1945–1970* (Washington: Congressional Quarterly Service, 1970) and *Biographical Directory of the American Congress 1774–1971* (Washington: Government Printing Office, 1971).

Explanation of Appendices 5 through 8

To predict waiting time for those committees simulated, Freshman X was appended to the bottom of each party's committee lists for the Ninty-second Congress. No simulation was made of the following standing committees, since they were either too recently formed or had too high a transfer rate for accurate prediction, or because they were not legislative committees: Senate Aeronautical and Space Sciences, District of Columbia, Rules and Administration, and Veterans' Affairs; and House Administration, Internal Security, Science and Astronautics, and Standards of Official Conduct.

Since X's progression to the chair depended upon the disappearance of those above him, it was necessary to compute the timing and likelihood of each cause of attrition as it applied to individual committee members. Five classes of attrition were chosen: death, retirement, promotion, defeat, and transfer from committee ("promotion" being defined as leaving one house to seek other public office).

All members of Congress serving from 1947 through 1972 were used as a data base for computing defeat, retirement, and promotion. From these data were computed the incidence of these causes by house, party, region, and length of tenure in that house. For transfer from committee, data were collected on the incidence of transfer by party for each committee for the Eightieth through Ninety-second Congresses. The incidence of transfer according to length of committee tenure was also determined and averaged for all committees. Life tables from the Statistical Abstract as modified by a Metropolitan Statistical Abstract Bulletin comparing longevity of congressmen to the adult American male population were used for death figures.

Using these five factors, twenty "Monte Carlo simulations" were performed for each party list for each committee. For House Democratic Agriculture, for example, the computer would first determine the attrition for 1973. Congressman W. R. Poage, the first on the list, is a southern Democrat, 74 years old, who has served in the House for 36 years. The computer would compare defeat, retirement, and promotion rates for southern Democratic Congressmen with 36 years' tenure to three random numbers. It would also compare the percentage of 74-year-olds who do not reach 76 to a random number, and the incidence of transfer from House Agriculture of Democrats with lengthy committee tenure to a random number. If for any one of these, the random number was less than the attrition figure computed, then Congressman Poage was eliminated from the committee. The computer then performed the same operation for all other Democratic members of the committee. If Congressman Poage remained on the committee in 1975, the same operation was performed, except that defeat, retirement, and promotion rates were based on southern Democratic Congressmen serving 38 years. Likelihood of death was recomputed with respect to a person of 78, using, however, a conditional-probability formula to take into account a start from age 74. Such operations were performed for all remaining members every two years, until Freshman X was the only remaining member.

Data for interim chairmen were averaged, since one cannot predict which current members will become chairmen.

Assistant Professor Richard Scamell from the University of Houston designed the program.

General Description

Program Congress is a Monte Carlo simulation that determines how long it takes a freshman congressman from the Ninety-third Congress, styled Freshman X, to become chairman or ranking minority member of selected committees based on the assumption that (1) Freshman X is always re-elected and (2) that he is initially assigned to the committee being studied and never transfers off this committee.

For each committee included in the study, Program Congress is governed by the general procedure described below.

1. The present composition of the committee is input. The following items are supplied to the program for each congressman:
   a. Name
   b. Geographical region (East, South, West, Midwest)
   c. Birth date
   d. Date congressman entered Congress
   e. Date congressman entered Committee
   f. Date up for re-election
2. Associated with each two-year session of Congress, a congressman can either
   a. lose in a bid for re-election,
   b. attempt to obtain a different elective or appointed office,
   c. retire from public office,
   d. transfer to another committee in Congress, or
   e. die.

   Each congressman currently on the committee under investigation, excluding Freshman X, is evaluated to determine if one of the five dispositions listed above, in 2, occurs. If none occurs, he remains on the committee for the next session of Congress. Otherwise, he is removed from the committee and the seniority of Freshman X is increased.
3. The simulation terminates for the committee under investigation when all congressmen with more seniority than Freshman X have been removed from the committee.

Program Flow

Program Congress is governed by the information pertaining to each congressman described in Section 1 and by data accumulated over the twenty-four years from 1947 to 1971 with respect to regional (1) defeat rates, (2) promotion rates, and (3) retirement rates. Each factor is depicted by a 25×4 matrix shown on page 226.

The data actually obtained indicated that these three factors differed significantly for the (1) House Appropriations Committee, (2) House Rules Committee, and (3) House Ways and Means Committee. All other committees in the House were grouped into a single classification because the three factors did not differ materially for these committees. Likewise all committees in the Senate were represented by a single classification. Therefore separate 25 × 4 matrices are employed

		Geographical Region			
		E	S	W	NW
	2				
	4				
	6				
	8				
	10				
Consecutive	.				
Years in	.				
Congress	.				
	30				
	.				
	.				
	.				
	50				

for each of the above divisions, making a total of 8 matrices (4 Democrats, 4 Republicans) for the House and 2 matrices (1 Democrat, 1 Republican) for the Senate.

Death was treated with the use of the *Life Table for White Males: United States* 1959–61, which specified the proportion of persons alive at the beginning of an age interval that die during the interval.

The direct use of the cumulative probabilities provided by this table, however, make it impossible for a person to live past age 72. Thus a heuristic technique is utilized to make it possible for a small number of congressmen to remain in office until their early nineties. Independent tests of the technique consistently resulted in an age of death between 71 and 74 with a lower limit in the late thirties and an upper limit in the middle nineties.

Separate transfer rates based on a study of all committee transfers since 1947 were used for each committee included in the study.

Program Congress is divided into six independent subroutines based on (1) the branch of Congress and (2) the system of seniority used.

· *Subroutine House—Present* simulates the House under the present system of seniority.

· *Subroutine House—Age* simulates the House under a system of seniority that prohibits a congressman from serving as a committee chairman if he is beyond a designated age.

· *Subroutine House—Age/Tenure* simulates the House under a system of seniority that prohibits a congressman from serving as a committee chairman if he (1) has been chairman for more than a specified number of years and/or (2) is beyond a designated age.

• *Subroutine Senate—Present* simulates the Senate under the present system of seniority.

• *Subroutine Senate—Age* simulates the Senate under a system of seniority that prohibits a senator from serving as a committee chairman if he is beyond a designated age.

• *Subroutine Senate-Age/Tenure* simulates the Senate under a system of seniority that prohibits a senator from serving as a committee chairman if he (1) has been chairman for more than a specified number of years and/or (2) is beyond a designated age.

Each subroutine contains the following four steps:

Step 1. The data applicable to the specific committee under investigation are obtained from temporary storage in three disk files.

Step 2. For a given two-year session of Congress, each current member of the committee under investigation is processed in order to determine if he (or she) (1) is defeated, or (2) is promoted, or (3) retires, or (4) transfers, or (5) dies, or (6) remains on the committee. During this process various statistics such as (1) the number of interim chairmen, (2) the ages when various men become chairman, (3) the length of tenure for chairmen, (4) the age of death for those members that die, and (5) the geographical region of all chairmen are calculated. This step terminates when Congressman X becomes chairman (or ranking minority member) of the committee.

Step 3. At the conclusion of Step 2, various accumulations are incremented. These are used in computing the averages described in Step 4.

Steps 1–3 are performed a designated number of times for each committee under investigation. Then control passes to Step 4.

Step 4. At this point the following over-all averages and totals are output for each specified committee.

a. The average year when the congressman under investigation becomes chairman or ranking minority member.

b. The standard deviation associated with the averages described in a.

c. The average age at which all interim chairmen obtain this post.

d. The average tenure of the chairmen described in c.

e. The average number of years served before becoming chairmen for the congressmen described in c and d.

f. A regional breakdown showing the geographical region of all chairmen of the committee under investigation during the entire simulation.

SAMPLE 1.
Predicted Waiting Time
(Years Necessary for Freshman, 93rd Congress
to Become Chairman/Ranking Minority Member*)
House of Representatives

Sample House Committees	Present System	Reforms												
		Limitation of Term			Limitation of Age		Limitation of Age and Tenure							
		2-year	4-year	6-year	Age 65	Age 70	2-65	2-70	4-65	4-70	6-65	6-70		
Appropriations (Dem.)	41.3	27.1	31.5	35.1	26.3	30.9	18.2	21.7	21.4	24.0	25.5	27.0		
Appropriations (Rep.)	38.1	21.7	26.6	27.5	23.5	26.4	16.0	18.8	20.7	23.0	21.8	24.1		
Armed Services (Dem.)	39.3	27.2	34.0	36.9	27.5	32.7	19.3	21.8	24.8	30.1	27.2	30.9		
Armed Services (Rep.)	31.4	18.8	23.4	27.6	18.8	24.6	13.7	16.4	18.6	21.6	19.7	22.6		
Banking and Currency (Dem.)	37.3	25.2	30.3	33.4	21.9	27.2	16.1	21.6	19.7	23.2	21.5	26.8		
Banking and Currency (Rep.)	39.9	18.7	29.3	34.3	23.7	27.7	16.3	19.2	22.4	25.7	23.6	27.4		
Public Works (Dem.)	39.2	25.4	33.3	35.3	23.8	28.2	19.5	21.6	23.0	27.5	23.5	28.2		
Public Works (Rep.)	36.1	17.1	27.5	29.5	22.7	28.7	15.2	16.8	19.3	21.0	21.6	26.3		
Rules (Dem.)	26.0	9.9	14.5	14.1	9.8	13.6	8.2	8.6	9.4	12.5	10.3	14.2		
Rules (Rep.)	21.4	6.6	10.5	10.2	11.0	12.3	5.0	6.0	8.2	8.2	9.5	11.2		
Ways and Means (Dem.)	37.7	17.4	23.7	26.8	24.8	27.2	11.7	15.2	14.8	18.8	18.1	20.8		
Ways and Means (Rep.)	28.4	13.2	17.5	19.6	13.5	17.7	10.9	13.2	12.6	15.9	13.2	17.3		

* The figures are an average based on twenty sample simulations of each reform for each committee. Present chair-man's years included

SAMPLE 2.

Predicted Tenure of Chairman/Ranking Minority Member
by Committee
House of Representatives*

Sample House Committees	Present System	Reforms										
		Limitation of Term			Limitation of Age		Limitation of Age and Tenure					
		2-year	4-year	6-year	Age 65	Age 70	2-65	2-70	4-65	4-70	6-65	6-70
Appropriations (Dem.)	10.0	2.4	4.2	5.4	6.2	7.4	2.6	2.5	3.9	4.2	4.6	4.8
Appropriations (Rep.)	10.4	2.5	4.1	5.2	7.0	6.5	2.7	2.6	4.3	4.0	5.0	5.1
Armed Services (Dem.)	7.9	2.0	3.7	5.2	4.1	4.5	2.0	2.0	3.2	3.4	3.8	4.0
Armed Services (Rep.)	10.7	3.3	5.0	6.5	7.6	6.8	3.8	3.5	5.7	5.1	6.7	6.2
Banking and Currency (Dem.)	9.5	2.6	4.2	5.6	6.7	7.6	2.9	2.7	4.7	4.6	5.8	6.1
Banking and Currency (Rep.)	14.4	2.6	4.2	5.8	8.3	9.4	2.7	2.6	4.4	4.2	5.7	5.1
Public Works (Dem.)	10.5	2.0	3.7	5.1	5.6	6.2	2.0	2.0	3.3	3.6	4.9	5.3
Public Works (Rep.)	14.6	2.0	3.7	5.3	8.4	10.1	2.0	2.0	3.6	3.7	4.5	5.3
Rules (Dem.)	8.0	2.7	4.0	4.5	5.5	6.2	2.8	2.7	4.1	4.0	4.5	4.7
Rules (Rep.)	12.9	3.2	4.6	5.4	8.5	7.7	3.4	3.2	4.7	4.7	5.0	5.7
Ways and Means (Dem.)	13.6	3.2	5.1	6.5	9.9	11.1	3.8	3.4	5.8	5.3	7.5	5.9
Ways and Means (Rep.)	13.8	3.0	4.7	6.0	6.3	7.4	3.2	3.0	4.4	4.1	5.9	4.7

* The figures are an average based on twenty sample simulations of each reform for each committee. The present chairman's tenure is included.

SAMPLE 3.
Predicted Waiting Time
(Years Necessary for Freshman, 93rd Congress
to Become Chairman/Ranking Minority Member*)
Senate

Sample Senate Committees	Present System	Limitation of Chairman's or RMM's Term			Limitation of Chairman's or RMM's Age		Limitation of Chairman's or RMM's Age and Tenure					
		2-year	4-year	6-year	Age 65	Age 70	2-65	2-70	4-65	4-70	6-65	6-70
Appropriations (Dem.)	28.5	15.8	22.1	24.5	14.8	19.0	10.9	13.8	12.4	16.9	13.7	16.6
Appropriations (Rep.)	22.3	12.6	16.3	19.0	10.8	13.4	5.0	8.4	8.4	9.9	10.1	11.6
Armed Services (Dem.)	27.0	11.0	17.7	21.3	12.8	16.5	7.8	9.4	11.5	14.2	12.5	14.6
Armed Services (Rep.)	21.8	8.3	12.7	15.6	15.0	18.8	6.2	7.7	8.1	11.4	10.4	13.3
Banking, Housing, and Urban Affairs (Dem.)	28.6	9.3	15.8	19.7	19.7	23.4	9.1	9.9	13.6	16.0	18.1	20.5
Banking, Housing, and Urban Affairs (Rep.)	22.0	5.8	9.6	11.8	16.1	18.2	6.3	6.0	8.2	9.5	11.8	11.3

Reforms

* The figures are averages based on twenty simulations of future events and include the present chairman and ranking minority member, for each committee above. The freshman senator is assigned to each committee in 1973.
† Limitation of chairman or ranking minority member by age and tenure is unusually low for this committee because only one senator is at present young enough to qualify under the age limitations.

Reforms

Sample Senate Committees	Present System	Limitation of Chairman's or RMM's Term			Limitation of Chairman's or RMM's Age		Limitation of Chairman's or RMM's Age and Tenure					
		2-year	4-year	6-year	Age 65	Age 70	2-65	2-70	4-65	4-70	6-65	6-70
Foreign Relations (Dem.)	25.5	11.5	17.2	21.6	14.5	19.8	7.5	8.4	10.7	14.1	11.1	15.8
Foreign Relations (Rep.)†	21.3	8.3	12.9	15.7	10.6	13.0	1.8	4.0	3.6	5.6	5.6	6.6
Interior and Insular Affairs (Dem.)	31.0	11.9	19.8	23.1	18.1	23.4	6.6	8.8	10.9	13.7	15.9	14.8
Interior and Insular Affairs (Rep.)	23.3	7.9	13.3	18.3	14.6	16.7	6.5	7.1	10.0	12.0	12.5	14.1
Public Works (Dem.)	30.2	9.1	16.0	19.2	21.0	24.4	9.4	7.7	13.7	14.1	17.1	18.7
Public Works (Rep.)	19.2	5.5	7.8	9.1	12.5	14.5	5.8	5.1	7.1	8.4	8.3	11.6

* The figures are averages based on twenty simulations of future events and include the present chairman and ranking minority member, for each committee above. The freshman senator is assigned to each committee in 1973.
† Limitation of chairman or ranking minority member by age and tenure is unusually low for this committee because only one senator is at present young enough to qualify under the age limitations.

SAMPLE 4.

Predicted Tenure of Chairman/Ranking Minority Member by Committee
Senate*

Sample Senate Committees	Present System	Reforms										
		Limitation of Chairman's or RMM's Term			Limitation of Chairman's or RMM's Age		Limitation of Chairman's or RMM's Age and Tenure					
		2-year	4-year	6-year	Age 65	Age 70	2-65	2-70	4-65	4-70	6-65	6-70
Appropriations (Dem.)	6.7	1.8	2.4	2.7	7.8	3.2	1.9	1.9	2.5	2.6	3.7	2.4
Appropriations (Rep.)	7.7	2.2	2.9	3.7	5.1	3.1	2.7	2.6	3.7	3.0	3.9	3.4
Armed Services (Dem.)	10.3	2.1	3.1	3.9	3.8	4.4	2.3	1.2	3.3	3.2	4.0	4.0
Armed Services (Rep.)	11.8	2.5	3.6	4.1	6.8	5.0	2.9	2.7	4.4	4.2	4.8	5.1
Banking, Housing, and Urban Affairs (Dem.)	10.4	2.5	3.8	5.0	5.5	6.3	2.6	2.6	4.2	3.9	5.4	5.2
Banking, Housing, and Urban Affairs (Rep.)	12.2	1.5	2.9	3.1	8.2	6.4	1.5	1.4	2.4	2.5	4.3	3.9

* The figures are averages based on twenty simulations of future events and include the chairman and ranking minority member, for each committee above. A freshman senator is assigned to each committee in 1973 and upon becoming chairman or ranking minority member establishes the "future" date (data concerning this senator are not included in the calculations).

Reforms

Sample Senate Committees	Present System	Limitation of Chairman's or RMM's Term			Limitation of Chairman's or RMM's Age		Limitation of Chairman's or RMM's Age and Tenure					
		2-year	4-year	6-year	Age 65	Age 70	2-65	2-70	4-65	4-70	6-65	6-70
Foreign Relations (Dem.)	14.0	3.5	4.5	5.5	12.4	12.4	4.5	4.2	6.5	5.9	7.0	7.4
Foreign Relations (Rep.)	7.0	2.0	2.8	3.0	6.5	4.8	2.9	2.6	3.8	3.0	4.6	3.1
Interior and Insular Affairs (Dem.)	14.5	3.0	3.9	4.9	9.0	8.3	3.8	3.4	4.8	5.0	5.5	5.4
Interior and Insular Affairs (Rep.)	11.1	2.2	3.0	4.0	4.2	5.5	2.1	2.1	3.1	3.2	3.4	3.9
Public Works (Dem.)	11.8	2.6	3.6	5.2	6.8	6.6	2.6	2.6	4.3	4.2	5.1	5.2
Public Works (Rep.)	14.5	3.5	4.6	5.6	4.7	6.6	3.5	3.6	3.9	5.1	4.2	5.9

* The figures are averages based on twenty simulations of future events and include the chairman and ranking minority member, for each committee above. A freshman senator is assigned to each committee in 1973 and upon becoming chairman or ranking minority member establishes the "future" date (data concerning this senator are not included in the calculations).

APPENDIX 5.

Waiting Time to Become Senate Chairman/Ranking Minority Member, by Committee, Party, Year
(From Chairman Serving in 1947 to Projected Accession by Freshman of 93rd Congress)

Democrats	Assigned to Committee	Became Chairman	Years Waited	Per cent Change
Agriculture and Forestry				
Thomas	1928	1945	17	—
Ellender	1937	1951	14	−18.6
Talmadge	1957	1971	14	0
Int. Chm.*			20.8	+48
Freshman X†	1973	1999.4	26.6	+27
Appropriations				
McKellar	1924	1946	22	—
Hayden	1928	1953	25	+13.6
Russell	1933	1969	36	+44.0
Ellender	1949	1971	22	−38.9
McClellan	1949	1972	23	+4.5
Int. Chm.*			27.9	+21
Freshman X†	1973	2001.5	28.5	+2

Republicans	Assigned to Committee	Became Chairman	Years Waited	Per cent Change
Agriculture and Forestry				
Capper	1919	1944	25	—
Aiken	1941	1949	8	−68.0
Miller	1965	1971	6	−25.0
Int. Chm.*			9.7	+31.7
Freshman X†	1973	1992.1	19.1	+96
Appropriations				
Bridges	1937	1945	8	—
Saltonstall	1947	1962	15	+87.5
Young	1949	1967	18	+20.0
Int. Chm.*			22.4	+24
Freshman X†	1973	1995.3	22.3	0

* Interim Chairmen: those serving between Chairman 92nd Congress and accession of hypothetical freshman, 93rd Congress, to the chairmanship.

† Freshman X: hypothetical freshman, 93rd Congress, who has the qualifications to become chairman—i.e., he never dies, retires, goes on to other public office, or is defeated.

Democrats

	Assigned to Committee	Became Chairman	Years Waited	Per cent Change
Armed Services				
Tydings	1927	1947	20	—
Russell	1933	1951	18	−10
Stennis	1959	1969	18	0
Int. Chm.*			24.5	+36
Freshman X†	1973	2000	27.0	+10
Banking, Housing, and Urban Affairs				
Wagner	1928	1937	9	—
Maybank	1943	1949	6	−33.3
Fulbright	1945	1955	10	+66.7
Robertson	1947	1959	12	+20
Sparkman	1947	1967	20	+66.7
Int. Chm.*			24.9	+36
Freshman X†	1973	2001.6	28.6	+14

Republicans

	Assigned to Committee	Became Chairman	Years Waited	Per cent Change
Gurney	1939	1947	8	—
Bridges	1937	1949	12	+50
Saltonstall	1945	1953	8	−33.3
Smith	1953	1966	13	+62.5
Int. Chm.*			15.8	+21
Freshman X†	1973	1994.8	21.8	+38
Tobey	1939	1941	2	—
Capehart	1945	1951	6	+200
Bennett	1951	1963	12	+100
Tower	1962	1971	9	−25
Int. Chm.*			11.1	+23
Freshman X†	1973	1995	22.0	+96

* Interim Chairmen: those serving between Chairman 92nd Congress and accession of hypothetical freshman, 93rd Congress, to the chairmanship.

† Freshman X: hypothetical freshman, 93rd Congress, who has the qualifications to become chairman—i.e, he never dies, retires, goes on to other public office, or is defeated.

Democrats

Democrats	Assigned to Committee	Became Chairman	Years Waited	Per cent Change
Commerce				
Johnson	1936	1947	11	—
Magnuson	1945	1955	10	−9.1
Int. Chm.*			25.2	+151
Freshman X†	1973	2001.7	28.7	+14
Finance				
George	1925	1942	17	—
Byrd	1933	1955	22	+29.4
Long	1953	1966	13	−40.9
Int. Chm.*			28.5	+119
Freshman X†	1973	2001.5	28.5	0

Republicans

Republicans	Assigned to Committee	Became Chairman	Years Waited	Per cent Change
Commerce				
White	1928	1937	9	—
Tobey	1939	1949	10	+11.1
Brecker	1949	1954	5	−50
Schoeppel	1953	1959	6	+20
Cotton	1957	1963	6	0
Int. Chm.*			19.5	+225
Freshman X†	1973	2000.9	27.9	+42
Finance				
Millikin	1943	1947	4	—
Martin	1947	1957	10	+150
Williams	1950	1959	9	−10
Bennett	1953	1971	18	+100
Int. Chm.*			14.3	−10
Freshman X†	1973	1993.8	20.8	+28

* Interim Chairmen: those serving between Chairman 92nd Congress and accession of hypothetical freshman, 93rd Congress, to the chairmanship.

† Freshman X: hypothetical freshman, 93rd Congress, who has the qualifications to become chairman—i.e., he never dies, retires, goes on to other public office, or is defeated.

Democrats	Assigned to Committee	Became Chairman	Years Waited	Per cent Change	Republicans	Assigned to Committee	Became Chairman	Years Waited	Per cent Change
Foreign Relations									
Connally	1922	1942	20	—	Vandenberg	1929	1947	18	—
George	1939	1953	14	−30	Wiley	1945	1952	7	−61.1
Greene	1949	1957	8	−42.9	Hickenlooper	1947	1963	16	+128.6
Fulbright	1950	1959	9	+12.5	Aiken	1954	1969	15	−6.2
Int. Chm.*			26.3	+191	Int. Chm.*			14.3	−4
Freshman X†	1973	1998.5	25.5	−2	Freshman X†	1973	1994.3	21.3	+48
Government Operations									
McClellan	1943	1947	4	—	Aiken	1942	1945	3	—
Ervin	1955	1972	17	+325	McCarthy	1947	1949	2	−33.3
					Mundt	1949	1958	9	+350
					Percy	1969	1972	3	−66.7
Int. Chm.*			24.4	+43	Int. Chm.*			14.1	+369
Freshman X†	1973	2000.7	27.7	+13	Freshman X†	1973	1989.1	16.1	+14

* Interim Chairmen: those serving between Chairman 92nd Congress and accession of hypothetical freshman, 93rd Congress, to the chairmanship.

† Freshman X: hypothetical freshman, 93rd Congress, who has the qualifications to become chairman—i.e., he never dies, retires, goes on to other public office, or is defeated.

Democrats

	Assigned to Committee	Became Chairman	Years Waited	Per cent Change
Interior and Insular Affairs				
Hatch	1934	1942	8	—
O'Mahoney	1934	1949	15	+87.5
Murray	1935	1953	18	+20
Anderson	1950	1961	11	−38.9
Jackson	1955	1963	8	−27.3
Int. Chm.*			28.8	+260
Freshman X†	1973	2004	31	+7
Judiciary				
McCarran	1934	1944	10	—
Kilgore	1942	1955	13	+30
Eastland	1944	1957	13	0
Int. Chm.*			25.1	+93
Freshman X†	1973	2009.9	36.9	+47

Republicans

	Assigned to Committee	Became Chairman	Years Waited	Per cent Change
Interior and Insular Affairs				
Butler	1941	1947	6	—
Cordon	1944	1955	11	+83.3
Malone	1947	1957	10	−9.1
Dworshak	1947	1959	12	+20
Kuchel	1953	1963	10	−16.7
Allott	1957	1969	12	+20
Int. Chm.*			20.9	+74
Freshman X†	1973	1999	26.3	+12
Judiciary				
Wiley	1939	1945	6	—
Langer	1941	1953	12	+100
Dirksen	1953	1963	10	−16.7
Hruska	1957	1970	13	+30
Int. Chm.*			16.9	+16.9
Freshman X†	1973	1999.4	26.4	+55

* Interim Chairmen: those serving between Chairman 92nd Congress and accession of hypothetical freshman, 93rd Congress, to the chairmanship.
† Freshman X: hypothetical freshman, 93rd Congress, who has the qualifications to become chairman—i.e, he never dies, retires, goes on to other public office, or is defeated.

Democrats	Assigned to Committee	Became Chairman	Years Waited	Per cent Change	Republicans	Assigned to Committee	Became Chairman	Years Waited	Per cent Change
Labor and Public Welfare									
Thomas	1928	1935	7	—	Taft	1939	1947	8	—
Murray	1947	1951	4	−42.8	Smith	1945	1953	8	0
Hill	1947	1955	8	+100	Goldwater	1953	1959	6	−25
Yarborough	1959	1969	10	+25	Javits	1959	1965	6	0
Williams	1959	1971	12	+20	Int. Chm.*			34.7	+328.3
Int. Chm.*			29.3	+143	Freshman X†	1973	2005.1	32.1	−7
Freshman X†	1973	2009.7	36.7	+25					
Post Office and Civil Service									
Chavez	1936	1946	10	—	Langer	1941	1947	6	—
Johnston	1947	1949	2	−80	Carlson	1951	1953	2	−66.7
Monroney	1951	1966	15	+650	Fong	1961	1969	8	+300
McGee	1963	1969	6	−60	Int. Chm.*			16.7	+108
Int. Chm.*			13.9	+131	Freshman X†	1973	1993.5	20.5	+22
Freshman X†	1973	1994.5	21.5	+54					

* Interim Chairmen: those serving between Chairman 92nd Congress and accession of hypothetical freshman, 93rd Congress, to the chairmanship.

† Freshman X: hypothetical freshman, 93rd Congress, who has the qualifications to become chairman—i.e., he never dies, retires, goes on to other public office, or is defeated.

Democrats	Assigned to Committee	Became Chairman	Years Waited	Per cent Change
Public Works				
Chavez	1936	1948	12	—
McNamara	1955	1963	8	−33.3
Randolph	1959	1967	8	0
Int. Chm.*			23.1	+188
Freshman X†	1973	2003.2	30.2	+30

Republicans	Assigned to Committee	Became Chairman	Years Waited	Per cent Change
Revercomb	1943	1947	4	—
Cain	1947	1949	2	−50
Martin	1947	1953	6	+200
Chase	1951	1959	8	+33.3
Cooper	1959	1963	4	−50
Int. Chm.*			14.6	+265
Freshman X†	1973	1992.2	19.2	+16

* Interim Chairmen: those serving between Chairman 92nd Congress and accession of hypothetical freshman, 93rd Congress, to the chairmanship.

† Freshman X: hypothetical freshman, 93rd Congress, who has the qualifications to become chairman—i.e., he never dies, retires, goes on to other public office, or is defeated.

APPENDIX 6.

Waiting Time to Become House Chairman/Ranking Minority Member, by Committee, Party, Year

(From Chairman Serving in 1947 to Projected Accession by Freshman of 93rd Congress)

Democrats	Assigned to Committee	Became Chairman	Years Waited	Per cent Change	Republicans	Assigned to Committee	Became Chairman	Years Waited	Per cent Change
Agriculture									
Flanigan	1932	1945	13	—	Hope	1928	1934	6	—
Cooley	1935	1949	14	+7.6	Anderson	1935	1957	22	+266.7
Poage	1941	1967	26	+85.7	Hoeven	1945	1959	14	−36.4
					Dague	1947	1965	18	+28.6
					Belcher	1951	1967	16	−11.1
Int. Chm.*			32.6	+25	Int. Chm.*			23.7	+47
Freshman X†	1973	2016.2	43.2	+32	Freshman X†	1973	2007.2	34.2	+44
Appropriations									
Cannon	1930	1942	12	—	Taber	1924	1933	9	—
Mahon	1939	1965	26	+116.7	Jensen	1943	1963	20	+122.2
					Bow	1953	1965	12	−40.0
Int. Chm.*			36.5	+40	Int. Chm.*			29.9	+148
Freshman X†	1973	2014.3	41.3	+13	Freshman X†	1973	2011.1	38	+27

* Interim Chairmen: chairmen projected to serve between current chairman and accession by freshman 93rd Congress.
† Freshman X: freshman assigned to committee 93rd Congress who is never defeated, retired, transferred, and does not die prior to accession to the chair.

Democrats

	Assigned to Committee	Became Chairman	Years Waited	Per cent Change
Armed Services				
Vinson	1917	1924	7	—
Rivers	1943	1965	22	+214.3
Hébert	1945	1971	26	+18.2
Int. Chm.*			32.6	+25.4
Freshman X†	1973	2012.3	39.3	+20
Banking and Currency				
Spence	1933	1945	12	—
Patman	1937	1963	26	+116.7
Int. Chm.*			31.9	+22
Freshman X†	1973	2010.3	37.3	+16
District of Columbia				
McMillan	1940	1946	6	—
Int. Chm.*			29.4	+404
Freshman X†	1973	2012.4	39.4	+34

Republicans

	Assigned to Committee	Became Chairman	Years Waited	Per cent Change
Armed Services				
Andrews	1933	1937	4	—
Short	1935	1949	14	+250
Arends	1935	1957	22	+57.1
Int. Chm.*			29.1	+32
Freshman X†	1973	2004.4	31.4	+8
Banking and Currency				
Wollcott	1933	1937	4	—
Talle	1942	1957	15	+275
Kilburn	1945	1959	14	-6.7
Widnall	1951	1965	14	0
Int. Chm.*			26.5	+89
Freshman X†	1973	2012.9	39.9	+50
District of Columbia				
Dirksen	1933	1935	2	—
Bates	1937	1949	12	+500
Simpson	1943	1950	7	-41.7
Auchincloss	1947	1959	12	+71.4
Broyhill	1953	1962	9	-25.0
Nelsen	1959	1965	6	-33.3
Int. Chm.*			24.7	+310
Freshman X†	1973	2002.7	29.7	+56.3

* Interim Chairmen: chairmen projected to serve between current chairman and accession by freshman 93rd Congress.
† Freshman X: freshman assigned to committee 93rd Congress who is never defeated, retired, transferred, and does not die prior to accession to the chair.

Democrats	Assigned to Committee	Became Chairman	Years Waited	Per cent Change	Republicans	Assigned to Committee	Became Chairman	Years Waited	Per cent Change
Education and Labor									
Lesinski	1933	1947	14	—	Hartley	1930	1947	17	—
Barden	1935	1951	16	+14.3	McConnell	1945	1949	4	−76.5
Powell	1945	1961	16	0	Gwinn	1945	1958	13	+225
Perkins	1949	1967	18	+12.5	Kearnes	1947	1959	12	−7.7
					Frelinghuysen	1953	1963	10	−16.7
					Ayres	1957	1965	8	−20.0
					Quie	1960	1971	11	+37.5
Int. Chm.*			37.2	+106	Int. Chm.*			35.4	+222
Freshman X†	1973	2015.0	42	+13	Freshman X†	1973	2015.3	42.3	+19
Foreign Affairs									
Bloom	1928	1940	12	—	Eaton	1925	1941	16	—
Kee	1933	1950	17	+41.7	Chiperfield	1939	1953	14	−12.5
Richards	1935	1952	17	0	Botton	1941	1963	22	+57.1
Gordon	1943	1957	14	−17.6	Adair	1953	1969	16	−27.3
Morgan	1946	1959	13	−7.1	Maillard	1961	1971	10	−37.5
Int. Chm.*			35.8	+175	Int. Chm.*			30.4	+204
Freshman X†	1973	2011.5	38.5	+7	Freshman X†	1973	2014.7	41.7	+36

* Interim Chairman: chairmen projected to serve between current chairman and accession by freshman 93rd Congress.
† Freshman X: freshman assigned to committee 93rd Congress who is never defeated, retired, transferred, and does not die prior to accession to the chair.

Democrats	Assigned to Committee	Became Chairman	Years Waited	Per cent Change	Republicans	Assigned to Committee	Became Chairman	Years Waited	Per cent Change
Government Operations									
Manasco	1942	1944	2	—	Hoffman	1935	1946	11	—
Dawson	1943	1949	6	+200	Riehlman	1947	1963	16	+45.5
Holifield	1949	1971	22	+266.7	Brown	1947	1965	18	+12.5
					Dwyer	1957	1966	9	−50.0
Int. Chm.*			34.9	+58	Int. Chm.*			28.8	+219
Freshman X†	1973	2014.7	41.7	+19	Freshman X†	1973	2012.8	39.8	+38
Interior and Insular Affairs									
Petersen	1933	1943	10	—	Welch	1928	1939	11	—
Murdock	1933	1951	18	+80	Crawford	1935	1950	15	+36.4
Engle	1944	1953	9	−50	Miller	1947	1953	6	−60.0
Aspinall	1949	1959	10	+11.1	Saylor	1950	1959	9	+50
Int. Chm.*			31.6	+215	Int. Chm.*			29.0	+222
Freshman X†	1973	2012.8	39.8	+175	Freshman X†	1973	2010.2	37.2	+28
Interstate and Foreign Commerce									
Lea	1921	1937	16	—	Wolverton	1925	1940	15	—
Crosser	1924	1949	25	+56.2	Bennett	1947	1959	12	−20
Priest	1943	1955	12	−52.0	Springer	1953	1965	12	0
Harris	1943	1957	14	+16.7	Int. Chm.*			31.2	+160
Staggers	1952	1967	15	+7.1	Freshman X†	1973	2012.4	39.4	+26
Int. Chm.*			35.8	+138					
Freshman X†	1973	2013.8	40.8	+13					

* Interim Chairmen: chairmen projected to serve between current chairman and accession by freshman 93rd Congress.
† Freshman X: freshman assigned to committee 93rd Congress who is never defeated, retired, transferred, and does not die prior to accession to the chair.

Democrats

	Assigned to Committee	Became Chairman	Years Waited	Per cent Change
Judiciary				
Celler	1930	1947	17	—
Int. Chm.*			32.0	+88
Freshman X†	1973	2013.4	40.4	+26
Merchant Marine and Fisheries				
Bland	1921	1933	12	—
Hart	1939	1951	12	0
Bonner	1942	1955	13	+8.3
Garmatz	1949	1966	17	+30.8
Int. Chm.*			30.1	+88
Freshman X†	1973	2013.3	40.3	+22
Post Office and Civil Service				
Murray	1943	1947	4	—
Dulski	1959	1967	8	+100
Int. Chm.*			30.9	+286
Freshman X†	1973	2011.6	38.6	+24

Republicans

	Assigned to Committee	Became Chairman	Years Waited	Per cent Change
Judiciary				
Michener	1921	1947	26	—
Reed	1937	1951	14	−46.2
Keating	1947	1957	10	−28.6
McCullough	1948	1959	11	+10.0
Int. Chm.*			28.3	+157
Freshman X†	1973	2011.5	38.5	+35
Merchant Marine and Fisheries				
Weichel	1943	1947	4	—
Tollefson	1947	1955	8	+100
Maillard	1953	1965	12	+50
Pelly	1955	1971	16	+33
Int. Chm.*			30.1	+88
Freshman X†	1973	2013.5	40.5	+34
Post Office and Civil Service				
Rees	1937	1947	10	—
Corbett	1945	1961	16	+60
Gross	1949	1971	22	+37.5
Int. Chm.*			25.2	+14
Freshman X†	1973	2011.5	38.5	+52

* Interim Chairmen: chairmen projected to serve between current chairman and accession by freshman 93rd Congress.
† Freshman X: freshman assigned to committee 93rd Congress who is never defeated, retired, transferred, and does not die prior to accession to the chair.

Democrats	Assigned to Committee	Became Chairman	Years Waited	Per cent Change	Republicans	Assigned to Committee	Became Chairman	Years Waited	Per cent Change
Public Works									
Mansfield	1920	1924	4	—	Dondero	1933	1941	8	—
Whittington	1925	1949	24	+500	McGregor	1940	1957	17	+112.5
Buckley	1947	1951	4	-84	Auchincloss	1943	1959	16	-5.9
Fallon	1946	1964	18	+350	Cramer	1955	1964	9	-43.8
Blatnik	1947	1971	24	+33.3	Harsha	1963	1971	8	-11.1
Int. Chm.*			36.5	+52	Int. Chm.*			27.2	+240
Freshman X†	1973	2012.2	39.2	+7	Freshman X†	1973	2009.1	36.1	+32
Rules									
Sabath	1930	1939	9	—	Allen	1939	1943	4	—
Smith	1933	1953	20	+20	Brown	1943	1961	18	+350
Colmer	1939	1967	28	+40	Smith	1961	1966	5	-72.2
Int. Chm.*			27.5	-1	Int. Chm.*			17.4	+248
Freshman X†	1973	1999	26	-5	Freshman X†	1973	1994.4	21.4	+23
Veterans' Affairs									
Rankin	1924	1930	6	—	Rogers	1926	1935	9	—
Teague	1947	1953	6	0	Ayres	1951	1961	10	+11.1
					Adair	1951	1965	14	+40.0
					Teague	1958	1969	11	-21.4
Int. Chm.*			33.3	+454	Int. Chm.*			22.2	+100
Freshman X†	1973	2003.8	30.8	-7	Freshman X†	1973	2003.2	30.2	+36

* Interim Chairmen: chairmen projected to serve between current chairman and accession by freshman 93rd Congress.
† Freshman X: freshman assigned to committee 93rd Congress who is never defeated, retired, transferred, and does not die prior to accession to the chair.

Democrats	Assigned to Committee	Became Chairman	Years Waited	Per cent Change	Republicans	Assigned to Committee	Became Chairman	Years Waited	Per cent Change
Ways and Means									
Doughton	1926	1933	7	—	Knutson	1933	1943	10	—
Cooper	1932	1953	21	+200	Reed	1933	1949	16	+60
Mills	1943	1959	16	−23.8	Simpson	1943	1959	16	0
Int. Chm.*			26.1	+63	Mason	1947	1961	14	−12.5
Freshman X†	1973	2010.7	37.7	+44	Byrnes	1947	1963	16	+14.3
					Int. Chm.*			22.0	+37
					Freshman X†	1973	2001.4	28.4	+28

* Interim Chairmen: chairmen projected to serve between current chairman and accession by freshman 93rd Congress.
† Freshman X: freshman assigned to committee 93rd Congress who is never defeated, retired, transferred, and does not die prior to accession to the chair.

APPENDIX 7.

Tenure of Senate Chairman/Ranking Minority Member, By Committee, Party, Year

(From Chairman Serving in 1947 to Future*)

Democrats	Became Chairman	Ended Chairmanship	Years Chairman	Republicans	Became Chairman	Ended Chairmanship	Years Chairman
Agriculture and Forestry							
Thomas	1945	1950	5	Capper	1944	1948	4
Ellender	1951	1970	19	Aiken	1949	1970	21
Talmadge	1971	—	2+	Miller	1971	—	2+
Interim Chm.*			16.1	Interim Chm.*			12.9
Appropriations							
McKellon	1946	1952	6	Bridges	1945	1961	16
Hayden	1953	1968	15	Saltonstall	1962	1966	4
Russell	1969	1970	1	Young	1967	—	6+
Ellender	1971	1972	1	Interim Chm.*			7.7
McClellan	1972	—	1+				
Interim Chm.*			6.7				
Armed Services							
Tydings	1947	1950	3	Gurney	1947	1948	1
Russell	1951	1968	17	Bridges	1949	1952	3
Stennis	1969	—	4+	Saltonstall	1953	1965	12
Interim Chm.*			10.3	Smith	1966	—	7+
				Interim Chm.*			11.8

* Interim Chairmen: chairmen projected to serve between current chairman and accession by freshman 93rd Congress.

Democrats	Became Chairmanship	Ended Chairmanship	Years Chairman	Republicans	Became Chairman	Ended Chairmanship	Years Chairman
Banking, Housing, and Urban Affairs							
Wagner	1937	1948	11	Tobey	1941	1950	9
Maybank	1948	1954	5	Capehart	1951	1962	11
Fulbright	1955	1958	3	Bennett	1963	1970	7
Robertson	1959	1966	7	Tower	1971	—	2+
Sparkman	1967	—	6+	Interim Chm.*			12.1
Interim Chm.*			10.4				
Commerce							
Johnson	1947	1954	7	White	1937	1948	11
Magnuson	1955	—	18+	Tobey	1949	1953	4
Interim Chm.*			14.5	Brecker	1954	1958	4
				Schoeppel	1959	1962	3
				Cotton	1963	—	10+
				Interim Chm.*			13
Finance							
George	1942	1954	12	Milliken	1947	1956	9
Byrd	1955	1965	10	Martin	1957	1958	1
Long	1966	—	7+	Williams	1959	1970	11
Interim Chm.*			9.4	Bennett	1971	—	2+
				Interim Chm.*			8.5

* Interim Chairmen: chairmen projected to serve between current chairman and accession by freshman 93rd Congress.

Democrats	Became Chairman	Ended Chairmanship	Years Chairman	Republicans	Became Chairman	Ended Chairmanship	Years Chairman
Foreign Relations							
Connally	1942	1952	10	Vandenberg	1947	1951	4
George	1953	1956	3	Wiley	1952	1962	10
Greene	1957	1958	1	Hickenlooper	1963	1968	5
Fulbright	1959	—	14+	Aiken	1969	—	4+
Interim Chm.*	—	—	14	Interim Chm.*	—	—	7
Government Operations							
McClellan	1947	1972	25	Aiken	1945	1948	3
Ervin	1972	—	1+	McCarthy	1949	1957	8
Interim Chm.*	—	—	17.8	Mundt	1958	1972	14
				Percy	1972	—	1+
				Interim Chm.*	—	—	16.3
Interior and Insular Affairs							
Hatch	1942	1948	6	Butler	1947	1954	7
O'Mahoney	1949	1952	3	Cordon	1955	1956	1
Murray	1953	1960	7	Malone	1957	1958	1
Anderson	1961	1962	1	Dwarshak	1959	1962	3
Jackson	1963	—	10+	Kuchel	1963	1968	5
Interim Chm.*	—	—	14.5	Allott	1969	—	4+
				Interim Chm.*	—	—	11.1

* Interim Chairmen: chairmen projected to serve between current chairman and accession by freshman 93rd Congress.

Democrats	Became Chairman	Ended Chairmanship	Years Chairman	Republicans	Became Chairman	Ended Chairmanship	Years Chairman
Judiciary							
McCarran	1944	1954	10	Wiley	1945	1952	7
Kilgore	1955	1956	1	Langer	1953	1954	1
Eastland	1957	—	16+	Dirksen	1963	1969	6
Interim Chm.*	—	—	17.4	Hruska	1970	—	3+
				Interim Chm.*			11.4
Labor and Public Welfare							
Thomas	1935	1950	15	Taft	1947	1952	5
Murray	1951	1954	3	Smith	1953	1958	5
Hill	1955	1968	13	Goldwater	1959	1964	5
Yarborough	1969	1970	1	Javits	1965	—	8+
Williams	1971	—	2+	Interim Chm.*			14
Interim Chm.*	—	—	15.1				
Post Office and Civil Service							
Chavez	1946	1948	2	Langer	1947	1952	5
Johnston	1949	1965	16	Carlson	1953	1968	15
Monroney	1966	1968	2	Fong	1969	—	4+
McGee	1969	—	4+	Interim Chm.*			14.7
Interim Chm.*	—	—	19.8				

* Interim Chairmen: chairmen projected to serve between current chairman and accession by freshman 93rd Congress.

Democrats	Became Chairman	Ended Chairmanship	Years Chairman	Republicans	Became Chairman	Ended Chairmanship	Years Chairman
Public Works							
Chavez	1948	1962	14	Revercomb	1947	1948	2
McNamara	1963	1966	3	Cain	1949	1952	5
Randolph	1967	—	6+	Martin	1953	1958	5
Interim Chm.*	—	—	11.8	Chase	1959	1962	3
				Cooper	1963	—	10+
				Interim Chm.*	—	—	14.5

* Interim Chairmen: chairmen projected to serve between current chairman and accession by freshman 93rd Congress.

APPENDIX 8.

Tenure of House Chairman/Ranking Minority Member, by Committee, Party, Year
(From Chairman Serving in 1947 to Future*)

Democrats	Became Chairman	Ended Chairmanship	Years Chairman	Republicans	Became Chairman	Ended Chairmanship	Years Chairman
Agriculture							
Flannigan	1945	1948	3	Hope	1934	1956	22
Cooley	1949	1966	17	Anderson	1957	1958	1
Poage	1967	—	6+	Hoeven	1959	1964	5
Interim Chm.*			11.1	Dague	1965	1966	1
				Belcher	1967	—	6+
				Interim Chm.*			12.3
Appropriations							
Cannon	1942	1964	22	Taber	1933	1962	29
Mahon	1965	—	8+	Jensen	1963	1964	1
Interim Chm.*			10	Bow	1965	—	8+
				Interim Chm.*			10.4
Armed Services							
Vinson	1924	1965	41	Andrews	1937	1948	11
Rivers	1965	1970	5	Short	1949	1956	7
Hébert	1971	—	2+	Arends	1957	—	16+
Interim Chm.*			7.9	Interim Chm.*			10.7

* Interim Chairmen: chairmen projected to serve between current chairman and accession by freshman 93rd Congress.

Democrats	Became Chairman	Ended Chairmanship	Years Chairman	Republicans	Became Chairman	Ended Chairmanship	Years Chairman
Banking and Currency							
Spence	1945	1962	17	Wallcott	1937	1956	19
Patman	1963	—	10+	Talle	1957	1958	1
Interim Chm.*	—		9.5	Kilburn	1959	1964	5
				Widnab	1965	—	8+
				Interim Chm.*	—		4.4
District of Columbia							
McMillan	1946	—	27	Dirksen	1935	1948	13
Interim Chm.*	—		14.8	Bates	1949	1949	<1
				Simpson	1950	1958	8
				Auchincloss	1959	1961	2
				Broyhill	1962	1964	2
				Nelson	1965	—	8+
				Interim Chm.*	—		12.1
Education and Labor							
Lesinski	1947	1950	3	Hartley	1947	1948	1
Barden	1951	1960	9	McConnell	1949	1957	8
Powell	1961	1966	5	Gwinn	1958	1958	<1
Perkins	1967	—	6+	Kearns	1959	1962	3
Interim Chm.*	—		10.1	Frelinghuysen	1963	1964	1
				Ayres	1965	1970	5
				Quie	1971	—	2+
				Interim Chm.*	—		14.9

* Interim Chairmen: chairmen projected to serve between current chairman and accession by freshman 93rd Congress.

Democrats	Became Chairman	Ended Chairmanship	Years Chairman	Republicans	Became Chairman	Ended Chairmanship	Years Chairman
Foreign Affairs							
Bloom	1940	1949	9	Eaton	1941	1952	11
Kee	1950	1951	1	Chiperfield	1953	1962	9
Richards	1952	1956	4	Botton	1963	1968	5
Gordon	1957	1958	1	Adair	1969	1970	1
Morgan	1959	—	14+	Maillard	1971	—	2+
Interim Chm.*	—	—	12.4	Interim Chm.*	—	—	10.9
Government Operations							
Manasco	1944	1948	4	Hoffman	1946	1962	16
Dawson	1949	1970	21	Riehlman	1963	1964	1
Holifield	1971	—	2+	Brown	1965	1965	<1
Interim Chm.*	—	—	10	Dwyer	1966	—	7+
				Interim Chm.*	—	—	12.5
Interior and Insular Affairs							
Petersen	1943	1950	7	Welch	1939	1949	10
Murdock	1951	1952	1	Crawford	1950	1952	2
Engle	1953	1958	5	Miller	1953	1958	5
Aspinall	1959	—	14+	Saylor	1959	—	14+
Interim Chm.*	—	—	10.6	Interim Chm.*	—	—	14.2

* Interim Chairmen: chairmen projected to serve between current chairman and accession by freshman 93rd Congress.

Democrats	Became Chairman	Ended Chairmanship	Years Chairman	Republicans	Became Chairman	Ended Chairmanship	Years Chairman
Interstate and Foreign Commerce							
Lea	1937	1948	11	Wolverton	1940	1958	18
Crosser	1949	1954	5	Bennett	1959	1964	5
Priest	1955	1956	1	Springer	1965	—	8+
Harris	1957	1966	9	Interim Chm.*	—		11.2
Staggers	1967	—	6+				
Interim Chm.*	—		9.8				
Judiciary							
Celler	1947	—	26+	Michener	1947	1950	3
Interim Chm.*	—		14.3	Reed	1951	1956	5
				Keating	1957	1958	1
				McCullough	1959	—	14+
				Interim Chm.*	—		13.3
Merchant Marine and Fisheries							
Bland	1933	1950	17	Weichel	1947	1954	7
Hart	1951	1954	3	Tollefson	1955	1964	9
Bonner	1955	1965	10	Maillard	1965	1970	5
Garmatz	1966	—	7+	Pelly	1971	—	2+
Interim Chm.*	—		12.1	Interim Chm.*	—		10.3

* Interim Chairmen: chairmen projected to serve between current chairman and accession by freshman 93rd Congress.

Democrats	Became Chairman	Ended Chairmanship	Years Chairman	Republicans	Became Chairman	Ended Chairmanship	Years Chairman
Post Office and Civil Service							
Murray	1947	1966	19	Rees	1947	1960	13
Dulski	1967	—	6+	Corbett	1961	1971	10
				Gross	1971	—	2+
Interim Chm.*			15.2	Interim Chm.*			16.5
Public Works							
Mansfield	1924	1948	24	Dondero	1941	1956	15
Whittington	1949	1950	1	McGregor	1957	1958	1
Buckley	1951	1963	12	Auchincloss	1959	1963	4
Fallon	1964	1970	6	Craner	1964	1970	6
Blatnik	1971	—	2+	Harsha	1971	—	2+
Interim Chm.*			10.5	Interim Chm.*			14.6
Rules							
Sabath	1939	1952	13	Allen	1943	1960	17
Smith	1953	1966	13	Brown	1961	1965	4
Colmer	1967	—	6+	Smith	1966	—	7+
Interim Chm.*			8	Interim Chm.*			12.9

* Interim Chairmen: chairmen projected to serve between current chairman and accession by freshman 93rd Congress.

Democrats	Became Chairman	Ended Chairmanship	Years Chairman	Republicans	Became Chairman	Ended Chairmanship	Years Chairman
Veterans' Affairs				**Veterans' Affairs**			
Rankin	1930	1952	22	Rogers	1935	1960	25
Teague	1953	—	20+	Ayres	1961	1964	3
Interim Chm.*	—	—	15.5	Adair	1965	1968	3
				Teague	1969	—	4+
				Interim Chm.*	—	—	14.1
Ways and Means				**Ways and Means**			
Doughton	1933	1952	19	Knutson	1943	1948	5
Cooper	1953	1958	5	Reed	1949	1958	9
Mills	1959	—	14+	Simpson	1959	1960	1
Interim Chm.*	—	—	13.6	Mason	1961	1962	1
				Byrnes	1963	—	10+
				Interim Chm.*	—	—	13.8

* Interim Chairmen: chairmen projected to serve between current chairman and accession by freshman 93rd Congress.

APPENDIX 9.

Members of the House Rules Committee (92nd Congress)

William M. Colmer (D., Miss.), chairman, *no subcommittees*
Ray Madden (D., Ind.)
James Delaney (D., N.Y.)
Richard Bolling (D., Mo.)
Thomas O'Neill (D., Mass.)
B. F. Sisk (D., Calif.)
John Young (D., Tex.)
Claude D. Pepper (D., Fla.)
Spark Matsunaga (D., Hawaii)
William Anderson (D., Tenn.)

H. Allen Smith (R., Calif.)
John Anderson (R., Ill.)
Dave Martin (R., Nebr.)
James H. Quillen (R., Tenn.)
Delbert Latta (R., Ohio)

*Members of the Senate Rules and Administration
Committee (92nd Congress)*

B. Everett Jordan (D., N.C.), chairman of the full committee and the
    Computer Services and Library Subcommittee
Howard W. Cannon (D., Nev.), chairman of the Subcommittee on
    Privileges and Elections
Robert C. Byrd (D., W. Va.), chairman of the Subcommittee on
    Standing Rules of the Senate
James B. Allen, (D., Ala.), chairman of the Subcommittee on
    Restaurants
Claiborne Pell (D., R.I.), chairman of the Subcommittee on the
    Smithsonian Institution

Winston Prouty (R., Vt.)
John Cooper (R., Ky.)

Hugh Scott (R., Pa.)
Robert Griffin (R., Mich.)

APPENDIX 10.
Sample House Rules Committee Resolutions

CONFERENCE REPORT ON H.R. 12931, RURAL DEVELOPMENT ACT OF 1972

MR. YOUNG of Texas. Mr. Speaker, by direction of the Committee on Rules, I call up House Resolution 1057 and ask for its immediate consideration.

The Clerk read the resolution as follows:

H. RES. 1057

Resolved, That upon the adoption of this resolution it shall be in order to consider the conference report on the bill (H.R. 12931) to provide for improving the economy and living conditions in rural America, and all points of order against the conference report for failure to comply with the provisions of clauses 2 and 3, rule XX and clause 3, rule XXVIII are hereby waived.

—*Congressional Record,* July 27, 1972, p. H6972–3

PUBLIC WORKS FOR WATER AND POWER DEVELOPMENT AND ATOMIC ENERGY COMMISSION APPROPRIATIONS, 1974

MR. YOUNG of Texas. Mr. Speaker, by direction of the Committee on Rules, I call up House Resolution 471 and ask for its immediate consideration.

The Clerk read the resolution, as follows:

H. RES. 471

Resolved, That during the consideration of the bill (H.R. 8947) making appropriations for public works for water and power development, including the Corps of Engineers—Civil, the Bureau of Reclamation, the Bonneville Power Administration and other power agencies of the Department of the Interior, the Appalachian regional development programs, the Federal Power Commission, the Tennessee Valley Authority, the Atomic Energy Commission, and related independent agencies and commissions for the fiscal year ending June 30, 1974, and for other purposes, all points of order against said bill for failure to comply with the provisions of clause 2, rule XXI, are hereby waived.

—*Congressional Record,* June 28, 1973, p. H5591.

APPENDIX 11.
Congress Project Survey of Five Bills and
Unanimous-Consent Requests

Civil Rights Bill of 1968

Unanimous-consent requests	*Uses*
For motion to consider a bill	4
To set time for reconvening (after that day's adjournment)	1
To insert material into the *Congressional Record*	9
For motion to postpone debate	1
To rescind call for quorum	54
For motion to proceed out of order	1
To have amendment and discussion printed	1
To consider message from House	1
For permission to make statement on nongermane subject	2
For motion to recess	2
To waive reading of amendment	24
To yield floor without losing right to floor	3
For extension of time of person who has floor	1
For scheduling of vote on an amendment	2
To permit additional senators to sign cloture motion during business day	1
To conduct morning business after cloture	1
For motion to amend	1
For motion to consider amendment at particular time	1
To recognize senator at close of morning business for purpose of moving for tabling of amendment	1
To conduct second cloture vote on specified day	1
To vote on pending amendment	1
To have name appended to cloture motion	1
To divide hour preceding cloture vote between minority and majority leaders	1
To recognize someone out of order during debate	2
To submit proposed amendments	1
To go into executive session	1
To clear chambers	8

That amendments be considered "en bloc"	2
To allow modification of an amendment	10
To permit name to be added to amendment	1
To vote on merits of an amendment	1
To allow secretary to make clerical and technical changes	1

Environmental Quality Council Bill of 1969

Unanimous-consent requests	*Uses*
For second reading of bill	1
For other senators to be named as cosponsors	1
For consideration of bill	1
For statement of differences between Senate and House versions of bill	1
To consider conference report	1
To print major changes in Senate bill with sectional analysis of bill	1
To insert material in the *Congressional Record*	3

Legislative Reorganization Act of 1970

Unanimous-consent requests	*Uses*
To insert material in the *Congressional Record*	13
To lay aside unfinished business (temporarily)	2
For personal privilege	2
To dispense with reading of amendment	10
To rescind order for quorum call	1
To print amendment to make it available for study	1
To set time of reconvening	1
To allow equal debate time on either side of amendment before vote	1
To vacate order for yeas and nays	2
To consider committee amendments *en bloc*	1
To limit time for debate	1
To vote on an amendment at a specific time, and if debate is concluded to take up other amendments but retain that vote	1
To proceed to consideration of another amendment	2

To permit someone to be absent for Senate proceedings
during time of vote on amendment   1

To set aside pending amendment and permit submission of
another one   1

To recess to a particular time   1

To vote on amendment   1

To permit secretary of Senate to make appropriate
technical changes in format of bill   1

To indefinitely postpone Senate bill (counterpart of
House-passed bill)   1

SST Appropriations

Unanimous-consent requests	*Uses*
To insert material into the *Congressional Record*	69
To request time in morning hour	1
To lay unfinished business before Senate	1
To set time for vote on amendment (and limiting time for debate)	1
To debate an amendment (for three hours)	1
To clear floor of staff members (until vote is announced)	1
To offer an amendment	1
To rescind order for quorum	7
To yield floor (without losing right to floor or be counted as second speech)	3
To ask questions of another senator and receive answers (without losing the floor or be counted as a second speech)	1
To temporarily hold presidential-veto message on desk until a specified time	1
For consideration of another bill	1
To lay aside pending business to consider conference report with the limitation	1
For consideration of a message from the House on another bill	1
To set time of reconvening	1
For personal privilege (permit staff members to remain)	1
To lay a conference report before the Senate	1
To stop further reading of amendment	1

To schedule a two-track system for consideration of the
  SST from 9:00 to 3:00 and other business from 3:00 on   1

Lockheed

Unanimous-consent requests	*Uses*
To insert material into the *Congressional Record*	36
To rescind order for quorum call	29
To yield the floor (in some cases, without losing right to floor)	9
To permit staff members to be on floor during debate	9
To suggest the absence of a quorum without time being charged to either side	3
To yield time without it being charged to either side	3
To dispense with further reading of an amendment	3
To not charge time consumed by quorum call to either side	1
To begin mandatory quorum call	1
To charge time consumed by two leaders against the hour	1
To charge time equally to both sides	2
To divide remaining time on pending amendments	1
To set aside time for debate on amendment	1
To temporarily lay aside pending business	3
To waive Rule XII	1
For extension of speaking time	1
To limit time on pending amendment	1
To vacate order for vote on a motion for cloture	1
To consider all amendments at the desk at the time of the cloture vote as having been read	2
To withdraw previously ordered yeas and nays	1
To withdraw earlier remarks regarding filing a cloture motion	1
To make an amendment the pending question following the disposition of the amendment immediately pending	2
To be included in list of signers of the cloture motion	1
To not apply rule of germaneness	1
To proceed to consider another bill	2
To change time of cloture vote	1
To change time of reconvening	2
For a roll-call vote on bill	1
To postpone indefinitely a bill	1

APPENDIX 12.

Complete List of Cloture Votes Since Adoption of Rule XXII

Following is a list of the 61 cloture votes since Rule XXII was adopted in 1917. Only 10 of these (shown in CAPITAL LETTERS) were successful. In the right-hand column is shown the vote necessary to invoke cloture under the proposed 3/5-majority vote. Nine additional cloture votes (shown in *italics*) would have been successful using the proposed change.

| | | | | Yea Votes Needed | |
| | | | | 2/3 | 3/5 |
Issue	*Date*		*Vote*	*Majority*	*Majority*
VERSAILLES TREATY	Nov. 15,	1919	78-16	63	56
Emergency tariff	Feb. 2,	1921	36-35	48	43
Tariff bill	July 7,	1922	45-35	54	48
WORLD COURT	Jan. 25,	1926	68-26	63	56
Migratory birds	June 1,	1926	46-33	53	47
BRANCH BANKING	Feb. 15,	1927	65-18	56	50
Disabled officers	Feb. 26,	1927	51-36	58	52
Colorado River	Feb. 26,	1927	32-59	61	55
D.C. buildings	Feb. 28,	1927	52-31	56	50
PROHIBITION BUREAU	Feb. 28,	1927	55-27	55	49
Banking Act	Jan. 19,	1933	58-30	59	53
Anti-lynching	Jan. 27,	1938	37-51	59	53
Anti-lynching	Feb. 16,	1938	42-46	59	53
Anti-poll tax	Nov. 23,	1942	37-41	52	47
Anti-poll tax	May 15,	1944	36-44	54	48
Fair Employment Practices Commision	Feb. 9,	1946	48-36	56	50
British loan	May 7,	1946	41-41	55	49
Labor disputes	May 25,	1946	3-77	54	48
Anti-poll tax	July 31,	1946	39-33	48	43
FEPC	May 19,	1950	52-32	64*	58*
FEPC	July 12,	1950	55-33	64*	58*
Atomic Energy Act	July 26,	1954	44-42	64*	58*
Civil Rights Act	March 10,	1960	42-53	64	57
Amend Rule XXII	Sept. 19,	1961	37-43	54	48
Literacy tests	May 9,	1962	43-53	64	58
Literacy tests	May 14,	1962	42-52	63	56

* Between 1949 and 1959 the cloture rule required the affirmative vote of two-thirds of Senate membership rather than two-thirds of senators who voted.

SOURCE: *Congressional Quarterly Almanac, 92nd Congress, 1st Session*, Vol. XXVII (Washington, D.C.: Congressional Quarterly Service, 1971), p. 14.

Issue	Date		Vote	Yea Votes Needed 2/3 Majority	3/5 Majority
COMSAT ACT	Aug. 14,	1962	63-27	60	54
Amend Rule XXII	Feb. 7,	1963	54-42	64	58
CIVIL RIGHTS ACT	June 10,	1964	71-29	67	60
Legislative reapportionment	Sept. 10,	1964	30-63	62	56
VOTING RIGHTS ACT	May 25,	1965	70-30	67	60
Right-to-work repeal	Oct. 11,	1965	45-47	62	55
Right-to-work repeal	Feb. 8,	1966	51-48	66	59
Right-to-work repeal	Feb 10,	1966	50-49	66	59
Civil Rights Act	Sept. 14,	1966	54-42	64	58
Civil Rights Act	Sept. 19,	1966	52-41	62	56
D.C. Home Rule	Oct. 10,	1966	41-37	52	47
Amend Rule XXII	Jan. 24,	1967	53-46	66	59
Open Housing	Feb. 20,	1968	55-37	62	55
Open Housing	Feb. 26,	1968	56-36	62	55
Open Housing	March 1,	1968	59-35	63	56
OPEN HOUSING	March 4,	1968	65-32	65	58
Fortas nomination	Oct. 1,	1968	45-43	59	53
Amend Rule XXII	Jan. 16,	1969	51-47	66	59
Amend Rule XXII	Jan. 28,	1969	50-42	62	55
Electoral College	Sept. 17,	1970	54-36	60	54
Electoral College	Sept. 29,	1970	53-34	58	53
Supersonic transport	Dec. 19,	1970	43-48	61	55
Supersonic transport	Dec. 22,	1970	42-44	58	52
Amend Rule XXII	Feb. 18,	1971	48-37	57	51
Amend Rule XXII	Feb. 23,	1971	50-36	58	52
Amend Rule XXII	March 2,	1971	48-36	56	50
Amend Rule XXII	March 9,	1971	55-39	63	57
MILITARY DRAFT	June 23,	1971	65-27	62	55
Lockheed Loan	July 26,	1971	42-47	60	54
Lockheed Loan	July 28,	1971	59-39	66	59
Lockheed Loan	July 30,	1971	53-37	60	54
MILITARY DRAFT	Sept. 21,	1971	61-30	61	55
Rehnquist nomination	Dec. 10,	1971	52-42	63	57
Equal Job Opportunity	Feb. 1,	1972	48-37	57	51
Equal Job Opportunity	Feb. 3,	1972	53-35	59	53

* Between 1949 and 1959 the cloture rule required the affirmative vote of two-thirds of Senate membership rather than two-thirds of senators who voted.

SOURCE: *Congressional Quarterly Almanac, 92nd Congress, 1st Session*, Vol. XXVII (Washington, D.C.: Congressional Quarterly Service, 1971), p. 14.

APPENDIX 13.

Key Votes on Cloture Motions (1949 to 1971)

Year	Vote		Issue Voted On
	For change in Rule XXII	*Against change in Rule XXII*	
1949	41	46	The applicability of Rule XXII to motions to consider.
1953	21	70	The tabling of a motion to consider the adoption of new rules.
1957	38	55	
1959	36	60	Motion to consider the adoption of new rules.
1961	37	43	To invoke cloture on discussion of rules change.
1963	42	53	Motion to submit the question to the Senate.
1965	No vote: Resolution reported from committee and placed on calendar where it stayed for rest of the session.		
1967	37	61	To table point of order against majority cloture on rules change.
1969	45	53	To overrule chair's ruling that a majority may invoke cloture on discussions of rules changes.
1971	37	55	To overrule chair's ruling that two-thirds vote necessary to invoke cloture on rules-change debate.

SOURCE: Information for years 1949 through 1967 is from articles by Parliamentarian Floyd Riddick each year from 1951 to 1968 in the *Western Political Quarterly* (Salt Lake City: University of Utah Press), Vols. 4–21. Information for years 1969 and 1971 is from the *Guide to the Congress of the U.S.* (Washington, D.C.: Congressional Quarterly Service, 1971), p. 35.

APPENDIX 14.

Sample Conference Report

CONFERENCE REPORT ON H.R. 6065, UNEMPLOYMENT COMPENSATION

(*Congressional Record*, Dec. 14, 1971, pp. H.12450–51)

MR. MILLS of Arkansas submitted the following conference report and statement on the bill (H.R. 6065) to amend section 903(c) (2) of the Social Security Act:

CONFERENCE REPORT (H. REPT. No. 92–749)

The committee of conference on the disagreeing votes of the two Houses on the amendments of the Senate to the bill (H.R. 6065) to amend section 903(c) (2) of the Social Security Act, having met, after full and free conference, have agreed to recommend and do recommend to their respective House as follows:

That the House recede from its disagreement to the amendment of the Senate to the text of the bill and agree to the same with the following amendments to the Senate engrossed amendment:

Page 3, line 3, strike out "extended".

Page 4, line 2, strike out "extended".

Page 4, line 9, strike out "extended".

Page 4, line 13, strike out "extended".

Page 4, line 21, strike out "6.0 per centum" and insert: "6.5 per centum".

Page 5, line 13, strike out "6.0 per centum" and insert: "6.5 per centum".

Page 5, line 16, strike out "insured employment" and insert: "insured unemployment".

Page 5, line 21, strike out "should be equal to—" and insert "is the percentage arrived at by dividing—".

Page 5, line 25, strike out "divided".

Page 6, line 25, strike out "100 per centum" and insert: "50 per centum".

Page 7, line 5, strike out "twenty-six" and insert: "thirteen".

Page 7, strike out lines 14, 15, and 16 and insert: "this Act. No emergency compensation shall ·be payable to any individual under such an agreement for any week ending after—

"(1) June 30, 1972, or

"(2) September 30, 1972, in the case of an individual who (for a week ending before July 1, 1972) had a week with respect to which emergency compensation was payable under such agreement."

Page 9, strike out line 5 and all that follows down through line 9 on page 10 and insert:

"(b) There are hereby authorized to be appropriated, without fiscal year limitation, to the extended unemployment compensation account, as repayable advances (without interest), such sums as may be necessary to carry out the purposes of this title. Amounts appropriated as repayable advances and paid to the States under section 203 shall be repaid, without interest, as provided in section 903(b) (3) of the Social Security Act.

"(c) Section 903(b) of the Social Security Act is amended by adding at the end thereof the following new paragraph:

" '(3) The amount which, but for this paragraph, would be transferred to the account of a State under subsection (a) or paragraph (1) of this subsection shall (after applying paragraph (2) of this subsection) be reduced (but not below zero) by the balance of that portion of the advances made under section 204(b) of the Emergency Unemployment Compensation Act of 1971 which was used for payments to such State under section 203 of such Act. An amount equal to the sum by which such amount is reduced shall be transferred to the general fund of the Treasury. Any amount transferred as a repayment under this paragraph shall be credited against, and shall operate to reduce, any balance repayable under this paragraph by the State to which (but for this paragraph) such amount would have been payable.' ".

Page 10, line 20, strike out "emergency extended" and insert: "emergency".

Page 10, line 23, strike out "emergency extended" and insert: "emergency".

Page 11, after line 4, insert: "For purposes of any State law which refers to an extension under Federal law of the duration of benefits under the Federal-State Extended Unemployment Compensation Act of 1970, this title shall be treated as amendatory of such Act."

Page 11, line 7, strike out "continuing and".

Page 11, line 16, strike out "after June 30, 1973" and insert: "after the period prescribed in section 202(f)".

Page 11, line 19, strike out "after June 30, 1973" and insert: "after the period prescribed in section 202(f)."

Page 11, line 20, strike out "July 1" and insert: "May 1".

Page 11, line 23, strike out "May 31" and insert: "March 31".

Page 12, line 4, strike out "after June 30, 1973" and insert: "after the period prescribed in section 202(f)".

And the Senate agree to the same.

That the House recede from its disagreement to the amendment of the Senate to the title of the bill and agree to the same.

> W. D. MILLS,
> AL ULLMAN,
> JAMES A. BURKE,
> *Managers on the Part of the House.*
> RUSSELL B. LONG,
> CLINTON ANDERSON,
> HERMAN TALMADGE,
> CARL T. CURTIS,
> *Managers on the Part of the Senate.*

JOINT EXPLANATORY STATEMENT OF THE
COMMITTEE ON CONFERENCE

The managers on the part of the House and the Senate at the conference on the disagreeing votes of the two Houses on the amendments of the Senate to the bill (H.R. 6065) to amend section 903(c) (2) of the Social Security Act, submit the following joint statement to the House and the Senate in explanation of the effect of the action agreed upon by the managers and recommend in the accompanying conference report:

The bill as passed by the House extended for an additional 10 years the period during which States may obligate, for administrative purposes, certain funds transferred from excess Federal unemployment tax collections.

The Senate amendment to the text of the bill made no change in the House provisions explained in the preceding paragraph but added a title II to the bill, relating to emergency unemployment compensation. Under the Senate amendment, any State, the State law of which provides for the payment of extended compensation in accordance with the requirements of the Federal-State Extended Unemployment Compensation Act of 1970, may enter into an agreement under which the agency of the State which administers the State unemployment compensation law will pay emergency compensation to individuals who have exhausted all rights to both regular compensation and extended compensation. The weekly benefit amount of the individual is determined in the same way as for regular compensation purposes; and the total amount of emergency compensation payable to an individual is an amount equal to the lesser of 100 percent of the regular compensation payable to him for the most recent benefit year or 26 times his average weekly benefit amount for his benefit year.

The emergency compensation payable under the amendment is payable only during an emergency extended benefit period. Such a period is triggered in a State when the rate of unemployment (which takes into account both the rate of insured unemployment and the rate of exhaustions of regular compensation) for such State for a 13-week period equals or exceeds 6.0 percent. Under the Senate amendment, emergency compensation is payable only for weeks of unemployment which begin more than 30 days after the date of the enactment of the bill (or, if later, after the week in which the State agreement is entered into). In addition, such compensation is payable only for weeks which end before July 1, 1973.

The Senate amendment provides for financing emergency benefits by increasing the rate of the Federal unemployment tax imposed by section 3301 of the Internal Revenue Code of 1954 on wages (as defined in section 3306(b) of such Code) paid during 1972 or 1973 from 3.2 percent to 3.29 percent.

The Senate amendment also provides for the Secretary of Labor to submit to Congress a full and complete report of the emergency compensation program on or before July 1, 1972.

The House recedes with amendments.

The conference agreement in general follows the Senate amendment with these major changes:

(1) Under the conference agreement, the total amount of compensation payable to an individual is the lesser of (A) 50 percent of the regular compensation payable to him with respect to the benefit year on the basis of which he most recently received regular compensation, or (B) 13 times his average weekly benefit amount for his benefit year.

(2) Under the conference agreement, the emergency benefit period is triggered in a State when the rate of unemployment (which takes into account both the rate of insured unemployment and the rate of exhaustions of regular compensation) for such State for a 13-week period equals or exceeds 6.5 percent.

(3) Under the conference agreement, no emergency compensation is payable for any week of unemployment which ends after June 30, 1972; except that, in the case of an individual who had a week of unemployment ending before July 1, 1972, for which emergency compensation was payable under a State agreement, the period for paying emergency compensation to that individual under the State agreement

will also include weeks of unemployment which end before October 1, 1972.

(4) Under the conference agreement, the emergency compensation will be payable out of the Federal extended unemployment compensation account. The agreement authorizes the appropriation to such account of repayable advances (which shall not bear interest) to carry out the emergency compensation program provided by the bill. The amounts paid to any State for benefits under this program are to be repaid by transferring to the general fund of the Treasury amounts equal to such benefits. These transfers are to be made out of amounts which would otherwise (but for the new section 903(b) (3) of the Social Security Act added by the bill) be paid over to such State out of excess Federal unemployment tax collections.

(5) The conference agreement also modifies the reporting provisions of the Senate amendment. Under the conference agreement, the Secretary of Labor is required to submit before May 1, 1972, a full and complete report of the emergency compensation program provided by the bill. The report is to cover the period ending on March 31, 1972, and is to contain recommendations of the Secretary with respect to the program, including (but not limited to) the operation and funding of the program and the desirability of extending the program beyond June 30, 1972.

W. D. MILLS,

AL ULLMAN,

JAMES A. BURKE,

Managers on the Part of the House.

RUSSELL B. LONG,

CLINTON ANDERSON,

HERMAN TALMADGE,

CARL T. CURTIS,

Managers on the Part of the Senate.

Like many other conference reports, this one was offered in the last six days of the session. The reading of the report on the floor was dispensed with by unanimous consent, for as Representative John Byrnes (R., Wis.) said, "It is perfectly clear that the reading, in many cases, is rather a meaningless operation." The members had very little opportunity to analyze this report before they had to vote on it. "The Members cannot understand the conference report just by the reading of the statement," Byrnes said.

Notes

CHAPTER 1. TOOLS OF THE TRADE

1. U.S., Congress, House, Committee on Rules, Special Subcommittee on Legislative Reorganization, *Legislative Reorganization Act of 1970: Hearings*, 91st Cong., 1st sess. (1969).
2. See *Senate Manual*, 92nd Congress, pp. 431–32.
3. *Congressional Record*, January 22, 1971, p. H.58.
4. Ibid., p. H.62.
5. Richard L. Lyons, "Panel on Policy Voted in House by Democrats," *Washington Post*, February 23, 1973, p. A6.
6. Richard Damon, "The Standing Rules of the U.S. House of Representatives" (unpublished doctoral dissertation, Columbia University, 1971), p. 27.
7. De Alva Stanwood Alexander, *History and Procedure of the House of Representatives* (Boston: Little, Brown, 1916), p. 111–112.
8. W. P. Cutler and J. P. Cutler (eds.), *Life, Journals and Correspondence of Richard Manasseh Cutler*, Vol. II (Cincinnati: Robert Clark and Co., 1888), pp. 186–89.
9. Nelson Polsby (ed.), *Congressional Behavior* (Kingsport, Tenn.: Kingsport Press, 1971), p. 18.
10. William Chapman, *Washington Post*, January 1, 1971, p. A2.
11. Richard Lyons, "Fishbait Miller Opens New Door in the House," *Washington Post*, November 24, 1972, p. A2.
12. Legislative Reorganization Act of 1970, Title I, Section 1021, 60 Stat, 831.
13. *Rules Adopted by the Committees of Congress*, pp. 34–35.

14. Bella Abzug with Mel Ziegler, *Bella! Ms. Abzug Goes to Washington* (New York: Bobbs-Merrill, 1970), p. 44.
15. *Washington Star*, July 28, 1971.
16. Interview with Dr. Doug Jones and Bill Hoffman, aides to Senator Mike Gravel, June 30, 1972.
17. Stephen Rich, *Washington Post*, July 1, 1971, p. A1.
18. George Goodwin, Jr., "The Seniority System in Congress," in Joseph S. Clark (ed.), *Congressional Reform* (New York: Thomas Y. Crowell, 1965), pp. 178–79.
19. Nelson W. Polsby, Miriam Gallagher, and Barry Spencer Rundquist, "The Growth of the Seniority System in the U.S. House of Representatives," *The American Political Science Review* (1969), pp. 790–91.
20. Champ Clark, *My Quarter Century of American Politics*, 2 vols. (New York: Harper's, 1920), I, p. 209.
21. Daniel M. Berman, *In Congress Assembled* (New York: Macmillan, 1964), p. 167; Estes Kefauver and Jack Levin, *A 20th Century Congress* (New York: Greenwood Press, 2nd edition, 1969), p. 135.
22. Goodwin, "The Seniority System in Congress," p. 185.
23. Interviewers in 1972 heard such estimates as these: David Cohen, chief lobbyist for Common Cause, believes that no more than ten members have a solid grasp of House rules; Majority Leader Thomas O'Neill (D., Mass.) believes that only twenty-five to thirty-five representatives truly know them; and the chief lobbyist for the United Auto Workers, Jack Beidler, says, "I don't think 10 per cent of the members of the House know that after a bill has been in conference committee for twenty days a privileged motion is in order. Most members don't even understand the difference between the hour rule and the five-minute rule in debate."
24. In Congress Project interviews, these members of Congress appeared to have an extensive knowledge of the rules: in the House, Carl Albert, Hale Boggs, Thomas O'Neill, Richard Bolling, B. F. Sisk, Spark Matsunaga, H. R. Gross, Durward Hall, Thomas Rees, William Steiger, and Bella Abzug; in the Senate, Mike Mansfield, Robert Byrd, James Allen, Sam Ervin, Marlow Cook, and Robert Packwood.
25. U.S., Congress, Joint Committee on the Organization of Congress, *Organization of Congress Hearings:* 89th Cong., 1st sess., 1965, pp. 514–15.
26. *Ibid.*, pp. 170–71.
27. *Ibid.*, p. 516.
28. Abzug with Ziegler, *Bella!*, p. 11.
29. Interview with Walter Kravitz, senior specialist in government of the Congressional Research Service, July 10, 1972.
30. Ralph Nader Congress Project, response to questionnaire by Glen H. Taylor, former member of Congress, 1972.

CHAPTER 2. THE PARLIAMENTARIANS

1. Nicholas Longworth, John N. Garner, Henry T. Rainey, Joseph W. Byrnes, William B. Bankhead, Joseph Martin, Sam Rayburn, John McCormack, and Carl Albert.
2. *Congressional Record*, March 4, 1963, p. H.3372.
3. Ibid.
4. Ibid.
5. *Congressional Record*, April 29, 1963, p. H.7256.
6. Ibid.
7. Ibid., p. H.7257.
8. U.S., Congress, House, Subcommittee on Legislative Appropriations, *Legislative Branch Appropriations Act: Hearings*, 89th Cong., 1st sess., pp. 527–28.
9. *Congressional Record*, Sept. 16, 1970, p. H.32213.
10. Ibid., p. H.32212.
11. Ibid.
12. Ibid., p. H.32213.
13. Ibid.
14. Representative Rees recalls a time when he was presiding over consideration of a bill to determine the width of buses. Before the proceeding, Representative Fred Schwengel (R., Iowa) informed Rees that he planned to propose an amendment from the floor. Rees was not warned that a point of order would be made against the amendment on the ground that it was not germane to the bill. When the point of order was made, the parliamentarian went to his office, checked the precedents, and in less than five minutes delivered a typed ruling to Rees via the sergeant-at-arms. Rees disagreed with the parliamentarian's ruling that the amendment was not germane, but after hesitating for a moment, he acquiesced to the ruling because he did not know the precedents on which to reject it.
15. *Congressional Record*, March 18, 1955, pp. H.3204–3205.
16. *Congressional Quarterly's Guide to the Congress of the United States* (Washington, D.C., 1971), p. 386.
17. *Congressional Quarterly*, March 11, 1965, pp. H.4785–86.
18. *Jefferson's Manual and the Rules of the House of Representatives*, 92nd Congress, House Document No. 439, Rule XXVIII, Clause 3. (Hereafter cited *House Manual*.)
19. Testimony of Representative William Steiger, House Rules Committee, August 2, 1971.
20. *House Manual*, Rule XXVIII, Clause 3.
21. Adam Klymer, *Baltimore Sun*, July 5, 1971.
22. Testimony of Steiger.
23. *New York Times*, August 3, 1971, p. 11.
24. *Baltimore Sun*, August 4, 1971, p. 7.

25. *Congressional Record*, June 8, 1971, pp. S.8543, S.8545, S.8547.
26. *Congressional Record*, November 10, 1971, p. H.10856.
27. *House Manual*, Rule XX, Clauses 1 and 3.
28. House Republican Policy Committee, *Committee Staff Manual on Legislative Procedure in the U.S. House of Representatives*, p. 84.
29. *House Manual*, Rule XX, Clauses 1 and 3.
30. *Congressional Record*, November 10, 1971, p. H.10856.
31. Ibid.
32. Ibid., p. 10857.
33. *House Manual*, p. 269.
34. Ibid., p. 271.
35. *Congressional Record*, November 10, 1971, pp. H.10857–58.
36. Ibid., p. H.10858.
37. Ibid., p. H.10859.
38. Ibid.
39. *Congressional Record*, March 3, 1970, p. H.5710.
40. *Congressional Record*, March 4, 1963, p. H.3372, quoted in Richard Bolling, *House Out of Order* (New York: Dutton, 1965), p. 153.
41. *Congressional Record*, Oct. 17, 1966, p. H.27096.
42. Comment by Deschler in *Congressional Quarterly Weekly Report*, January 14, 1963. Also see *Congressional Quarterly Weekly Report*, March 11, 1965, p. 4785, where Deschler says he has been appealed ten times.
43. *Congressional Record*, March 3, 1970, p. H.5710.
44. Bolling, *House Out of Order*, pp. 110–13.
45. Charles Clapp, *The Congressman—His Work as He Sees It* (Washington, D.C.: Brookings Institution, 1963), pp. 128–29.
46. Interview with Dr. Floyd Riddick, Senate parliamentarian, July 18, 1972.
47. U.S., Congress, Joint Committee on the Organization of Congress, Hearings, 89th Congress, 1st sess., June 2, 3, 4, 1965, part 4, pp. 635–36. (Hereafter cited "1965 Joint Committee on Organization Hearings.")
48. 1965 Joint Committee on Organization Hearings, p. 636.
49. 1965 Joint Committee on Organization Hearings, p. 635.
50. *Congressional Record*, Nov. 23, 1971, p. S.19477.
51. Ibid., p. S.19489.
52. *Congressional Record*, July 15, 1972, p. S.9520.
53. *Congressional Record*, July 19, 1971, p. S.11467.
54. U.S., Congress, Senate, *Senate Procedure, Precedents and Practices*, S. Doc. 44, 88th Cong., 1st sess., 1964, by Charles L. Watkins and Floyd M. Riddick.
55. *Congressional Record*, Sept. 30, 1971, p. S.15595.
56. Ibid., pp. S.15595–96.
57. Ibid., p. S.15596.
58. *Congressional Record*, Feb. 24, 1972, p. S.2569.
59. Ibid., p. S.2568.
60. 1965 Joint Committee on Organization Hearings, p. 635.

61. Automated Legislative Record Keeping, February 19, 1972, Senate Subcommittee on Computer Services, Senate Rules and Administration, p. 124.
62. Floyd M. Riddick, *The United States Congress, Organization and Procedure* (Boston: Chapman and Guiness, 1941), pp. 142–43.

CHAPTER 3. TWENTIETH-CENTURY LORDS AND FIEFDOMS: CHAIRMEN AND THEIR COMMITTEES

1. Woodrow Wilson, *Congressional Government* (N.Y.: Meridian, 1956), p. 66.
2. Bella Abzug with Mel Ziegler, *Bella! Ms. Abzug goes to Washington* (New York: Bobbs-Merrill, 1970), p. 17.
3. Nicholas Masters, "Committee Assignments in the House of Representatives," in Joseph S. Clark (ed.), *Congressional Reform* (New York: Thomas Y. Crowell, 1965), p. 210.
4. *Congressional Record*, Jan. 28, 1971, p. S.405.
5. *Rules of the House of Representatives*, 92nd Congress (Washington, D.C.: Government Printing Office, 1971), pp. 331–32.
6. *Congressional Record*, Feb. 4, 1971, pp. H.427–34.
7. George Goodwin, Jr., "The Seniority System in Congress," in Clark, *Congressional Reform*, p. 180.
8. Ibid., p. 179.
9. Joseph Clark, *The Sapless Branch* (New York: Harper & Row, 1965), p. 178.
10. Ibid.
11. William S. White, "The Kernel of the Power," in Clark, *Congressional Reform*, p. 235.
12. Abzug with Ziegler, *Bella!*, pp. 26–27.
13. *Congressional Quarterly Weekly Report*, "Increase in Female House Members in 1971 Expected," July 10, 1970, p. 1748.
14. Ibid.
15. George Goodwin, Jr., *The Little Legislatures* (Amherst, Mass.: University of Massachusetts Press, 1972), p. 68.
16. Goodwin, "The Seniority System in Congress," in Clark, *Congressional Reform*, p. 170.
17. Goodwin, *The Little Legislatures*, p. 89.
18. *New York Times*, Feb. 22, 1972, p. 82.
19. Randall Ripley, *Power in the Senate* (New York: St. Martin's Press, 1969), p. 137.
20. *Congressional Quarterly Weekly Report*, Jan. 29, 1971, p. 257.
21. Ripley, *Power in the Senate*, p. 134.

22. Ibid., p. 197.
23. Masters, "Committee Assignments," p. 213.
24. Charles Clapp, *The Congressman—His Work as He Sees It* (Washington, D.C.: Brookings Institution, 1963), p. 20; Masters, "Committee Assignments," p. 224.
25. Clapp, *The Congressman*, pp. 189–90.
26. Clapp, *The Congressman*, p. 196; Masters, "Committee Assignments," p. 227.
27. Clapp, *The Congressman*, p. 193.
28. Goodwin, *The Little Legislatures*, p. 78
29. Masters, "Committee Assignments," p. 227.
30. Clapp, *The Congressman*, p. 205.
31. *Congressional Quarterly Weekly Report*, Jan. 27, 1973, p. 136.
32. Letter from Josephine Wilson, clerk of the Republican Committee on Committees, to the Congress Project.
33. Interview with Representative Jerry Pettis.
34. Donald G. Tacheron and Morris K. Udall, *The Job of a Congressman* (New York: Bobbs-Merrill, 2nd ed., 1970), pp. 165–66.
35. *Preamble and Rules Adopted by the Democratic Caucus*, Addendum, Sec. 5, 6. Revised Jan. 24, 1973.
36. Ibid., p. 22.
37. Goodwin, "The Seniority System in Congress," p. 602.
38. Nine House and five Senate committees explicitly permit chairmen to create *ad hoc* subcommittees. See *Rules Adopted*, pp. 6, 10, 34, 35, 46, 61, 76, 78, 106, 118, 123, 126.
39. *Congressional Quarterly Weekly Report*, June 24, 1971, p. 179.
40. *Rules Adopted*, pp. 6, 10, 13, 18, 22, 36, 45, 55, 69, 70, 77, 78, 123, 130.
41. Interview with Tom Gallagher, legislative assistant to Senator John Tunney, June 29, 1972.
42. Goodwin, "The Seniority System in Congress," p. 602.
43. Ibid.
44. Interview with Representative Thomas O'Neill, Jr., and Linda Melconian, legislative assistant, June 26, 1972.
45. Tacheron and Udall, *The Job of a Congressman*, p. 174; Ripley, *Power in the Senate*, p. 112.
46. Goodwin, "The Seniority System in Congress," p. 600.
47. *Rules Adopted*, p. 9.
48. Donald Matthews, *U.S. Senators and Their World* (Chapel Hill: The University of North Carolina Press, 1960), pp. 59–60.
49. Floyd Riddick, *Congressional Procedure* (Boston: Chapman and Grimes, 1941), p. 112; Richard F. Fenno, Jr., "The Internal Distribution of Influence: The House," in *Congress and America's Future*, The American Assembly, Columbia University (New Jersey: Prentice-Hall, Inc., 1965), p. 53; Matthews, *U.S. Senators and Their World*, pp. 159–60.
50. Matthews, *U.S. Senators and Their World*, p. 160.

51. Tacheron and Udall, *The Job of a Congressman*, p. 174.
52. *Rules Adopted*, p. 157.
53. Jack Kneece, (Washington) *Evening Star*, Sept. 29, 1972.
54. Confidential interview.
55. Robert Bendiner, *Obstacle Course on Capitol Hill* (New York: Mc-Graw-Hill, 1964), p. 61.
56. Ibid.
57. Clapp, *The Congressman*, p. 221.
58. Matthews, *U.S. Senators and Their World*, p. 161.
59. Woodrow Wilson, *Congressional Government*, p. 76.
60. Matthews, *U.S. Senators and Their World*, p. 162.
61. William S. White, "The Kernel of the Power," pp. 233–34.
62. Tacheron and Udall, *The Job of a Congressman*, pp. 177–78.
63. Roy Reed, "Arkansans Voting in Runoff," *New York Times*, June 14, 1972, p. 36.
64. 376 U.S. 1 (1964).
65. All data concerning committee appointments and accession to chairmanships were garnered from comparison of *Congressional Directories*. No direct source exists for appointments other than those to fill special vacancies. For convenience, committee lists from the *Congressional Directories* rather than from the *Congressional Record* were compared.
66. The 79th–92nd Congresses were studied. Dates of members' service were compiled from *Congressional Quarterly, Members of Congress 1945–1970* (1971). Causes for leaving were drawn from the *Biographical Directory of the American Congress 1774–1971*, 15 S. Doc. No. 92–8, 92nd Congress, 1st Session (1971). Date on "total" turnover and mean tenure in the House of Representatives for the years through 1963 were drawn from Nelson Polsby, *The Institutionalization of the House of Representatives*, 62 *American Political Science Review*, 144 (1968). The turnover data were collected with the help of fifty members of Professor Alan Sager's Government 610(b) course at the University of Texas. Michael Pelfrey and William Bennett of Austin, Texas, programed the data, and George Avery, also of Austin, helped design the tables. (See "Explanation of Appendix 5 and 6" in the Appendix for the program and sample output.)
67. Eighty-plus-year-old chairmen in the 92nd Congress included Emanuel Celler (D., N.Y.), born in 1888; William M. Colmer (D., Miss.), and John L. McMillan (D., S.C.), born in 1890; and George P. Miller (D., Calif.) and Allen J. Ellender (D., La.), 1891. Other chairmen born before the turn of the century and serving in the 92nd Congress were Wright Patman (D., Tex.), 1893; Clinton P. Anderson (D., N.M.), 1895; Wayne N. Aspinall (D., Colo.), 1896; John L. McClellan (D., Ark.), 1896; W. R. Poage (D., Tex.), 1899; and John J. Sparkman (D., Ala.), 1899.

CHAPTER 4. THE HOUSE RULES COMMITTEE AND THE SENATE RULES AND ADMINISTRATION COMMITTEE

1. *House Manual*, p. 361.
2. Walter Kravitz, "A Short History of the Development of the House Committee on Rules," Library of Congress, Legislative Reference Service, Feb. 17, 1969.
3. *Congressional Record*, July 14, 1955, p. H.10609.
4. "Couldn't Make It for Vote—Bolling," *Washington Post*, December 3, 1970, p. A12.
5. *Congressional Quarterly Weekly Report*, April 15, 1972, p. 843.
6. *Congressional Record*, June 21, 1972, p. H.5869.
7. David Dennis (R., Ind.), *Congressional Record*, June 21, 1972, p. H.5873.
8. Ralph Nader Congress Project, response to questionnaire, Representative Marvin Esch (R., Mich.), 1972.
9. Ralph Nader Congress Project, response to questionnaire, Representative Bella Abzug (D., N.Y.), 1972.
10. *Congressional Record*, Jan. 22, 1971, p. H.67.
11. Ibid., p. H.59.

CHAPTER 5. UNANIMOUS-CONSENT AGREEMENTS: ALMOST ANYTHING GOES

1. George Goodwin, Jr., *The Little Legislatures*, (Amherst, Mass.: University of Massachusetts Press, 1972), pp. 230–31.
2. Ibid., p. 231.
3. *Congressional Record*, June 2, 1971, p. S.8029.
4. Ibid.
5. Donald G. Tacheron and Morris K. Udall, *The Job of a Congressman* (New York: Bobbs-Merrill, 2nd ed., 1970), p. 260.
6. Carol L. Buck, "Committee Jurisdictional Overlap," Congressional Research Service, March 6, 1972, p. 2 (emphasis added).
7. Bella Abzug with Mel Ziegler, *Bella! Ms. Abzug Goes to Washington* (New York: Bobbs-Merrill, 1972), p. 254.
8. Democratic Study Group, House of Representatives, "Some Delaying Tactics Possible in House of Representatives" (undated).

CHAPTER 6. FLOOR DEBATING AND VOTING: RULES
FOR TUESDAY–THURSDAY CLUBS

1. Neil MacNeil, *Forge of Democracy* (New York: David McKay, 1963), p. 253.
2. Samuel W. McCall, *The Business of Congress* (Boston: Little, Brown, 1911), p. 65.
3. Representative Clem Miller (R., Ohio), newsletter, August 15, 1961.
4. Richard Damon, "The Standing Rules of the U.S. House of Representatives" (unpublished doctoral dissertation, Columbia University, 1971), pp. 208–209.
5. Joseph S. Clark, *Congress: The Sapless Branch* (New York: Harper & Row, 1964), p. 192.
6. Ibid.
7. Lewis A. Froman, Jr., *The Congressional Process* (Boston: Little, Brown, 1967), p. 114.
8. *Congressional Record*, Aug. 3, 1972, p. S.12605.
9. George B. Galloway, *The Legislative Process in Congress* (New York: Thomas Y. Crowell, 1953), p. 543.
10. Clarence Mitchell, speaking in favor of Rule XXII reform in hearings before the Special Bipartisan Committee on Senate Reform, Jan. 19, 1971.
11. *Congressional Record*, Jan. 29, 1971, p. S.390.
12. *Congressional Quarterly Weekly Report*, Oct. 14, 1972, p. 2697.
13. John Bilby and Roger Davidson, *Capitol Hill: Studies of the Legislative Process* (New York: Holt, Rinehart & Winston, 1967), p. 119.
14. *Congressional Record*, Jan. 29, 1971, p. S.566.
15. Ibid., p. S.557.
16. Ibid., p. S.486.
17. U.S., Congress, Senate, *Final Report of the Joint Committee on the Organization of Congress*, S. Con. Res. 2, 89th Cong., 2nd sess., 1966, pp. 8–9.
18. Legislative Reorganization Act of 1970, p. 7.
19. Ibid., pp. 7–8.
20. Randall Ripley, *Power in the Senate* (New York: St. Martin's Press, 1969), p. 118.
21. *Final Report of the Joint Committee on the Organization of Congress*, pp. 8–9.
22. Froman, *The Congressional Process*, p. 123.
23. Ibid., p. 122.
24. "Senate Amends Job Equity Bill," *Washington Post*, Feb. 22, 1972.
25. "The First Year of Record Teller Voting," special report, Democratic Study Group, Jan. 27, 1972.

26. David S. Broder, "SST: Hill Reform Victim," *Washington Post*, March 23, 1971, p. A19.
27. *Congressional Record*, Feb. 9, 1972, p. S.1528.
28. Froman, *The Congressional Process*, pp. 126–27.
29. Ibid., p. 136.
30. *Congresisonal Record*, Jan. 22, 1972, p. H.59.

CHAPTER 7.   RUNS SILENT, RUNS DEEP: THE CONFERENCE COMMITTEES

1. Lewis A. Froman, Jr., *The Congressional Process* (Boston: Little, Brown, 1967), pp. 158–68.
2. Ada McCown, *The Congressional Conference Committee* (New York: Columbia University Press, 1927), p. 1.
3. Ibid., p. 69.
4. Ibid., p. 33.
5. *Congressional Record*, June 8, 1971, p. S.8544.
6. Ibid., p. S.8552.
7. Ibid., p. S.8545.
8. *Congressional Record*, Oct. 13, 1972, p. H.9877.
9. *Congressional Record*, July 16, 1959, p. S.8019.
10. *Congressional Record*, Sept. 1, 1965, p. H.21629.
11. House Republican Policy Committee, *Committee Staff Manual of Legislative Procedure*, p. 111.
12. *Congressional Record*, May 12, 1959, p. S.7975.
13. Ibid.
14. House Republican Policy Committee, *Committee Staff Manual of Legislative Procedure*, p. 112.
15. *Congressional Record*, March 8, 1972, p. H.1840.
16. *Hinds' and Cannon's Precedents of the House of Representatives* (Government Printing Office, 1936), Volume VIII, p. 3736.
17. Phil Casey, *Washington Post*, June 2, 1962, p. A17.
18. "Legislator Is Taught How Congress Works," *Washington Star*, March 12, 1964, p. 1.
19. Richard F. Fenno, Jr., *The Power of the Purse: Appropriations in Congress* (Boston: Little, Brown, 1966), p. 625.
20. McCown, p. 55.
21. Ibid., p. 57.
22. Spencer Rich, "Hill Plays 'Chicken' on Draft End-the-War Amendments," *Washington Post*, July 19, 1971, p. A14.
23. *Congressional Quarterly Almanac* (1971), p. 293.
24. John Manley, *The Politics of Finance* (Boston: Little, Brown, 1970), p. 266.

25. Ibid.
26. Neil MacNeil, *Forge of Democracy* (New York: David McKay, 1963), p. 127.
27. Representative Edith Green (D., Ore.), *Congressional Record*, March 9, 1972, p. H.1843.
28. Ralph Nader Congress Project, *Citizens Look at Congress*, Profile of Representative Wilbur Mills by Stephen A. Merrill (Washington, D.C.: Grossman Publishers, 1972), p. 9.
29. Manley, *The Politics of Finance*, p. 264.
30. Representative Clem Miller, newsletter, August 15, 1961.
31. Manley, *The Politics of Finance*, p. 300.
32. *Congressional Record*, June 30, 1972, p. H.6460.
33. Ibid., p. H.6494.
34. Ibid., p. H.6507.
35. Ibid., p. H.6510.

CHAPTER 8. EXCHANGING TOOLS

1. Richard Damon, "The Standing Rules of the U.S. House of Representatives" (unpublished doctoral dissertation, Columbia University, 1971), pp. 10–11.
2. Ibid., p. 12.
3. Charles S. Hyneman, *A Second Federalist* (Columbia: University of South Carolina Press, 1970), p. ix.
4. Roger H. Davidson, *Congress in Crisis* (Belmont, Calif.: Wadsworth Publishing Co., 1966), p. 79.
5. *Congressional Record*, March 9, 1972, p. H.1843.

CHAPTER 9. CONCLUSIONS

1. See study prepared by Legislative Reference Service in Hearings, Joint Committee on the Organization of Congress (1965), 89th Cong., 1st sess., part 1, pp. 132–65.
2. Joe Evins, *Understanding Congress* (New York: Clarkson N. Potter, 1963), p. 103.
3. Joseph Clark, *The Sapless Branch* (New York: Harper & Row, 1965), pp. 182–84.
4. George Goodwin, Jr., *The Little Legislatures* (Amherst, Mass.: University of Massachusetts Press, 1972), pp. 122–23.
5. Albert Gore, "The Conference Committee: Congress' Final Filter," *The Washington Monthly*, Vol. 3, No. 4 (June 1971), p. 48.

Index

285